Fundamentals
of Computer-Aided
Engineering

Fundamentals of Computer-Aided Engineering

Benny Raphael and Ian F. C. Smith

Swiss Federal Institute of Technology (EPFL),
Lausanne, Switzerland

WILEY

Other Wiley Editorial Offices

John Wiley & Sons Inc., 111 River Street, Hoboken, NJ 07030, USA

Jossey-Bass, 989 Market Street, San Francisco, CA 94103-1741, USA

Wiley-VCH Verlag GmbH, Boschstr. 12, D-69469 Weinheim, Germany

John Wiley & Sons Australia Ltd, 33 Park Road, Milton, Queensland 4064, Australia

John Wiley & Sons (Asia) Pte Ltd, 2 Clementi Loop #02-01, Jin Xing Distripark, Singapore 129809

John Wiley & Sons Canada Ltd, 22 Worcester Road, Etobicoke, Ontario, Canada M9W 1L1

Wiley also publishes its books in a variety of electronic formats. Some content that appears in print may not be available in electronic books.

British Library Cataloguing in Publication Data

A catalogue record for this book is available from the British Library

ISBN 0-471-48709-0 (HB)
ISBN 0-471-48715-5 (PB)

Typeset in 10/12pt Times by Laserwords Private Limited, Chennai, India
Printed and bound in Great Britain by TJ International, Padstow, Cornwall
This book is printed on acid-free paper responsibly manufactured from sustainable forestry in which at least two trees are planted for each one used for paper production.

Contents

Foreword

S. Fenves, University Professor Emeritus, Carnegie Mellon University, USA

During the past four decades, computers and computer-based information technologies have penetrated into every aspect of our daily lives and have profoundly changed the way we perform many of our daily activities. Computers have also changed every aspect of engineering practice and research. In practice, engineers would have found it difficult, if not impossible, to respond to increased pressures without the support of computers. These pressures include, among others, the increased scope and complexity of the artefacts and projects that engineers design, produce and manage, accelerated schedules, growing regulatory and environmental demands, and the globalization of the profession – increasing opportunities for collaboration as well as competition. In engineering research, much of the experimental work that is aimed at a better understanding of physical phenomena has been translated into expanded simulation models. In parallel, the increased computerization of engineering processes has brought about research on the fundamental nature of these processes themselves.

The trends have brought about a fundamentally changed view of computing. The initial view of computing as a means for calculating has given way to viewing computing as a means for generating, communicating and sharing data, information and knowledge. Computing in this broad sense is the subject of this book.

Within the general trends sketched above, there have been a series of major changes in the way engineers acquire and use computing aids. Computer hardware has undergone three generations, defined by mode of access: from sequential batch processing, through time-shared access, to ubiquitous computing on desktop computers. More relevant to this book are the generational changes in how engineers acquire and use software. Initially, every engineer who wanted to use the computer was his or her own programmer. Later, program development groups emerged within each engineering organization, developing and maintaining the organization's software in-house or through contracted custom programming, with possibly some support from user groups. Out of these two sources, in-house and contract development groups, there emerged a highly competitive marketplace of commercial software products. Today the vast majority of engineers use commercial software.

The near-total dependence of practising engineers on commercial software has stratified their roles with respect to computing. The largest stratum consists of engineers who are users of software developed by others. A much smaller stratum is the information technology (IT) staffs of engineering organizations, the successors to the in-house development staffs, responsible for selecting, adapting, and integrating hardware, networks and software for the organizations. A second small stratum works for the commercial software companies, developing, upgrading and maintaining that software. Computing in research may be somewhat more fluid with respect to these three strata, but it generally follows the same pattern.

The computing component of engineering education, for future engineers and existing practitioners, has had to adapt to these changing use patterns. Initially, many of us argued that programming was an excellent pedagogic device for teaching engineering concepts. This view turned out to be too limited: the effort to craft a program embodying a concept, say, in statics, turned out to be counterproductive to learning the concept. While there was a preponderance of engineer-programmers, procedural programming was a skill needed for practice. Today productivity tools such as spreadsheets and equation solvers, courseware, and an array of commercial software are all available to support and augment a student's coursework. There is actually a concern about students' overdependence on such tools. In today's environment the educational value of a procedural programming course for all engineering students is being questioned. Nevertheless, in today's curriculum dominated by analysis courses, the design of a program provides one of the few opportunities for students to synthesize an artefact.

How should engineering education respond to the stratification in engineering computing? For the two smaller strata, several universities provide specialized graduate-level tracks. These two strata appear to be adequately served: as a fraction of the total number of graduates in engineering, the number of graduates on these tracks appears to be roughly in proportion to the fraction of the two strata in the engineering population at large. But there is no consensus on the educational foundations in computing needed by all students.

In this book, Raphael and Smith provide an innovative proposal: they present a carefully selected, well-integrated set of topics that constitute the core of computer-aided engineering, presented at a level suitable for engineering undergraduates. Many of the chapters in the book correspond to one or more courses in computer science, but this should not to be seen as making the book shallow. On the contrary, the contents of the book reflect its multiple purposes: for future users of computing aids and for casual programmers, it is intended to provide self-sufficiency in the basics of computing and self-confidence in the use of their software; for future IT and commercial software development staff, it provides motivation and structure for further study; and for current practitioners it offers a means of self-study.

The authors have been careful to choose topics that will retain their relevance for some time, and which will not age prematurely. Will the book hold up to the future and have a reasonably long shelf life? Over the years, I have repeatedly demonstrated that I am not a reliable forecaster of computing trends. However, it is clear that there will be many further innovations in information technology and in software, and that engineers will continue to adapt and exploit these new developments. At the same time, entirely novel engineering applications of computing are to be expected. If anything, the rate of change will accelerate further. The topics included in this book have demonstrated their applicability and longevity over many previous changes, and can be expected to provide the basis for further developments as well. The science base of computer-aided engineering is likely to continue growing by spawning sub-disciplines, as has already been demonstrated by topics in the book such as database theory and computational geometry.

The net result will be the progressive deepening of the topics presented, rather than the addition of brand-new topics.

There is one aspect of computing that I can predict with reasonable certainty. For the largest stratum of engineers, very substantial changes in human–computer interaction, visual programming tools, a host of other support disciplines, and in the nature of engineering practice will have to occur before there can be a large-scale return from the engineer-user of today to the engineer-programmer of the past. Until these changes occur, if they ever do, I expect this book to provide the essentials of computer-aided engineering. I recommend the book to all future and present engineers and to their teachers.

It has been a pleasurable and informative experience to review early drafts of this book. I acknowledge Carnegie Mellon University and the National Institute for Standards and Technology for allowing me the time to do this, and the staff of the Swiss Federal Institute of Technology, Lausanne, for hosting me.

Steven J. Fenves
Lausanne, Switzerland
May 2002

Preface

What makes computer-aided-engineering software a good return on investment? This is a more difficult question to answer than it seems; astonishingly, not many practising engineers have given it much consideration. The term 'engineering software' is used in this book to include commercial software as well as software that is developed by engineers at their place of work to do specific tasks. Let us briefly evaluate the returns on investment that are currently observed by practising engineers for both types of engineering software.

In-house engineering software is often written by engineers who have little or no formal training in computer science. Furthermore, development of this software often finishes before they acquire an adequate understanding of the task. Under such circumstances, software usually works correctly for a short time only and only in the presence of its developers. When developers leave the organization, utilization drops and new people have to start again. Even if key people are still present, changes in requirements may make software obsolete and difficult to revise. Such software rarely provides a good return on investment. Over the past decades, redevelopment of software has been repeated countless times in engineering firms and industries at a tremendous cost.

The use of commercial software packages is commonplace in engineering practice. University educators also employ software packages to support teaching of concepts and practical aspects related to topics such as analysis, drafting and design. Learning to use engineering software is seldom easy and often exacerbated by regular releases of new versions. What is the best software package to use for a given task? Why is one package better than others? Which package is most likely to adapt to changing needs? Such questions are usually answered only by installing a trial version and testing it.

While these activities are essential, a more fundamental knowledge of software attributes does help to avoid costly mistakes. Poor application of commercial software can often be traced to a lack of understanding of the fundamentals of computer-aided engineering. When one considers the number of computer-aided engineering products that have been proposed over the years, it is easy to conclude that few commercial software products currently provide a positive return on investment, either in the classroom or in practice. Some practitioners have commented that the best investment they have ever experienced has provided only a marginally positive return on initial costs and operating expenses.

This situation is somewhat troubling. Many current engineering applications are defective and the understanding of fundamental concepts by users and commercial software developers is low. Nevertheless, the use of computers in engineering is growing exponentially. Advances are feeding an unstoppable trend, advances in areas such as internet applications, multimedia, computer-aided design, model-based diagnosis, autonomous computing, speech recognition and synthesis, adaptive control, wearable computing, concurrent engineering, robotics, computer vision and visualization, including augmented and virtual reality. Therefore, this situation may become even worse. Also, this list is hopelessly incomplete; there are many more areas that are contributing to a vast, multidimensional array of potentially useful software for engineers.

The objective of this book is to present fundamental computing concepts that have an impact on engineering tasks in all areas of traditional engineering. Here 'traditional' refers to those engineering areas that do not have a direct relationship with electrical and computing engineering. Examples in this book are drawn mostly from elementary engineering mechanics because this is common domain knowledge within a wide range of traditional engineering disciplines. Particular attention is given to aspects of fundamental computing that are independent of specific tasks. For those who wish to go further into individual topics, this book will clarify terminology and the basic concepts, making it easier to continue studying.

This book does not contain information related to programming languages and commercial software. It has no availability lists and product comparisons. The information that is expected to remain relevant for a long time, perhaps throughout a career. Also, the topics are presented according to the engineering context. For example, the chapter on knowledge systems does not cover knowledge acquisition and representation in detail since successful systems in engineering are developed by domain specialists who work with knowledge representations that are mostly predefined.

Raphael would like to thank the late C. S. Krishnamoorthy and S. Rajiv (Indian Institute of Technology, Madras) for introducing him to the field of computer-aided engineering and to B. Kumar (Glasgow Caledonian University) and I. MacLeod (University of Strathclyde) for many discussions that have contributed to the development of several themes in the book. He also gratefully acknowledges that the knowledge of software engineering practices he acquired while working at Infosys Technologies, Bangalore, has significantly influenced certain concepts.

Smith is indebted to several people who provided support over many years. M. A. Hirt and J.-C. Badoux originally placed their faith in several initial studies in the 1980s and helped obtain the first of many research contracts and industrial collaborations. In the early 1990s B. Faltings accepted Smith, coming from a traditional engineering field, into his laboratory in the Computer Science Department for a five-year period. That experience initiated some of the themes in this book. In particular, key concepts in Chapters 1, 2, 7 and 9 come from teaching and research activities carried out in collaboration with B. Faltings; some examples in Chapters 2 and 7 are taken from course notes. Finally, many insights came from collaboration with G. Schmitt (Swiss Federal Institute of Technology in Zurich) during ten years of projects.

The authors are grateful to several people who contributed directly and indirectly to this book. K. Shea (Cambridge University) contributed to the first set of lectures on these topics. S. Fenves (Carnegie Mellon University and US National Institute of Standards) reviewed most chapters and provided valuable comments. He also inspired some examples. A few examples and exercises were prepared by Y. Robert-Nicoud. T. Schumacher proofread chapters and also provided technical input. M. Jirasek contributed to concepts in Chapter 6. J.-L. Guignard prepared the final versions of all the figures. Many others at the Applied Mechanics and Computing Laboratory of the Swiss Federal Institute of Technology, Lausanne (EPFL) provided comments and suggestions.

The need for this book was identified after discussions with colleagues from around the world revealed that fundamental knowledge of important aspects of computing was hindering successful applications in traditional engineering fields. We would like to recognize the International Association for Bridge and Structural Engineering, the American Society of Civil Engineers and the European Group for Intelligent Computing in Engineering for organizing meetings where many of these discussions took place.

Benny Raphael and Ian F. C. Smith
EPFL, Lausanne
November 2002

1
Fundamental Logic and the Definition of Engineering Tasks

The success of computer software in engineering rarely depends on the performance of the hardware and the system-support software. Computer applications have to match engineering needs. Although the principal objective of this book is to introduce fundamental concepts of computing that are relevant to engineering tasks, it is essential to begin with the fundamental concepts of engineering that are relevant to computing. This is the objective of this first chapter and key concepts are described in the following sections.

1.1 THREE TYPES OF INFERENCE

From the perspective of fundamental logic, engineering reasoning is categorized into the following three types of inference: deduction, abduction and induction. The best way to understand inference types is through an example. Consider a bar of length L and area A that is fixed at one end and loaded at the other with a load Q (Figure 1.1).

From fundamental solid mechanics and assuming elastic behaviour, when a load Q is applied to a prismatic bar having a cross-sectional area A this bar deforms axially (elongates) by an amount $\delta = QL/AE$ where E is the Young's modulus of the material. Thus, for a given bar, we have the following items of information:

- two facts: Q and δ;
- one causal rule: if Q then δ.

A causal rule has the form *if cause then effect*. The difference between deduction, abduction and induction originates from what is given and what is inferred. *Deduction* begins with one fact Q and the causal rule. With these two items as given information, we infer that a deformation δ occurs. *Abduction* begins with the effect δ and the causal rule. Starting with these two items, we infer that a load Q is present. *Induction* begins with the two facts, Q and δ, and then infers the causal rule. Table 1.1 summarizes the important elements of these three types of inference.

Logically, deduction is the only legal inference type in an open world. The use of abduction and induction requires a closed-world hypothesis. A closed-world hypothesis

---

Fundamentals of Computer-Aided Engineering   B. Raphael and I. F. C. Smith
© 2003 John Wiley & Sons, Ltd   ISBNs: 0-471-48709-0 (HB); 0-471-48715-5 (PB)

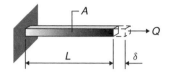

Figure 1.1   An axially loaded bar

Table 1.1   Three types of inference

Type of inference	Given information	Inferred information
Deduction	Cause and rule	Effect
Abduction	Effect and rule	Cause
Induction	Cause and effect	Rule

assumes that all facts and all rules are known for a given task. Such hypotheses are typically found at the beginning of mathematical proofs using statements such as 'for all $x \ldots$' and 'y is an element of $\ldots$'.

For illustration, refer to the example of the loaded bar. We can state with some confidence that if there is a load Q and when the causal rule *if Q then δ* is known, we can infer that a deformation δ is expected (deduction). However, when we know the rule and only that a deformation δ is observed, we cannot necessarily say in an open world that this deformation was caused by a load Q (abduction). For example, the deformation may have been caused by an increase in temperature. Similarly, just because we observe there is a load Q and a deformation δ, we cannot necessarily formulate the rule *if Q then δ* (induction). Other facts and contextual information may justify the formulation of another rule. Abduction and induction become valid inferences for the example only when we make the closed-world hypothesis that the only relevant items of information are the two facts and one rule.

Scientists and mathematicians frequently restrict themselves to closed worlds in order to identify in a formal manner kernel ideas related to particular phenomena. Also, the closed-world idea is not limited to research. Job definitions in factories, offices and many other places often only require decision making based on closed, well-defined worlds. However, engineers (as well as other professionals such as doctors and lawyers) are not allowed to operate only in closed worlds. Society expects engineers to identify creative solutions in open worlds. For example, engineers have to consider social, economic and political aspects of most of their key tasks before reaching decisions. Such aspects are difficult to define formally. Moreover, attempts to specify them explicitly, even partially, are hindered by environments where conditions change frequently.

Therefore, engineers must proceed carefully when they perform abductive and inductive tasks. Since a closed-world hypothesis is not possible for most of these tasks, any supporting software needs to account for this. For example, engineering software that supports abductive tasks has to allow for frequent user interaction in order to accommodate open-world information. This is the root of a fundamental difference between traditional computer software, such as those used for bookkeeping, and some tasks in computer-aided engineering (CAE). The next section will expand on this theme through providing a classification of engineering tasks according to their type of inference.

1.2   ENGINEERING TASKS

Among the important engineering tasks are simulation, diagnosis, synthesis and interpretation of information. All of these tasks transform one type of information to another through inference. Some more terminology is needed. In this discussion the word *structure* refers to information that is commonly represented in drawings, such as dimensions, location, topography and other spatial information, as well as properties of materials and environmental influences such as temperature, humidity and salinity of the air. This category also includes the magnitude, direction and position of all loading that is expected to be applied to the object. The word *behaviour* is used to include parameters that describe how the structure reacts, such as deformations, stresses, buckling, shrinkage, creep and corrosion.

In *simulation*, causes are applied to particular structures in order to observe effects (or more precisely, behaviour). For example a factory process is simulated to observe output and other aspects, such as sensitivity to breakdown of a machine. *Analysis* is a special case of simulation. Analysis is performed when behavioural parameters are required for a given physical configuration in a particular environment (the word 'structure' is used loosely to define this information). For example, bridges are analysed for various loading (such as wind, truck and earthquake) in order to determine behaviour that is expressed in terms of stresses and deflections. These transformations are summarized in Figure 1.2.

We can think of *diagnosis* as the reverse of simulation. For this task, observed effects are considered with the physical configuration and the environment to infer causes. For example, maintenance engineers observe the vibrations of motors in order to identify the most likely causes. Similarly, from an information viewpoint, *synthesis* is the reverse of analysis, where target behaviour is used to infer a physical configuration within an environment. For example, engineers design building structures to resist many types of loading in such a way that stresses and deflections do not exceed certain values.

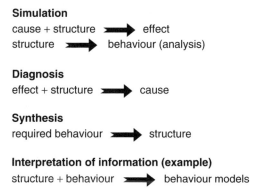

Simulation
cause + structure ➤ effect
structure ➤ behaviour (analysis)

Diagnosis
effect + structure ➤ cause

Synthesis
required behaviour ➤ structure

Interpretation of information (example)
structure + behaviour ➤ behaviour models

Figure 1.2   Four common engineering tasks. The arrows indicate transformation of information through inference

The *interpretation of information* includes a wide range of engineering activities. For example, interpretation of information refers to tasks that infer knowledge from activities such as load tests, commissioning procedures and laboratory experiments. Test results in the form of values of behavioural parameters are combined with known structure to infer models of behaviour. The form of the model may already be known; in such cases, testing is used for model calibration. For example, engineers test aircraft components in laboratories to improve knowledge of strength against fatigue cracking. These results are often used to improve models that predict behaviour of other components. Although such models are usually expressed in terms of formulas, they are transformable into causal rules, as in Figure 1.1.

Each arrow in Figure 1.2 refers to an inference process where the left-hand side is the input, and the right-hand side is the output. Reviewing the definitions for deduction, abduction and induction that are given in Section 1.1, a classification of engineering tasks in terms of inference types becomes possible. Since deduction begins with known causes and causal rules to infer effects, analysis and simulation are examples of deduction. Abduction begins with known effects and causal rules to infer causes, therefore diagnosis and synthesis are abductive inferences. Interpretation of information begins with known causes and known effects to infer causal rules (models of behaviour), therefore this task is an example of induction. Results are summarized in Table 1.2.

Therefore, important engineering tasks of diagnosis, synthesis and interpretation of information involve logical inferences that are not reliable in open worlds (abduction and induction). This result has a very important impact on requirements for software intended to support such tasks. This classification also provides clues to an explanation for the early success of analysis and simulation software. Nevertheless, it can be argued that engineering tasks which provide the greatest added value to society are mostly abductive and inductive. Therefore, the potential gain with appropriate computer-aided engineering support is correspondingly greater as well. It is just harder to do things correctly.

Indeed failure to recognize logical differences between engineering tasks has been a central reason for failures of software such as early artificial intelligence applications (expert systems) proposed during the last quarter of the last century. See Chapter 7 for further discussion. More generally, software applications that support abduction and induction in open worlds are much more sensitive to changing knowledge and contexts. Therefore, maintaining such software over long periods is more difficult than software that supports deduction.

Table 1.2 Engineering tasks classified into inference types

Engineering task	Inference type
Analysis	Deduction
Simulation	Deduction
Diagnosis	Abduction
Synthesis	Abduction
Interpretation of information	Induction

1.3   A MODEL OF INFORMATION AND TASKS

In Section 1.2 we explained that inference processes transform information from one type, such as structural information, to another type, such as behavioural information. How many types of information are there? What is the best way to organize engineering information so that we can obtain the most support from computer-aided engineering?

These questions have been the subject of much discussion. A framework that has been thoroughly discussed by CAE researchers and has stood the test of time is the function–behaviour–structure schema. In this schema, information is divided into the three categories that are part of its name. Information in the *function* category includes functional requirements such as design criteria, specifications, desires of society and purpose. The categories of *behaviour* and *structure* have been defined in the previous section.

The transformations associated with these categories of information have been collected into a schema that was initially proposed by Gero (1990). For the purpose of describing this schema systematically, a design example is used in the following discussion. Subsequent discussion demonstrates the importance of this schema for a range of engineering activities.

At the beginning of a design activity, engineers identify functional requirements for future objects through contacts with clients and meetings with other people that could influence design decisions. Engineers then transform these requirements into required behaviour. For example, the functional requirement of a building to provide safe shelter for its occupants leads to behaviour requirements related to strength and stability. Behaviour requirements are different from functional requirements because behavioural parameters are explicitly mentioned. Other requirements for occupant comfort lead to serviceability requirements such as maximum beam deflections. This transformation is a task called formulation and it is shown schematically in Figure 1.3.

In the second stage of design, parameters associated with the required behaviour, along with environmental parameters such as loading, are used to generate spatial information within the structure category. For example, the foundations and load-carrying elements of the building are chosen and sized during this stage. This transformation is called synthesis and is described schematically in Figure 1.4.

Once the as-designed structural information has been completed, the structure is then analysed to obtain predicted behaviour. In the building example, the structural configuration would be analysed to determine lateral deflections.[1] Such predicted behaviour is then compared during an evaluation with required behaviour. Analysis and comparison tasks are included in Figure 1.5.

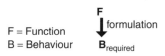

Figure 1.3   Formulation

---

[1] There is often more than one synthesis–analysis cycle. For example, once the element layout is determined and section properties are estimated for a building in a synthesis task, this may be analysed to determine bending moments which are then used to fix the cross-sectional dimensions of elements. This information is then used to reanalyse the structure to obtain values for additional behavioural parameters such as deflections.

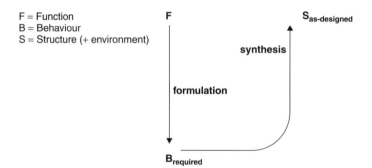

Figure 1.4   Synthesis added to Figure 1.3

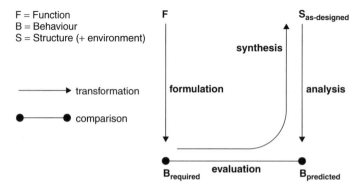

Figure 1.5   Analysis and evaluation

Results of the evaluation may lead to a new formulation or to new synthesis tasks and new analyses. These additional tasks are particularly likely if the evaluation reveals that predicted behaviour is unsatisfactory. For example, if predicted building deflections exceed the maximum deflections fixed during formulation, designers may reformulate the required behaviour, redo the synthesis so that the building is stiffened, or rework the analysis to provide a more accurate prediction. These three actions are often not equivalent in their ease of application and their effectiveness. For example, if the formulated requirements are parts of legal documents (such as building codes), reformulating required behaviour is not possible. Also, reworking the analysis may not provide the necessary correction to the calculations. The best course of action is usually to redo the synthesis step. If the designer is satisfied with the results of all the evaluations, the construction task is begun. Adding this to the schema results in Figure 1.6.

At this point, engineers are often motivated to question the applicability of two general assumptions. The first assumption is that the as-built structure is the same as the as-designed structure. Since structural information in this schema includes information related to the environment, including loading, such an assumption is notoriously risky. The second assumption is that the results of the analysis task are sufficiently accurate for the comparison with required behaviour. Accuracy implies other more specific assumptions related to material properties (e.g. homogeneity, isotropy, linear elastic behaviour), deflections and boundary conditions such as perfect pins and absolute fixity.

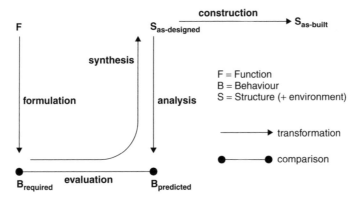

Figure 1.6   Adding the construction task

Often these two general assumptions are not acceptable. For example, engineering products are often not built exactly as they are designed: real loading may be very different from design loading; material may be non-homogeneous; deflections could lead to geometric non-linearities; finally, engineers know that all connections between elements are neither perfectly rigid nor perfectly free. Indeed the evaluation task in Figure 1.6 may seem dangerously far away from the as-built structural information in many practical situations.

When too much doubt surrounding these assumptions exists and when engineers determine that such uncertainties may have an important influence on subsequent decisions, the structure might be monitored. The monitoring task provides a third type of behaviour, measured behaviour, and this is compared with predictions from analysis to improve models as well as the accuracy of values of parameters that quantify environmental effects. Finally, more accurate structural information may be used to improve predictions of structural behaviour. These tasks are described in Figure 1.7.

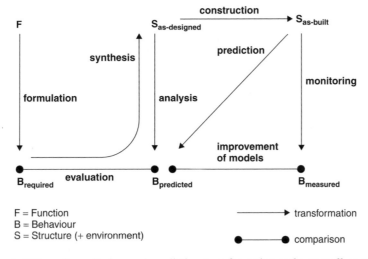

Figure 1.7   Addition of monitoring and prediction transformation tasks as well as an additional comparison task to improve models

Opportunities for increasing the details related to required behaviour, such as more specific constraints related to functional requirements arise when predicted values of behaviour are more reliable. Such activities are often known as performance-based engineering.

1.4 ANOTHER TASK DEFINITION

In 1960 Newell introduced another classification of tasks that accounts for how well tasks were defined.[2] Well-defined tasks are

- carried out in closed worlds;
- defined by goals explicitly and unambiguously expressed using, for example, a mathematical formula (this may be used as an objective function, see Chapter 8);
- described by algorithms that lead to identification of solutions.

Many engineering tasks are decomposed into well-defined tasks in order to simplify matters. This strategy is a common engineering tactic. When applied judiciously, reasonable solutions to complex tasks are possible. However, when simplification is not possible, engineering tasks are usually poorly defined. Poorly defined tasks occur when at least one of the following aspects is important to the nature of the solution:

- open-world conditions prevail;
- goals are defined only partially;
- definitions of solutions and their forms are incomplete;
- procedures for obtaining solutions are not known completely.

In reality, most engineering tasks are poorly defined. Accommodating such conditions while being able to perform useful tasks is the job of engineers. Requirements for software that support engineering tasks are subsequently more challenging for poorly defined tasks when compared with well-defined tasks.

1.5 THE FIVE ORDERS OF IGNORANCE

When tasks begin, engineers are often not able to appreciate every subtlety associated with aspects such as requirements, interdependencies, goals and contextual information. Armour (2000) believes that the core value-added activities are those of acquiring knowledge and reducing ignorance. While much discussion has centred on acquiring knowledge, little attention has been given to its corollary, reducing ignorance. Armour proposes a classification of ignorance into the following five orders:

- Zeroth-order ignorance (0OI) is *lack of ignorance*. This means that answers are available and skills for completing tasks exist. For example, most engineers know how to find the roots of a polynomial equation in one variable.

---

[2] Newell used the terms 'well structured' and 'ill structured' to classify tasks. For the purposes of avoiding ambiguity in terminology, the word 'structured' is replaced by the word 'defined' in this text. Also, for clarity, the word 'ill' is replaced by the word 'poorly'.

- First-order ignorance (1OI) is *lack of knowledge*. This shortfall is exactly quantifiable, tasks required to overcome it are known and skills exist to complete the tasks. For example, engineers who have learned one programming language can easily learn another and thereby satisfy their 1OI related to the new language.

- Second-order ignorance (2OI) is *lack of awareness*. This is when it is not known what is not known. For example, having 1OI and not knowing it is 2OI. Some engineers, thinking that computers are just big calculators, suffer from 2OI regarding the topics discussed in this book. They are not aware that computing is a science and not a skill.

- Third-order ignorance (3OI) is *lack of process*. This order occurs when it is not known how to go about finding out what is not known. For example, there are people who do not realize that going to university is the best way to find out what is not known (2OI) about important aspects of engineering knowledge and methodologies.

- Fourth-order ignorance (4OI) is *meta ignorance*. 4OI occurs when one is unaware of the other four orders of ignorance. If you have read and understood this far, then you no longer suffer from 4OI.

The first four orders have a generality that exceeds the boundaries of computer-aided engineering. Nevertheless, they are particularly pertinent for developing and using computer-aided engineering software. Engineers need mechanisms to identify and organize knowledge that is important for the task. Now that 4OI is no longer present, the goal of this book is to provide readers with capabilities to overcome 3OI, 2OI and 1OI when confronted with tasks that involve computers in engineering.

1.6 SUMMARY

- Inference is the basis of engineering reasoning.

- There are three types of inference: deduction, abduction and induction.

- Use of conclusions from abduction and induction implicitly requires a closed-world assumption.

- Engineers work in open worlds.

- Engineers deal with three categories of information: function, behaviour and structure.

- Many important engineering tasks involve the transformation of this information from one category to another.

- Although engineers are required to carry out well-defined and poorly defined tasks, the added value to society is usually greater when poorly defined tasks are successfully completed than when well-defined tasks are successfully completed.

- Development of engineering software is a process of information design and construction. This process involves setting up mechanisms where developers become able to discover the existence of information.

REFERENCES

Armour, P. G. 2000. The five orders of ignorance. *Communications of the ACM*, **43**, 10, 17–20.

Gero, J. S. 1990. Design prototypes: a knowledge representation schema for design. *AI Magazine*, **11**, 4, 26–48.

EXERCISES

1.1 Find an example of (a) deduction, (b) abduction and (c) induction in engineering.

1.2 For the abduction example in Exercise 1.1, formulate another causal rule that would make abduction ambiguous.

1.3 Identify two engineering tasks that would be hard to carry out with a closed-world hypothesis.

1.4 Should a computer give only one answer when supporting the engineering tasks identified in Exercise 1.3?

1.5 In Figure 1.7 which tasks are deductive, abductive and inductive?

1.6 Name three tasks that are well defined.

1.7 Name three tasks that are poorly defined.

1.8 Which tasks add the most value to society when performed successfully, well-defined tasks or poorly defined tasks?

2
Complexity

Complexity is a central theme in computer science and an important topic in computer-aided engineering (CAE). Indicators of complexity are used to determine whether or not, and if so how well, a task can be performed by a computer. The following three types of complexity are relevant:

- computational complexity;
- descriptive complexity;
- cognitive complexity.

Computational complexity is of interest for well-defined tasks (Chapter 1) when the goal is to find a solution efficiently. Although efficiency can be measured in terms of use of memory and hardware resources, algorithms are traditionally classified according to factors that influence trends in execution time. Such trends are generally independent of hardware characteristics.

Descriptive complexity classifies levels of difficulty associated with providing descriptive structures to information. While much engineering information can be assigned descriptive structures without difficulty (Chapter 3), it is often not easy to describe and classify information describing things such as music, paintings, economic climate and parameters related to politics. Complex engineering tasks also involve descriptive complexity challenges. For example, engineering product and process models have been standardized for only a few subdomains. The descriptive complexity of the remainder is too great to allow standardization.

Cognitive complexity metrics classify difficulties related to describing and simulating human thought for various activities. For example, the ease of simulating many tasks performed by bank tellers is demonstrated by the increased use of machines by clients wishing to perform transactions. On the other hand, tasks performed by professionals such as those in medicine, law and engineering are not easily simulated. Although this is partly due to the 'open world' characteristics of their tasks (Chapter 1), professional people are required to consider aspects such as multiple criteria, complex constraints and highly coupled parameters within environments that are changing and difficult to predict. The cognitive complexity associated with such professional activity is high.

This chapter describes fundamental concepts of the first type of complexity only – computational complexity. The other two types of complexity do not yet have fixed and generally accepted classification schemas. Nevertheless, they are both important areas of computer science and many aspects are important to engineers.

Fundamentals of Computer-Aided Engineering   B. Raphael and I. F. C. Smith
© 2003 John Wiley & Sons, Ltd   ISBNs: 0-471-48709-0 (HB); 0-471-48715-5 (PB)

This chapter uses a standard notation called the 'big oh' notation to represent trends in execution time with respect to changes in task parameters. Through the use of examples, it is demonstrated that a small change in an engineering task can result in important changes in computational complexity. The final section identifies a category of hard tasks and describes a fundamental research problem that is yet to be solved.

2.1 PROGRAM EXECUTION TIME VERSUS TASK SIZE

The execution time of a program depends on factors such as task formulation, desired results, algorithm optimality, hardware capacity and operating environment. The first factor is important; a task may be modelled in an unnecessarily complex way resulting in inefficiency. As will be seen in this chapter, results might not be possible within a lifetime whereas by using a better algorithm a solution could be found within seconds. For example, several algorithms exist for general tasks such as the sorting of numbers. Some are very efficient, while the time taken by others could be several orders of magnitude higher. The most important hardware characteristic that influences execution time is the clock speed of the computer. Other characteristics are available memory, the number of central processors (CPUs) and disk access rate. The operating environment may also affect a program's execution time. For example, if every piece of data required by the program needs to be downloaded over the network, input and output operations might consume most of the time.

The relationships between most of these factors and execution time cannot be quantified or expressed in mathematical equations. Moreover, their effects are likely to change with inevitable improvements in hardware and software. However, there is one factor that is likely to remain constant. This factor is the *relative influence* of the size of input and the time taken for the algorithm to terminate. In other words, *trends* in execution time with respect to the size of the task as modelled by the algorithm are largely independent of the technology employed. Certain problems are inherently complex. No amount of improvement in hardware and software is able to reduce the complexity. The following examples provide a qualitative understanding of the relationship between the size of the task and the execution time of a program.

2.1.1 Estimating the Execution Time of a Program

A standard task of minimization is considered here to illustrate the influence of the size of the task and the execution time of a program. The function chosen here is *Griewank's function*, which is used to test the performance of optimization algorithms described in Chapter 8. The model of the task is stated as follows.

Given the function $F(x) = 1 + x^2/4000 - \cos x$, find the value of x in the range $[-10,10]$ such that the value of $F(x)$ is the minimum. To avoid an infinite number of points in the range, we shall assume that x takes only 21 discrete values at regular intervals within the specified range.

The function is plotted on a grid consisting of 21 points (20 intervals) in Figure 2.1. The global minimum is at $x = 0.0$. Other local minima differ by a small amount. In

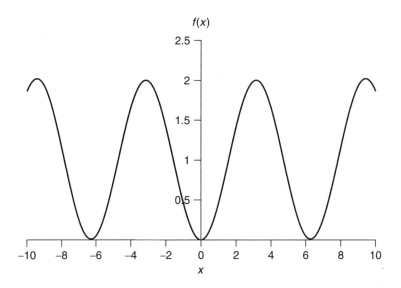

Figure 2.1   Griewank's function in a single variable

one dimension the solution is easily found by evaluating all the points and selecting the minimum. The global minimum is approximated by evaluating 21 points. The general form of Griewank's function for n dimensions is

$$f(x_{i|i=1,N}) = 1 + \sum_{i=1}^{N} \frac{x_i^2}{4000} - \prod_{i=1}^{N} \cos(x_i/\sqrt{i}) \qquad (2.1)$$

In two dimensions the function is

$$f(x_1, x_2) = 1 + \frac{x_1^2}{4000} + \frac{x_2^2}{4000} - \cos(x_1)\cos(x_2/\sqrt{2}) \qquad (2.2)$$

Here the grid consists of 21×21 points. A total of 441 evaluations are required to find the minimum. In three dimensions the function is

$$f(x_1, x_2, x_3) = 1 + \frac{x_1^2}{4000} + \frac{x_2^2}{4000} + \frac{x_3^2}{4000} - \cos(x_1)\cos(x_2/\sqrt{2})\cos(x_3/\sqrt{3}) \qquad (2.3)$$

Here the grid consists of $21 \times 21 \times 21$ points. Generalizing, 21^n evaluations are required to find the minimum of the function in n dimensions. The number of evaluations required for completing the task with 8 variables is more than 1 billion. Assuming it is possible to perform 1 billion floating-point operations per second, this problem would require more than a century to complete the task for 15 variables.

Discussion   *We conclude from this example that the execution time for finding the minimum value of a function in n variables using the method of evaluating all the points on a grid of fixed size increases exponentially with respect to the number of variables. Hence this approach cannot be used in practical engineering tasks. However, better algorithms* *exist for certain cases. For example, the partial derivatives of the function may be set to zero, and in special cases they may be solved directly.*

2.2 'BIG OH' NOTATION

The relationship between the size of the task and the execution time is of fundamental importance in determining the feasibility of an algorithm. This relationship can be expressed in mathematical terms. Several schemes have been suggested, including this one proposed by Wilf (1986):

- little oh, o;
- big oh, O;
- theta, θ;
- asymptotic, $\sim$;
- omega, Ω.

These notations are used to express relationships between the size of input and the amount of computational resources required. Since the big oh notation is the most widely used for analysing computational complexity, it is described in more detail here.

The principal interest is how fast a function grows, rather than the actual values of the function. For example, the time taken to solve a problem with n variables is not very important here. Whether the time taken increases as fast as n or n^3 or 2^n is of greater interest since this determines how the algorithm scales up to tasks that involve greater values of n. This determines whether the algorithm is feasible for solving practical tasks, since most practical tasks involve large values of n.

2.2.1 Definition of the Big Oh Notation

Define $f(n) = O(g(n))$ if there exists a positive integer n_0, and a positive real number constant c such that

$$|f(n)| \leq c\ g(n)$$

$$\text{for all } n \geq n_0 \tag{2.4}$$

In the context of analysing computational complexity, n represents the task size (positive integer); $f(n)$ is the amount of computational resource required (execution time) and $g(n)$ is a reference function to compare the rate of growth of $f(n)$. $f(n)$ is called the real function and $g(n)$ the reference function. The big oh notation provides an indication of the order of magnitude of the computational resources required to carry out the task.

For example, consider a polynomial function

$$f(n) = 4n^2 + 4n + 1$$

We can say that $f(n) = O(n^2)$ because for all $n \geq 1$ there exists a positive real number constant, here $c = 9$, such that

$$|f(n)| \leq 9n^2 \tag{2.5}$$

To verify this result, we proceed as follows. For $n \geq 1$ the left-hand side (LHS) of (2.5) is positive, hence we may drop the absolute value symbol and write the expression to be proven as

$$4n^2 + 4n + 1 \leq 9n^2$$
$$(2n + 1)^2 \leq (3n)^2 \quad \text{(using algebraic expansion)}$$
$$2n + 1 \leq 3n \quad \text{(since both sides are positive)}$$
$$1 \leq n \quad \text{(subtracting } 2n \text{ from both sides)}$$

This inequality is valid for all $n \geq 1$, hence (2.5) is verified. This is generalized in Section 2.2.2.1.

By using the big oh notation, we omit many details of the function and concentrate on the orders of magnitude of values. Also, we are not interested in specific *values* of c and n_0, provided these values exist. Omitting these details allows classification of the level of complexity of an algorithm into categories such as linear, polynomial and exponential. This classification is described in more detail in Section 2.2.3.

2.2.2   Big Oh and Tightness of Bound

A constant a is said to be the *upper bound* of a function $f(x)$ if the value of the function is not greater than a for all values of x in a given range. The term *tightness* refers to how close the upper bound is to the maximum of the function. A function $g(x)$ is said to be an upper bound of $f(x)$ if for all x in the specified range, $g(x) > f(x)$. A constant a is said to be the *lower bound* of a function $f(x)$ if the value of the function is never smaller than a for all values of x in a given range.

Upper and lower bounds of functions are estimated through mathematical analyses without finding the maximum and minimum of the function in a given range. (Finding the maximum of a function is a difficult task.) For example, consider the function $f(x) = x - x^3 + 5x^5$ in the range $(-1 < x < +1)$. A loose upper bound is found by taking the absolute value of the maximum of each term in the expression. That is,

$$f(x) = x - x^3 + 5x^5$$
$$\leq |x - x^3 + 5x^5| \quad \text{(since the expression may be negative)}$$
$$\leq |x| + |x^3| + |5x^5| \quad \text{(since } x \text{ may be negative)}$$
$$\leq \max(|x| + |x^3| + |5x^5|) \quad \text{(taking the maximum value of the expression)}$$
$$\leq \max(|x|) + \max(|x^3|) + \max(|5x^5|)$$
$$\leq 1 + 1 + 5 \times 1$$
$$\leq 7$$

Thus an estimate of the upper bound of the function is 7. The real maximum of the function in this range is 5. Through other procedures it is possible to find upper bounds that are closer to the real maximum.

2.2.2.1   Big oh and upper bound

The big oh notation provides an upper bound for a function's rate of growth. That is, the rate of growth is certain not to exceed a value. However, the definition of big oh does not place any restriction on how close the real function is to the reference function. The difference between the real function and the reference function is the tightness of the bound. For example, the linear function $f(n) = n$ may be written as $O(n^2)$ (a polynomial function) as well as $O(2^n)$ (an exponential function). However, for practical purposes, it is best to express O in terms of a function having the lowest possible rate of growth. That is, we are interested in a 'tight' upper bound. The following examples demonstrate important details in complexity analysis. Although these mathematical proofs can be skipped, their results should be noted since they are used later in this chapter.

Example 2.1

Show that the following relation holds:

$$n^q = O(n^{q+r}) \qquad (2.6)$$

where q, r are integers greater than or equal to zero.

Solution

Using inequality (2.4), we need to show that

$$|n^q| \le cn^{q+r} \qquad (2.7)$$

That is,

$|n^q| \le cn^q n^r$

$\quad n^q \le cn^q n^r \qquad$ (since the LHS is always positive)

$\qquad 1 \le cn^r \qquad$ (dividing by n^q, since n^q is always positive and non-zero for $n > 0$)

If c is arbitrarily chosen to be greater than 1, this relation is always true for $n \ge 1$. Hence the verification is complete.

Using equation (2.6), the following big oh notations are valid:

- $1 = O(n)$, $\qquad (q = 0, r = 1)$
- $n = O(n)$ $\qquad (q = 1, r = 0)$
- $n = O(n^2)$ $\qquad (q = 1, r = 1)$
- $n = O(n^3)$ $\qquad (q = 1, r = 2)$
- $n^2 = O(n^{10})$ $\qquad (q = 2, r = 8)$

Discussion   *This example demonstrates that a polynomial of a lower degree can be written as big oh of a polynomial of higher degree. That is, big oh notation does not provide any indication about how close the rate of growth of the function is to the reference function.*

Example 2.2

Show that for a polynomial of degree q,

$$P^q(n) = O(n^q) \tag{2.8}$$

Solution

$P^q(n)$ can be written in its general form as

$$a_0 + a_1 n + a_2 n^2 + \cdots + a_q n^q \tag{2.9}$$

Using inequality (2.4), we need to show that

$$|p^q(n)| \le cn^q \tag{2.10}$$

That is,

$$|a_0 + a_1 n + a_2 n^2 + \cdots + a_q n^q| \le cn^q \tag{2.11}$$

Examine the LHS of this inequality

$$|a_0 + a_1 n + a_2 n^2 + \cdots + a_q n^q|$$
$$\le |a_0| + |a_1 n| + |a_2 n^2| + \cdots + |a_q n^q|$$

(since some of the a_i could be negative)

$$\le |a_0| + |a_1| n + |a_2| n^2 + \cdots + |a_q| n^q \quad \text{(since } n \text{ is positive)}$$
$$\le |a_0| n^q + |a_1| n^q + |a_2| n^q + \cdots + |a_q| n^q$$

(since $|a_0| \le |a_0| n^q$, $\quad |a_1| n \le |a_1| n^q$, etc., for all $n \ge 1$)

$$\le (|a_0| + |a_1| + |a_2| + \cdots + |a_q|) n^q \quad \text{(taking out common factors)}$$
$$\le cn^q \quad \text{where } c = |a_0| + |a_1| + |a_2| + \cdots + |a_q|$$

Hence equation (2.10) is verified. Using this equation the following big oh notations are valid:

- $2.5x = O(x)$
- $x^2 + 4x + 2 = O(x^2)$
- $125x^5 + 22.2 = O(x^5)$

Discussion   *Complexity analysis is simplified by using a single-term expression instead of a complex polynomial expression.*

Example 2.3

Show that the following relation holds:

$$n^q = O(a^n) \text{ where } q > 1 \text{ and } a > 1 \tag{2.12}$$

Solution

Using inequality (2.4), we need to show that

$$|n^q| \le ca^n \tag{2.13}$$

Expanding the right-hand side (RHS) using the binomial theorem leads to an expression of a polynomial in n. This polynomial contains the term n^q, hence the expansion is greater than a constant times n^q. This is developed below.

Consider the factor a^n in the RHS of (2.13):

$$a^n = (1 + (a-1))^n = 1 + C_1^n(a-1) + C_2^n(a-1)^2 + \cdots + C_n^n(a-1)^n$$

where C_1^n, C_2^n, etc., are binomial coefficients. For $n > 2q$ the expansion contains the term $P^q(n)$, where

$$P^q(n) = C_q^n(a-1)^q$$

This is a polynomial in n of degree q. Since all the terms in the binomial expansion are positive for $a > 1$,

$$
\begin{aligned}
a^n &> P^q(n) \\
&> C_q^n(a-1)^q \tag{2.14} \\
&> C_q^n c_2 \quad \text{(where c_2 is a positive constant)}
\end{aligned}
$$

Consider C_q^n:

$$C_q^n = n(n-1)\cdots(n-q+1)/q!$$

There are q factors in the above expression and all are greater than or equal to $(n-q+1)$. So

$$
\begin{aligned}
C_q^n &> \frac{(n-q+1)^q}{q!} \\
&> \left(1 - \frac{q-1}{n}\right)^q \frac{n^q}{q!} \quad \text{(dividing by n and taking out n^q)} \\
&> c_1 n^q \text{ for all } n > n_0 \tag{2.15}
\end{aligned}
$$

where c_1 is any arbitrarily chosen positive real number less than 1, n_0 can be evaluated using the relation

$$\left(1 - \frac{q-1}{n}\right)^q \frac{1}{q!} > c_1$$

That is,

$$n > \frac{q-1}{1 - (c_1 q!)^{1/q}} \quad \text{(by rearranging the terms)}$$

Combining (2.14) and (2.15),

$$a^n > c_1 c_2 n^q$$

or by reversing the inequality,

$$n^q \leq ca^n \quad \text{where } c = 1/c_1 c_2$$

$$\Rightarrow |n^q| \leq ca^n \quad \text{(since } n \text{ is positive)}$$

Hence (2.13) is verified. With this equation, the following expressions are valid:

- $n = O(2^n)$ $(a = 2, q = 1)$
- $n^2 = O(2^n)$ $(a = 2, q = 2)$
- $n^{25} = O(2^n)$ $(a = 2, q = 25)$
- $n^5 = O(300^n)$ $(a = 300, q = 5)$

Discussion   *This example demonstrates that an exponential relationship is an upper bound to all polynomial relationships. An exponential function grows much faster than a polynomial function; nevertheless, we may write a polynomial function as the big oh of an exponential function. This illustrates that the big oh notation does not provide any indication about the tightness of the bound.*

Example 2.4

Show that for a real number $a > 0$,

$$n^q + a^n = O(a^n) \tag{2.16}$$

Solution

Using inequality (2.4), we need to show that

$$|n^q + a^n| \leq ca^n \tag{2.17}$$

The LHS can be written as

$$|n^q + a^n| = |n^q| + |a^n| \quad \text{(since both terms are positive)}$$

$$\leq c_1 a^n + a^n \quad \text{(from 2.13)}$$

$$\leq (c_1 + 1)a^n \quad \text{(taking out the common factor)}$$

$$\leq ca^n \quad \text{(where } c = c_1 + 1)$$

Hence (2.17) is verified. With this inequality, the following expressions are valid:

- $2^n + n^2 = O(2^n)$
- $2^n + n^{23} = O(2^n)$
- $5^n + n^4 + 3n^2 = O(5^n)$

Discussion   *The sum of an exponential function and a polynomial is big oh of an exponential function.*

2.2.3 Classification of Functions

The big oh notation provides an indication of the trend of increasing time taken by an algorithm as the size n of the task increases, hence it is used to classify the complexity of the algorithm. The following classification is useful to denote the way an algorithm scales up with increasing values of n:

- logarithmic, $O(\log n)$;
- linear, $O(n)$;
- polynomial, $O(n^q)$;
- exponential, $O(a^n)$;
- factorial, $O(n!)$;
- double exponential, $O(n^n)$.

The growth rates of these functions are shown in Figure 2.2. A logarithmic function remains almost constant for large task sizes. The practical implication of this is that after a certain value of n, the time taken remains almost constant. This behaviour is exploited extensively in many successful software applications. The rate of growth (derivative) of a linear function is constant, hence linear algorithms lead to solutions for many practical tasks. The rate of growth of polynomial functions increases with the degree of the polynomial. An algorithm that provides answers in a lower-degree polynomial function is better than an algorithm in a higher-degree polynomial. Exponential and factorial algorithms are not usually feasible for practical tasks.

A task that permits the use of a reasonable or polynomial-time algorithm is said to be tractable. If the formulation of a task permits only the use of algorithms of exponential complexity or higher, the task formulation is called intractable. There are many engineering task formulations that are considered to be intractable. There are others that are considered to be tractable and for which very efficient algorithms have already been found. Examples of both categories are described in the following sections.

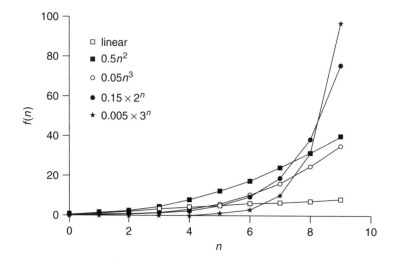

Figure 2.2 Growth rate of functions

2.2.4 Examples

2.2.4.1 Binary search

Searching for an item in a list is a common task in engineering and non-engineering contexts. We search for information such as telephone numbers in directories, addresses in Yellow Pages, book titles in library catalogues, etc. From experience, we know that searching in an ordered list is much simpler than searching in an unordered list. In this example it will be shown that the task of searching in an ordered list has the tightest complexity of $O(\log n)$, where n is the number of items in the list. Searching in an unordered list has complexity $O(n)$ (Section 2.2.4.2).

Consider an ordered list (sorted in ascending order) as shown in Figure 2.3. Suppose we are interested in finding out whether the number 65 exists in the list. The binary search algorithm works as follows. Compare the number against the one in the middle of the list. Since there is an even number of elements in this list, take the last element in the first half of the list, i.e. the number 57 at position 10. Since 65 is greater than 57, we only need to search in the second half of the list. For the subsequent search, we consider the list as consisting of only elements from positions 11 to 20 (second half of the original list). The next comparison is made against the middle element of the new list, i.e. the number 79 at position 15. Since 65 is less than 79, the next list is selected as the elements in the first half of the current list, i.e. from positions 11 to 15. This procedure is continued until a single element remains in the list. All the comparisons required in this search are tabulated in Table 2.1. Only five comparisons are required to infer that the number does not exist in the list.

To analyse the complexity of the binary search algorithm, we need to count the number of comparisons required to find out whether the number exists in the list. Starting with a list size of n, we keep on dividing the list into two parts until we reach a list consisting of a single element. After the first division, there are $n/2$ elements in the new list; after the second division, $(n/2)/2$, and so on. After the ith division there are $n/2^i$ elements in

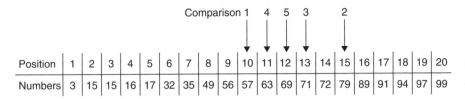

Figure 2.3 Binary search in an ordered list

Table 2.1 Comparisons required to search in an ordered list

Comparison	Position	Number	New list selected
1	10	57	11–20
2	15	79	11–15
3	13	71	11–12
4	11	63	12
5	12	69	–

the list. Therefore the number of divisions required to reach a list size of 1 is computed as follows:

$$\frac{n}{2^i} = 1$$

i.e. $n = 2^i$ or $i = \log_2 n$

This is the number of comparisons required in the worst case. Therefore the algorithm is $O(\log n)$. The base of the logarithm is omitted since the big oh does not change with the base of the logarithm. This is illustrated by the following equations:

$$\log_2(n) = \frac{\log_{10} n}{\log_{10} 2} = \frac{\log_{10} n}{0.301}$$

The logarithm to a different base differs only by a constant factor, which is not important in the big oh notation. The binary search algorithm is arguably the most important algorithm in computer science. It is used for tasks in most database applications, spell checking, graphics and constraint solving. Without binary search, it is doubtful that computers would be used as much as they are today.

2.2.4.2   Searching in an unordered list

Suppose the list in the previous example were unordered, then it would not be possible to perform a binary search and it would be necessary to compare each and every element in the list. In the worst case, n comparisons are required, where n is the size of the list. This algorithm has complexity $O(n)$. The time required to search for a number increases linearly with the size of the list.

2.2.4.3   Solving a system of linear equations

Solving a system of linear equations is a common task in numerical analysis and other types of simulation. Gaussian elimination is a standard technique to solve a system of linear equations. To illustrate this method, consider the following system of equations:

$$3x + 2y + z = 6 \tag{1}$$

$$x + 2y + z = 4 \tag{2}$$

$$x + y + 2z = 4 \tag{3}$$

The term containing the variable x in equations (2) and (3) is eliminated by multiplying these equations by 3 and subtracting from equation (1). After this operation we have

$$4y + 2z = 6 \tag{4}$$

$$y + 5z = 6 \tag{5}$$

The term containing y in equation (5) is eliminated by multiplying the equation by 4 and subtracting it from equation (4). This yields

$$18z = 18 \tag{6}$$

$$z = 1 \tag{9}$$

Substituting (9) in (5) yields

$$y = 1 \tag{10}$$

Substituting (9) and (10) in (1) yields

$$x = 1 \tag{11}$$

The values of all variables are obtained. Generalizing this procedure, the algorithm for solving a set of simultaneous equations by the method of Gaussian elimination consists of two parts: (a) elimination of coefficients in equations (4) to (9) and (b) back substitution in equations (10) and (11). The general form of the method is described below.

Let n be the number of variables, let A be the $n \times n$ matrix containing the coefficients of all variables in the system of equations, let Y be the constants on the RHS of equations, let X be the array containing the values of the variables to be solved for. The equations can be written in matrix form as

$$A_{(n,n)}X_{(n,1)} = Y_{(n,1)}$$

Equations (3), (4) and (5) are written in this form as

$$\begin{bmatrix} 3 & 2 & 1 \\ 1 & 2 & 1 \\ 1 & 1 & 2 \end{bmatrix} \begin{bmatrix} x \\ y \\ z \end{bmatrix} = \begin{bmatrix} 6 \\ 4 \\ 4 \end{bmatrix} \tag{12}$$

In the first part of the algorithm (reduction or elimination of coefficients), the coefficients in the lower triangle of the matrix A are made zero. This is done by subtracting equations from one another after multiplying them by appropriate factors. At the end of this process, the last equation has only one variable and its value is determined directly. Using this procedure, equation (12) reduces to

$$\begin{bmatrix} 3 & 2 & 1 \\ 0 & 4 & 2 \\ 0 & 0 & 18 \end{bmatrix} \begin{bmatrix} x \\ y \\ z \end{bmatrix} = \begin{bmatrix} 6 \\ 6 \\ 18 \end{bmatrix}$$

In the second part of the algorithm, the variables that have already been solved for are substituted into other equations. This procedure starts from the last equation and continues to the top. Since all the coefficients below the diagonal are zero, there is at most one unknown variable in each equation and it is solved directly.

The procedure for the first part of the algorithm (elimination of coefficients) is given in the following pseudocode. The numbers down the left-hand side are line numbers.

```
1  Repeat for i = 1 to n-1 {                          This is the loop to eliminate
                                                           the coefficients of all
                                                           variables i
2    Repeat for j = (i+1) to n {                      This is the loop to subtract
                                                           jth equation from the ith
                                                           equation
3      Repeat for k = j to n {                        This is the loop to modify
                                                           all the coefficients A[j,k]
                                                           of the jth equation
4        A[j,k] = A[j,k]-A[i,k] * A[j,j]/A[i,i]       Modifying the coefficient
5      }                                               End of loop in k
6      Y[j] = Y[j] - Y[i] * A[j,j]/A[i,i]             Modifying the RHS of
                                                           equation j
7    }                                                 End of loop in j
8  }                                                   End of loop in i
```

To find the time taken to complete the process, it is necessary to count the number of computations involved. For simplicity we assume that the majority of the time is taken by floating-point operations, that is, the expressions in lines 4 and 6. Times taken for updating the counters in the loops are ignored. Since the number of times the inner loops are executed varies with the values of the counters in the outer loops, the expression for the exact number of computations is complex. However, an upper bound may be estimated by noting that the inner loops will not be repeated more than n times within each iteration of the outer loop. More specifically, in lines 2 and 3 the maximum number of repetitions occurs when i and j have the value 1. Thus line 4 will not be executed more than $n \times n \times n$ times. Similarly, line 6 will not be executed more than $n \times n$ times. Assuming that both statements take at most k seconds for computation, the total computation time will be less than $k \times (n \times n \times n + n \times n)$. This is $O(n^3)$ (from Example 2.2).

A similar analysis can be performed for the back substitution. It may be verified that the back substitution operation is $O(n^2)$. Thus the entire algorithm is $O(n^3)$, since adding a lower-order polynomial does not increase the order of the higher-order polynomial.

Gaussian elimination procedures having similar forms as described above were used within early numerical analysis programs. Subsequent generation of these programs increased efficiency through taking advantage of characteristics such as the presence of zeros in the coefficient matrix (equation 12). In the best case, when all non-diagonal coefficients are zero, the complexity is linear. Even though this case is unrealistic, banded matrices are common in engineering. In banded matrices, coefficients of the matrix far away from the diagonal are always zero. The term 'bandwidth of the matrix' refers to the maximum distance from the diagonal at which coefficients are non-zero. In the worst case, the bandwidth is the same as the dimension of the matrix and algorithms for solving the set of linear simultaneous equations are $O(n^3)$.

2.2.4.4 Assignment of tasks to workers

The first part of the example considered here involves a task allocation problem. The goal is to construct a brick wall with three workers. The following tasks are involved:

1. Bring bricks to site.
2. Prepare foundation.
3. Prepare mortar.
4. Bring bricks to where wall is to be built.
5. Build wall.
6. Finish wall.

Two sets of requirements will be considered to illustrate how different requirements change the nature of the task and its complexity. Here is the first set:

- A worker can only perform one task at a time.
- A task is only performed by one worker.
- All workers can perform all tasks.
- All tasks should start and finish at the times shown in Figure 2.4.

A solution is found by iterating over all tasks and assigning the first free worker to the current task. This is possible because all workers can perform all tasks. The final solution is shown in Table 2.2. The procedure for finding a solution is illustrated in Table 2.3.

To analyse the complexity of this procedure, it is enough to count the total number of options to be considered for allocating all tasks. For each task, we need to check a maximum of m workers for availability, hence the total number of options considered for n tasks is $m \times n$. This is linear with respect to n, hence the complexity is $O(n)$. The complexity with respect to the number of workers is also linear; that is, the time taken for task allocation increases linearly with respect to the number of workers and the number of tasks.

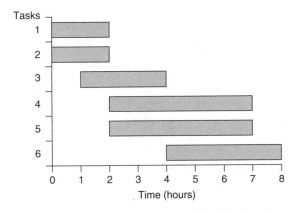

Figure 2.4   Required start and finish time for tasks

Table 2.2   Task allocation solution

Worker	Tasks
1	1, 4
2	2, 5
3	3, 6

Table 2.3   Task allocation procedure in the absence of constraints

Step	Task considered	Worker considered	Remarks	Worker assigned
1	1	1	free	1
2	2	1	not free	2
		2	free	
3	3	1	not free	3
		2	not free	
		3	free	
4	4	1	free	1
5	5	1	not free	2
		2	free	
6	6	1	not free	3
		2	not free	
		3	free	

Modified task allocation

Here is the same task allocation with a slightly different set of requirements. Instead of all workers being able to perform all tasks, workers can only perform specified tasks as given in Table 2.4.

Consider the design of an algorithm to find a solution; as before, we consider each task one by one. We assign the current task to the next free worker who is able to perform the task. If there is no free worker capable of carrying out the task, we backtrack and change the earlier assignment of tasks to workers. We need to do this because all workers are not equivalent and a different task assignment might result in freeing a worker who is capable of carrying out the current task. This procedure is illustrated in Table 2.5. The final solution is shown in Table 2.6.

To analyse the complexity of the procedure, it is necessary to compute the number of options that are considered in the worst case. In the worst case, we need to consider m workers for the first task followed by m workers for the next task, and so on. This happens when every decision has to be reversed through backtracking. Hence the total number of possibilities considered is $m \times m \times \cdots \times m = m^n$. This is an exponential function in n, therefore it has exponential complexity with respect to the number of tasks. Exponential complexity is frequently encountered in tasks that require backtracking. Note that the complexity is polynomial with respect to the number of workers for a given number of tasks.

If we assume that it takes 0.1 second to solve the problem for 6 tasks, we can evaluate the constant in the exponential relation and can show that it takes 2176 centuries to solve

Table 2.4   Tasks performed by workers

Worker	Title	Tasks
1	Foreman	1,2,4,5,6
2	Bricklaying specialist	1,3,6
3	Non-specialist	1,4,6

Table 2.5 The worker assignment procedure

Step	Task considered	Worker considered	Remarks	Worker assigned
1	1	1	free, capable	1
2	2	1	not free	none
		2	free, not capable	
		3	free, not capable	
			Backtrack to step 1	
3	1	2	free, capable	2
4	2	1	free, capable	1
5	3	1	not free	none
		2	not free	
		3	free, not capable	
			Backtrack to step 4	
6	2	2	not free	none
		3	free, not capable	
			Backtrack to step 3	
7	1	3	free, capable	3
8	2	1	free, capable	1
9	3	1	not free	2
		2	free, capable	
10	4	1	free, capable	1
11	5	1	not free	none
		2	not free	
		3	free, not capable	
			Backtrack to step 10	
12	4	2	not free	3
		3	free, capable	
13	5	1	free, capable	1
14	6	1	not free	2
		2	free, capable	

Table 2.6 Task allocation solution (constrained)

Worker	Tasks
1	2, 5
2	3, 6
3	1, 4

35 tasks. This happens in the worst case when every task assignment needs to be reversed until every combination of workers is considered for all tasks. A more powerful computer is not a practical solution; no increases in computing power are capable of counteracting an exponential function. According to Moore's law, processing power of computers doubles every 18 months. If this trend continues for 30 years, we might have computers that are a million times faster than today's. Even with computers that are a million times faster than today's, the time taken will be several centuries for 50 tasks (Table 2.7). Therefore, for large values of n, increasing the computation power does not help.

Table 2.7   Estimate of execution time

Number of tasks	Time	Time for a computer 10^6 times faster
6	0.1 s	10^{-7} s
10	8.1 s	10^{-6} s
15	32.8 min	0.002 s
20	5.5 days	0.5 s
25	3.7 years	1.9 min
30	9 centuries	7.9 h
35	2176.2 centuries	79.4 days
50		31 200 centuries

Is it possible to use a different algorithm in order to reduce the complexity? We may start with specialized tasks with maximum restrictions. In this example, tasks 1 and 5 can only be done by the foreman and task 3 can only be done by the bricklaying specialist (Table 2.4). Since we do not have any other options, we could assign these tasks to the corresponding workers first. Even with this simplification, the execution time is reduced by a factor that depends on specific characteristics of the problem. Let us assume that in the general case we are able to assign p tasks to workers without having to consider multiple options. We are still left with $(n - p)$ tasks to be assigned to m workers. The number of options to be considered in the worst case is m^{n-p}. The complexity of this procedure is $O(m^n)$ since

$$m^{n-p} = \frac{m^n}{m^p} = cm^n$$

where $c = 1/m^p$ is constant. In special cases p may be equal to n or $n - 1$, so the complexity is $O(\text{constant})$. Therefore this problem is often assigned a complexity of 'asymptotically' linear. While in the general case the algorithm is exponential with respect to the number of tasks, this example demonstrates that problem-specific information may reduce complexity. Use of such information is often referred to as heuristics. In this case the heuristic is to assign tasks first to workers that are most constrained.

Conclusions from this example

- Some problems are exponential; then it is not possible to find solutions in a reasonable amount of time.
- Increasing computer power does not help when the value of n is high.
- Presence of well-defined algorithms is not the only criterion for computability.
- Use of heuristics and other techniques that rely on problem-specific characteristics reduces complexity in certain cases.

2.2.4.5   Repair plan for a stretch of road

A certain stretch of road of length 3 kilometres needs to be repaired between 1000 and 1600 hours on a particular day. The repair has to be carried out in three stages of 2 hours each. During each stage, a 1 kilometre stretch of road is blocked from traffic. The indirect

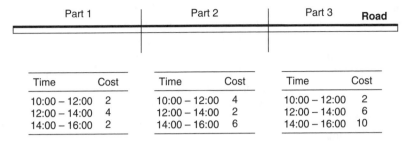

Figure 2.5 Indirect costs for closing down different parts of a road

Table 2.8 Indirect costs for each repair sequence. The numbers in the first column indicate the parts of the road that are repaired at 10:00, 12:00 and 14:00 hours

Sequence	Cost
1, 2, 3	$2 + 2 + 10 = 14$
1, 3, 2	$2 + 6 + 6 = 14$
2, 1, 3	$4 + 4 + 10 = 18$
2, 3, 1	$4 + 6 + 2 = 12$
3, 1, 2	$3 + 4 + 6 = 13$
3, 2, 1	$2 + 2 + 2 = 6$

costs of blocking traffic at different times of the day for each stretch of the road are given in Figure 2.5.

It is necessary to find the best sequence of repairs so that indirect costs are minimized. Since the size of the task is small, we enumerate all possibilities, evaluate them and select the best. This is shown in Table 2.8.

The optimal solution is the sequence 3, 2, 1; that is, part 3 of the road is repaired at 1000 hours, part 2 at 1200 hours and part 1 at 1400.

In the general case of finding the optimal repair sequence for n road parts, the number of possibilities is $n!$ (n factorial). This is because there are n possibilities for selecting the first part, $(n - 1)$ for the second part, and so on. Hence the complexity is $O(n!)$. Complexity of $O(n!)$ is higher than standard exponential algorithms. Its complexity lies between $O(a^n)$ and $O(n^n)$.

2.2.5 Tractability and Algorithm Optimality

When algorithms of different complexity are possible for the same task, the optimality of an algorithm becomes important. An algorithm is said to be optimal if the big oh of the task is equal to the big oh of the algorithm.

A method of proving the optimality of an algorithm is to estimate the lower bound of the complexity of the task through theoretical considerations. If we can rigorously prove that a solution cannot be found by any algorithm having complexity less than $O(g(n))$, we say $O(g(n))$ is the lower bound to the complexity of the task. For certain tasks, it has been possible to prove the existence of a lower bound. For example, theorems from graph theory (Chapter 3) have been used in establishing lower bounds. Hence it is possible to prove the optimality of an algorithm by showing that the order of the algorithm is equal to the best known lower bound. When lower bounds cannot be established, as in many problems, it is impossible to prove the optimality of algorithms. Then an important challenge is to show non-optimality through the identification of another algorithm having a lower order of complexity.

2.3 PRACTICAL METHODS FOR DETERMINING THE COMPLEXITY OF ALGORITHMS

An upper bound of the level of complexity is estimated by counting the number of elementary operations carried out for completing the algorithm in the worst-case scenario. Since we consider only the worst case, the actual time taken in specific cases might be much less. In searching a number in an unordered list (Section 2.2.4.2), the worst-case scenario involved comparing every number. In some cases the number might be found in the first comparison. However, when the number is at the end of the list, all numbers have to be compared, hence the algorithm is of type $O(n)$, where n is the number of elements in the list.

Counting the number of elementary operations is difficult in practice because it depends on the definition of elementary operations in a given model of computation and expressing each high-level operation in terms of elementary operations. For example, certain function calls may be considered to be elementary operations, while others are not. Simplifications are made to the analysis by concentrating on key control structures such as loops and recursive function calls. In Section 2.2.4.3 we counted the number of times the statement in the innermost loop was executed. All other operations were ignored.

Counting the number of computations is easy when there are nested loops containing simple arithmetic expressions. However, counting becomes more difficult when there are recursive function calls. Recursion is a common technique used in structured programming. Using this technique, complex operations may be performed with very few lines of code. Recursion is carried out by calling the same function within itself until the task is complete. Here is an example of a recursive function, the factorial:

```
1    Function factorial(n){
2        if n is equal to 1, return 1
3        else return n*factorial(n-1)
4    }
```

To understand how the function operates, consider the computation of 3 factorial. The function is called with a value of 3; that is, $n = 3$ when the function starts. In line 2 the `if` condition is not satisfied, and the `else` part in line 3 is executed. In line 3 the function calls itself (first recursive call) with the argument `(n-1)=2`. The factorial of 2 is computed in this recursive call. The value returned by this call is multiplied by 3 and the resulting number is returned by the function. The first recursive call to the function (with argument 2) internally results in another recursive call of the same function with argument 1 (second recursive call). The call with argument 1 returns the value 1 since the condition in line 2 is satisfied.

Many recursive functions have exponential complexity. However, the above function is $O(n)$. This may be established by carefully counting the number of operations. The function calls itself at most n times. Within each call, it performs at most one multiplication and one subtraction. By ignoring the time taken for other computations such as comparison, the total number of operations performed is $2n$. Thus, it has complexity $O(n)$.

Now we will consider another recursive function which indeed has double-exponential complexity. The objective of this function is to print all permutations of a set of symbols stored in an array A[n]. For example, let A contains the symbols {a,b,c}. The function should print the following:

1. abc
2. acb
3. bac
4. bca
5. cab
6. cba

An algorithm that carries out this task is shown in Figure 2.6. Let B be an array of dimension n representing the current sequence at any time. To start, B contains the symbols {a,b,c} representing the sequence *abc*. The recursive function printAll prints all permutations obtained by modifying the current sequence. The argument to this function is a parameter, startPosition, which signifies the position in the array B from which changes have to be made. Elements before startPosition are left unchanged and elements from startPosition on are permuted. If startPosition is 1, it modifies symbols at all positions in the sequence. If it is 2, it modifies symbols at all positions starting from 2, and so on. Here is the function printAll in pseudocode:

```
1      Function printAll (startPosition){
2          if startPosition is greater than n then {
3              the last position has been reached, nothing else to modify
4              print the sequence B
5              return
6          }
7
8          Repeat for j = 1 to n {
9              If A[j] is not present in B at a position less than
                   startPosition, then {
10                 B[startPosition] = A[j]; to assign the symbol at the
                       current position
11                 call printAll(startPosition+1); to change the rest of the
                       sequence
12             }
13         }
14     }
```

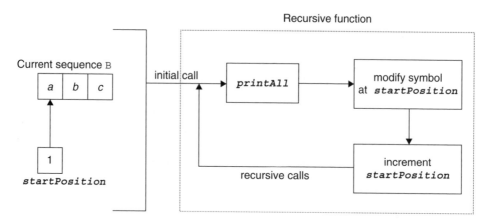

Figure 2.6   Illustration of a recursive function to print all permutations of a set of symbols. (All details are not shown)

The function is initially called with `startPosition` = 1. The condition in line 2 is not satisfied, hence it enters the loop beginning at line 8. In each iteration of this loop a different symbol is assigned to position 1 in the sequence B. In the first iteration of the loop, the symbol a is assigned to B[1]. After that, the same function is called again with `startPosition` = 2. In the second entry to the function, the loop at line 8 is executed once again. In the first iteration of this loop it checks whether the symbol a is already present in the sequence B. Since it is present, it continues with the next iteration without making any assignment. In the second iteration, the symbol b is assigned to B[2], and `printAll` is called a third time with `startPosition` = 3. In the third call, the symbol c is assigned to B[3], and `printAll` is called a fourth time with `startPosition` = 4. This time the condition in line 2 is satisfied and the sequence is printed. The events that happen upon each call to the `print-All` function are tabulated in Table 2.9 (iterations that do not result in any effects are not shown).

If the time taken for all operations except printing the sequence is ignored, the algorithm has factorial complexity since the number of sequences printed will be $n!$. However, if the time taken to perform the check in line 9 is significant, it becomes difficult to count the number of operations. Alternatively, we may compute a 'loose' upper bound by noting that the condition in line 9 will not be satisfied more than n times for each call to the function. Each time the condition is satisfied, the same function is called again and line 9 will be executed a maximum of n times. The maximum level of recursion is $n + 1$, since the recursion terminates when `startPosition` is greater than n. Thus the maximum number of times line 9 is executed is

$$n \times n \times n \times \cdots \times n = n^n$$

This function has double-exponential complexity. This example illustrates the difficulty in estimating the complexity of even simple recursive functions.

Table 2.9 Effects of different iterations in multiple calls to the function `printAll`

Call number				Argument (startPosition)	Iteration (j)	Effects
1				1	1	B[1]=a
	2			2	2	B[2]=b
		3		3	3	B[3]=c
			4	4	–	print abc
	2			2	3	B[2]=c
		5		3	2	B[3]=b
			6	4	–	print acb
1				1	2	B[1]=b
	7			2	1	B[2]=a
		8		3	3	B[3]=c
			9	4	–	print bac
	7			2	3	B[2]=c
		10		3	1	B[3]=a
			11	4	–	print bca
1				1	3	B[1]=c
	12			2	1	B[2]=a
		13		3	2	B[3]=b
			14	4	–	print cab
	12			2	2	B[2]=b
		15		3	1	B[3]=a
			16	4	–	print cba

2.4 P, NP AND NP-COMPLETENESS

It is useful to categorize problems into equivalence classes using criteria of complexity. Complexity criteria are applied to the generation of solutions and to the verification that the solution is valid. In the previous section we found that task allocation in the presence of constraints has exponential complexity. In fact, there are more than 1000 problems in computer science for which the best known algorithms have exponential complexity. They share the following characteristics:

- They all have exponential-time algorithms and none of them are known to have polynomial-time algorithms.

- No one has been able to prove that polynomial-time solutions are *not* possible.

- The best known lower bounds for execution are $O(n)$, meaning it is conceivable that they admit linear-time algorithms (even though no one has been able to find one).

- Their verification algorithms are polynomial.

- All problems can be transformed to each other in polynomial time. The implication of this is that if anyone is able to find a polynomial time solution to one problem, every problem in this set can be solved in polynomial time.

This class of problems is called NP-complete, or NP-C. NP stands for non-deterministic polynomial, in comparison with P (polynomial), the set of problems that can be solved in polynomial time. To find out whether a problem belongs to this class, we proceed as follows. We select a reference problem that is known to be NP-complete. For simplicity, a particular problem called ZOIP (zero-one integer programming) is chosen. This problem is described in Section 2.4.1. If we are able to transform the current problem into ZOIP and vice versa in polynomial time, the problem belongs to NP-C. Remember from Example 2.4 that adding a polynomial-time algorithm to an exponential algorithm does not modify its big oh complexity. Here is a formal definition of NP-C:

- A problem is NP-complete if it belongs to NP and is also NP-hard (defined below).
- A problem belongs to NP if it can be transformed to the ZOIP problem in polynomial time (Figure 2.7).
- A problem is NP-hard if the ZOIP problem can be transformed to it in polynomial time.

Relationships between the sets P, NP and NP-C are shown in Figure 2.8. Problems in P also belong to NP. That is because an easy problem can also be posed as a difficult problem. It is possible to transform a problem in P to ZOIP in polynomial time. However, it has not so far been possible to transform ZOIP to a problem in P. Hence problems in NP-C do not belong to P. Figure 2.8 does not show the category of algorithms that produce results which cannot be verified in polynomial time. Such algorithms are of interest in cryptography and other fields.

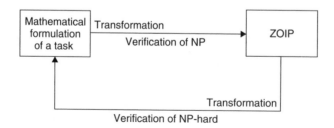

Figure 2.7   Verifying whether a problem (mathematical formulation of a task) belongs to NP-Complete. If a problem can be converted to ZOIP (upper arrow) it is a member of the class NP. If ZOIP can be converted into the problem (lower arrow), it belongs to the set of NP-hard. If a problem belongs to NP and NP-hard, it belongs to NP-Complete

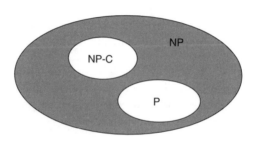

Figure 2.8   P, NP and NP-C

2.4.1   Zero-One Integer Programming Problem

2.4.1.1   Definition

Given the $m \times n$ matrix A, the constant vectors $\mathbf{b}$ and $\mathbf{c}$, and the vector $\mathbf{x}$ that contains the set of unknown variables, minimize $\mathbf{cx}$ subject to the set of m constraints

$$A\mathbf{x} = \mathbf{b} \tag{2.18}$$

such that each component of $\mathbf{x}$ takes on only the value 0 or 1. The function $\mathbf{cx}$ is known as the objective function.

2.4.1.2   Example

Minimize

$$2u - v + w \tag{2.19}$$

such that

$$u + v + w = 2 \tag{2.20}$$

where u, v and w take on only the values 0 or 1. This problem can be stated in the form given by equation (2.18). Minimize

$$\begin{bmatrix} 2 & -1 & 1 \end{bmatrix} \begin{bmatrix} u \\ v \\ w \end{bmatrix}$$

subject to

$$\begin{bmatrix} 1 & 1 & 1 \end{bmatrix} \begin{bmatrix} u \\ v \\ w \end{bmatrix} = [2]$$

Comparing with equation (2.18):

$$\mathbf{x} = \begin{bmatrix} u \\ v \\ w \end{bmatrix} \quad \mathbf{c} = \begin{bmatrix} 2 & -1 & 1 \end{bmatrix} \quad A = \begin{bmatrix} 1 & 1 & 1 \end{bmatrix} \quad \mathbf{b} = [2]$$

This example in three variables is solved quite easily. From equation (2.20) the only possible solutions are when one of the variables is zero and the others are 1. The objective function has the minimum value when the negative term, $-v$, is non-zero and the term with bigger positive coefficient, $2u$, is zero. Hence the solution is $v = w = 1$ and $u = 0$.

In the general case, equation (2.18) permits many combinations of values for the variables. Finding the optimum involves evaluating all possible combinations, hence the problem is exponential with respect to the number of variables. Formulations of many important tasks do not have closed-form solutions. Different permutations and combinations of values lead to a large number of possible solutions. In the worst case, all possible solutions have to be generated and evaluated with respect to the objective function and constraints. This observation provides an intuitive reason for the equivalence of ZOIP to other NP-C problems.

2.4.2 Classes of NP-complete Problems

Instances belonging to the NP-complete set are found in various branches of engineering and science. The following domains have many examples:

- graph Theory;
- design;
- modelling;
- sequencing and scheduling;
- mathematical programming;
- algebra and number theory;
- games and puzzles;
- non-monotonic logic;
- natural language processing;
- image recognition;
- optimization.

2.4.2.1 Current status and practical implications

The best known algorithms for all NP-complete problems have a complexity that is exponential with the problem size. We are unable to prove that an algorithm for an NP-complete problem is optimal. The best practical lower bound that we know for the NP-complete equivalence class is linear, but no one has found an algorithm in polynomial time that has solved an NP-complete problem for all input values. Since exponential-time algorithms are not suitable for practical engineering tasks, one or more of the following approaches are often adopted:

- use of heuristics;
- relaxation of requirements;
- careful choice of objects to be searched;
- guidance through user interaction.

The study of strategies for solving NP-complete problems is part of research in artificial intelligence (AI) and operations research (OR). These strategies have resulted in many successful engineering applications.

2.5 SUMMARY

- The big oh notation is useful for characterizing computational complexity.
- Levels of complexity include logarithmic, linear, polynomial, exponential and factorial.
- Problems having exponential and factorial complexity lead to excessive execution times for large problem sizes.
- Problems having a high computational complexity cannot be solved by using faster computers.

- Classifying problems as P, NP and NP-complete helps algorithm design and guides the use of approximate methods.
- Methodologies in operations research and artificial intelligence assist in finding solutions to NP and NP-complete problems

REFERENCE

Wilf, H. S. 1986. *Algorithms and Complexity*. Englewood Cliffs NJ: Prentice Hall.

FURTHER READING

Aho, A. and Ullman, J. 1992. *Foundations of Computer Science*. New York: W. H. Freeman.
Bertsimas, D. and Tsitsiklis, J. N. 1997. *Introduction to Linear Optimization*. Belmont MA: Athena Scientific.
Garey, M. and Johnson, D. 1979. *Computers and Intractability: A Guide to the Theory of NP-Completeness*. New York: W. H. Freeman.
Harel, D. 1987. *Algorithmics: The Spirit of Computing*. London: Addison-Wesley.

EXERCISES

2.1 A design task involves finding values for three variables. Each variable can take two values. How many solutions are possible? If each solution requires 1 second to be evaluated on a computer, how long does it take to evaluate all solutions? If the number of variables increases to 30, how long does it take to evaluate all solutions?

2.2 A mathematical problem involves finding values for N continuous variables such that a certain function (the objective function) is a minimum. The bounds of variables (minimum and maximum) of all variables are known. An algorithm for finding an optimal solution requires evaluation of all corner points of the domain (i.e. solutions containing the minimum or maximum values of all variables). What is the complexity of this algorithm?

   (a) $O(N)$
   (b) $O(N^2)$
   (b) $O(2^N)$
   (c) $O(N^N)$

2.3 Which of the following statements are true if n, a and b are positive constants such that $a > b$?

   (a) $n = O(n)$
   (b) $n = O(n^3)$
   (c) $n = O(a^n)$
   (d) $a^n = O(n^n)$
   (e) $n^n = O(n)$
   (f) $a^n = O(b^n)$
   (g) $n^2 + n = O(n^2)$
   (h) $a^n + n = O(n)$

(i) $a^n + b^n = O(a^n)$

(j) $n^3 - n^2 = O(n^2)$

(k) $n^4 - a^n = O(n^4)$

(l) $n^2 = O(2 \log n)$

(m) $\log n = O(n)$

2.4 Arrange the following functions according to their order of complexity. Indicate all functions that have the same order of complexity.

(a) $f(n) = 2000n$

(b) $f(n) = 2n^2 - 20\,000n$

(c) $f(n) = 2n^2 + 20\,000n$

(d) $f(n) = 2^n + n$

(e) $f(n) = 2^{2n}$

(f) $f(n) = 3^n$

(g) $f(n) = 2^n$

2.5 The bubble sort algorithm involves comparing adjacent elements in a list and swapping them if they are not in the correct order. For example, in the list (2,1,3) the numbers 2 and 1 are swapped since they are not in the correct order. This procedure is repeated till all adjacent elements are in the correct order. What is the complexity of this algorithm with respect to the number of elements in the list?

2.6 Look at the following pseudocode. What is the complexity of the algorithm with respect to n?

```
sum =0
repeat for i = 0 to n {
   repeat for j = 0 to 2 {
            repeat for k = 0 to n {
                    sum = sum+ a(i)*b(j)*c(k)
            }
   }
}
```

2.7 Which of these statements are true?

(a) If a problem can be converted to ZOIP in polynomial time, it belongs to the NP-complete set.

(b) ZOIP can be transformed into any problem belonging to the NP-complete set in polynomial time.

(c) If a problem X can be transformed to ZOIP and ZOIP can be transformed to X in polynomial time, then X belongs to NP-complete.

(d) A solution to any NP-complete problem may only be verified in exponential time.

2.8 A logistics task: rectangular boxes containing mechanical components need to be transported to a site. Every box has the same width and height (60 cm × 10 cm). Lengths of boxes vary from 10 cm to 60 cm. All boxes need to be packed into a large container of dimensions $60\,cm \times 60\,cm \times 60\,cm$. In a certain shipment the boxes have the following lengths L.

Box	B1	B2	B3	B4	B5	B6	B7	B8	B9	B10
L (cm)	40	60	30	10	5	10	40	40	30	30

How can the boxes be packed in the container? Any empty space within the container could be filled with packing material. Design an algorithm for handling the task for n boxes of variable lengths. What is the complexity of this algorithm (see Figure 2.9)?

2.9 For the task in Exercise 2.8, a new constraint is added: heavier boxes should not be placed over lighter boxes. The weight W of each box is as follows.

Box	B1	B2	B3	B4	B5	B6	B7	B8	B9	B10
W (kg)	9	9	8	1	1	10	7	6	1	1

Find an algorithm to arrange boxes in the container. What is the complexity of the new algorithm?

2.10 Consider the following variation of the task allocation example in Section 2.2.4.4. The goal is to construct a brick wall using three workers. The following tasks are involved:

1. Bring bricks to site.
2. Prepare foundation.
3. Prepare cement.
4. Bring bricks to wall.
5. Build wall.
6. Perform finishing tasks.

And these are the requirements:

- A worker can only perform one task at a time.
- All tasks should start and finish at the times shown in Figure 2.4.
- A task is only performed by at most two workers. If two workers carry out a task, the time taken is only half of that shown in Figure 2.4.
- All workers can perform all tasks.

What is the complexity of this problem with respect to the number of tasks?

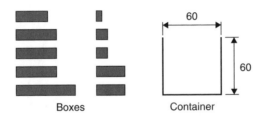

Boxes   Container

Figure 2.9   How can the boxes be packed in the container?

2.11 Show that $a^n = O(n!)$ and $n! = O(n^n)$. Hint: use the following inequality for the proof:

$$n! = n(n-1)(n-2)\cdots 1$$
$$\leq n \times n \times \cdots \times n \quad \text{(replacing } n-1, n-2, \text{ etc., by } n\text{)}.$$
$$\leq n^n$$

3
Data Structures

3.1 INTRODUCTION

The previous chapter focused on characteristics of algorithms that manipulate information; this chapter deals with possibilities available for representing information. We call such possibilities data structures. The identification of the most appropriate data structures is an important step in the development of every engineering application.

Data structures determine how efficiently information is treated in a program and therefore they may be important for determining computational complexity. Even if complexity is not affected by the choice of data structure, good data structures are easy to understand by users and lead, for example, to the development of good user interfaces. Also, well-designed data structures facilitate subsequent modifications and thereby help contribute to the robustness, maintenance and durability of computer-aided engineering (CAE) software.

In some engineering fields, work has concentrated on standardizing data structures. Data structure standardization helps contribute to better communication between engineers during complex engineering tasks. Such standardization also increases compatibility between software products. Increases in productivity that are linked to such efforts could result in better, faster and cheaper engineering activities.

This chapter presents and describes fundamental types of data structure. Knowledge of these types is important for understanding the material presented in subsequent chapters on object-oriented programming (Chapter 4), database concepts (Chapter 5), constraint-based reasoning (Chapter 7) and optimization and search (Chapter 8).

3.2 DEFINITIONS

The term 'data structure' refers to the organization of data within software applications. Properly organized data are easy to understand and maintain. Consider the list of variables shown in Figure 3.1(a). Compare it with the structured form of the same data shown in Figure 3.1(b). In structured form, logically related data are grouped together. Such structure helps understanding, thereby increasing the reliability of appropriate data use and modifications.

Data structures often involve hierarchies, called decomposition hierarchies, where data are organized into attributes of systems, components and sub-components. In this chapter the term 'object' will be used informally to refer to a collection of data organized into

Fundamentals of Computer-Aided Engineering   B. Raphael and I. F. C. Smith
© 2003 John Wiley & Sons, Ltd   ISBNs: 0-471-48709-0 (HB); 0-471-48715-5 (PB)

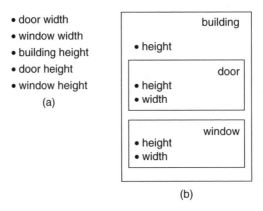

Figure 3.1   Data structures group related information together: (a) a flat list of unorganized data, (b) structured data

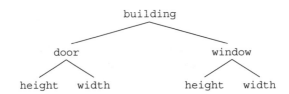

Figure 3.2   A partial decomposition of building information

attributes. The term 'attribute' is used in a generic sense to denote characteristic aspects of objects (properties) as well as components of objects. Thus an attribute might itself be an object consisting of sub-attributes. Figure 3.2 illustrates the decomposition of the data structure in Figure 3.1(b).

3.3   DERIVED DATA TYPES

Most programming languages support simple data types such as integers and real numbers; these are called basic or primitive data types. Earlier languages such as Fortran did not support grouping of primitive data types to create more complex data types. Such grouping of data is needed to represent data structures so there is a close correspondence between real objects and their representations in a programming language. For example, the object called Door in Figure 3.2 might be represented by a structure consisting of two primitive data types, height and width. Data types that are created by grouping primitive data types are called derived data types.

3.3.1   Examples of Derived Data Types

The difference between a basic data type and a derived data type depends on the programming language. What is considered to be a primitive data type in one language may not be primitive in another language. For example, arrays and strings are useful derived data types even though in some languages they may be considered to be basic data types.

3.3.1.1 Arrays

Arrays represent a collection of data of the same type. Arrays may be composed of integers, real numbers and character strings. Figure 3.3 illustrates the representation of an array. An array may be viewed as a piece of paper divided into a number of rows. Each data item is stored in a row. The size of each element (number of bits used to represent the data item) is constant. Each element has an index in the array. Indices are integers and they usually start from 0. It is common to have arrays of constant dimensions; that is, the maximum number of elements in the array is specified a priori and cannot be changed during the execution of a program. This is analogous to a piece of paper having a fixed size and hence containing a fixed number of rows. If the size of the data is known a priori, arrays can be used efficiently. However, in many situations the size of data changes dynamically. In such situations, abstract data types such as linked lists are more appropriate.

Operations on arrays

The most essential array operator is the subscript operator. The subscript operator is used to refer to a particular element in the array. The subscript operator is usually denoted by square brackets []. For an array variable myArray, myArray[0] refers to the first element, myArray[1] to the second element, and so on. The following assignments are applicable if myArray is an array of integers:

- myArray[0] = 3
- myArray[1] = 4

Use of arrays

Arrays are used when there are multiple data of the same type. Instead of having multiple variables to represent each data item, it is possible to have a single variable with variable

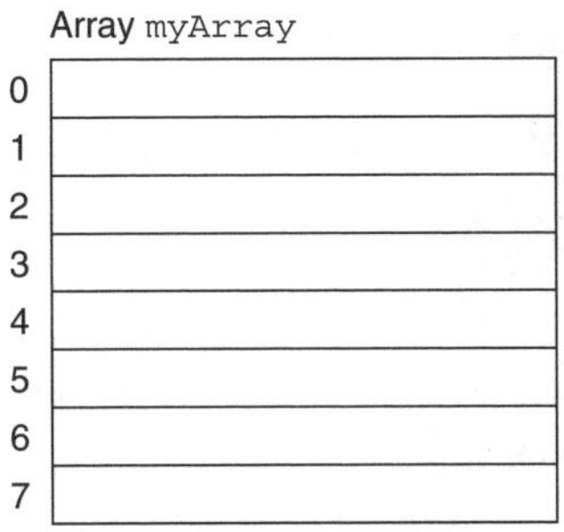

Figure 3.3 Illustration of an array. Each element of an array is referenced by an index that usually starts from zero

subscripts. Another important use is to repeat a set of computations for all elements of a set. For example, instructions to print all elements of an array x may be expressed as follows:

```
repeat for i = 0 to n {
    print x[i]
}
```

This code is more convenient than, for example,

```
print x0
print x1
print x2
print x3
    ⋮
print xn
```

3.3.1.2 Multidimensional arrays

Multidimensional arrays are the equivalent of matrices in mathematics. A two-dimensional array organizes data in the form of rows and columns. Arrays having more than two dimensions are difficult to visualize. They are best understood as arrays stored within arrays. This idea is illustrated by the following example.

An array Load stores the total load acting on the floor slab of each room in a two-storey building. The building consists of two identical blocks, with two rooms on each floor. Therefore, Load is defined as a three-dimensional array such that Load[i][j][k] refers to the load on the ith block, jth floor and kth room (Figure 3.4). Load[i] is a

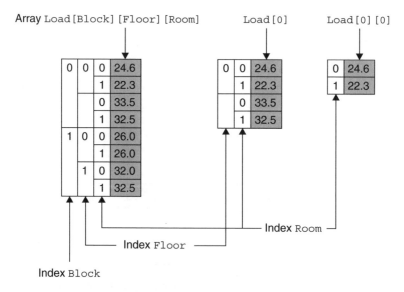

Figure 3.4 Viewing a multidimensional array as an array of arrays

two-dimensional array storing the loads in each room of the ith block. `Load[i][j]` is a one-dimensional array that stores the loads in each room of the ith block and jth floor. Multidimensional arrays help to organize data into groups that correspond to the semantics of the application.

3.3.1.3 Strings

A string is an array of characters and is usually enclosed within double quotes. `''A small string''`, `''A big string''`, etc., are examples of strings. Three common string operators are `substring`, `concatenate` and `length`:

- `substring` extracts a part of a string.
- `concatenate` combines two strings.
- `length` returns the number of characters in a string.

Strings play an important role in modern engineering applications. Conventionally, computers have been used in engineering applications mainly for manipulating numbers. However, computers are used effectively for tasks such as communication, collaboration, decision support, diagnosis, scheduling, control and design. These tasks involve reasoning with symbols (which have string representations) as well as numbers.

3.3.2 User-Defined Data Types

User-defined data types form the core of structured programming. New data types are defined by developers in order to represent the structure of entities more realistically. Attributes of such data types themselves might belong to user-defined types, resulting in a decomposition hierarchy as discussed earlier.

However, not all data structures have simple hierarchical decompositions such as those shown in Figure 3.2. Complex relationships might exist between parts of the data. Figure 3.5(a) is a representation of two rooms in a building. The representation of a room contains the following attributes:

- `wall1`
- `wall2`
- `wall3`
- `wall4`

The data structure of a wall includes attributes `wallType` and `thickness`. The decomposition hierarchy of the rooms in Figure 3.5(a) is shown in Figure 3.5(b). Wall `wall4` is shared between two rooms, `room1` and `room2`; therefore, both `room1` and `room2` share the same data. There is a link between attributes of two objects. In practical applications such links are common and they increase the complexity of data structures (this is representational complexity, not computational complexity).

A pointer or a reference data type is used in situations where an object is part of several objects. A pointer is a link to another object that is not directly contained within the parent object.

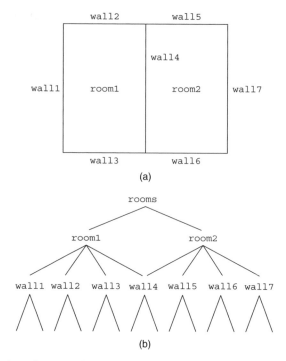

Figure 3.5 Illustration of a non-hierarchical decomposition: (a) plan of part of a building, (b) decomposition

3.4 ABSTRACT DATA TYPES

An *abstraction* is a generalization that involves removing detailed information. When sufficient amounts of detail are left out, groups of data possess similar structures. The term 'abstract data type' is used to refer to such data structures. Examples of abstract data types are

- linked lists;
- graphs;
- trees;
- stacks;
- queues.

Each abstract data type has a set of standard attributes. The operations performed on these data types are also standard. Standard operations performed on primitive data types such as numbers include addition, multiplication and division. Although these operations are not valid for abstract data types, their generality is comparable to operations performed on abstract data types. Table 3.1 gives some examples of operations on abstract data types.

An advantage of using abstract data types is that their operations are generic, therefore they may be reused for a variety of applications. Just as arithmetic operators are employed everywhere, operations on abstract data types may also be used in diverse situations. Another advantage is that it is possible to employ a standard terminology (vocabulary) to communicate between programmers and engineers. Engineers need to be

Table 3.1 Standard operations on abstract
data types

Abstract data type	Operations
Linked lists	Add, delete
Stacks	Push, pop
Queues	Enqueue, dequeue

familiar with the terminology and basic concepts that are related to data structures and abstract data types. With this knowledge they are in a better position to understand how data are organized in applications, therefore they are better able to communicate their requirements to computer specialists.

3.4.1 Linked Lists

The conventional data structure for storing a collection of objects is the array. But arrays have two drawbacks: (a) the array size is usually fixed a priori, and (b) inserting and deleting elements is difficult. The character array in Figure 3.6(a) represents the string ``engineer''. Suppose that the string needs to be changed to ``an engineer''. Three characters need to be inserted at the beginning. During this process all elements are 'pushed' to the bottom of the array, as shown in Figure 3.6(b), thereby changing the indices of all elements. The procedure to insert an element at the pth position of an array A is shown in the following pseudocode:

```
repeat for i = p to length of array{
     A[i+1] =A[i]
}
A[p] = x
```

Similarly, deleting an element from an array requires a loop for bringing elements to the top. A more efficient representation for a group of data items is a linked list. A linked

(a)   (b)

Figure 3.6 Inserting elements in an array requires moving all the elements below it: (a) initial array, (b) after insertion

Figure 3.7 A linked list. Elements are linked to next elements by references

list consists of a sequence of elements called links or nodes. Each link consists of a piece of data and a reference to the next element, as shown in Figure 3.7. A linked list may be viewed as a chain with each link in the chain connecting adjacent parts of the chain. Schematically, a link is represented by two attributes, `data` and `next`. The attribute `next` points to the next link in the list. The list itself is represented by an attribute `head`, which points to the first link. The attribute `next` of the last link is `NULL`. (`NULL` is used to denote a pointer that does not point to anywhere.) To insert a new element in a linked list, it is enough to change the pointers; this is illustrated in Figure 3.8. The attribute `next` of link A is assigned to the new link D, and the attribute `next` of link D is assigned to link B. A loop to push elements down, as would be the case for an array, is not required. Upon data deletion (Figure 3.8(b)), the attribute `next` in link A is assigned to link C, and the link B is deleted. An array would require a loop to pull elements up, but a linked list has no need for this.

Even though it is easy to insert elements and delete elements, some operations are more difficult than with arrays. For example, locating the `i`th element in the list involves a loop to traverse from the head of the list until the `i`th element is reached. This procedure is shown in the following pseudocode:

```
set link = head
set counter = 0
repeat while link is not NULL {
    if counter is equal to i, then return data in the link
```

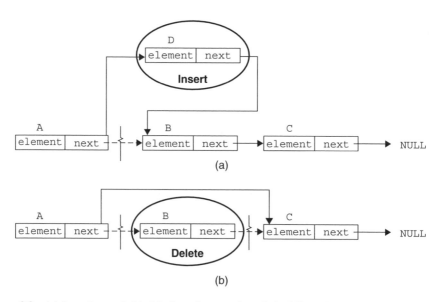

Figure 3.8 (a) Inserting and (b) deleting elements in a linked list. Elements may be inserted or deleted at any position in a linked list by reassigning the reference to the next element

```
        set link = next pointer of current link
          increment counter
}
```

The complexity of this operation is $O(n)$ where n is the number of elements in the list. Accessing the ith element of an array has complexity $O(1)$.

3.4.1.1 Applications

The concept of a linked list is employed for more than programming. It is useful in information representation. Imagine a teacher using this textbook for a course. The preferences of the teacher related to covering chapters may be treated as a linked list. For example, one teacher employs the following sequence of chapters to teach a class: 1, 2, 3, 4, 5, 6, 7, 8, 10. Another teacher might omit Chapters 4, 5, 6, 11 and 12. The lists would appear as `Linked list 1` and `Linked list 2` in Figure 3.9. Chapters in the book do not change; only the links are different.

3.4.1.2 Path finding

Consider a road network that connects islands as shown in Figure 3.10. Places are denoted as n1, n2, ..., n11. Solid lines indicate places that are connected. How does one represent all the paths from n1 to n6 that involve crossing the bridge?

Solution

The solution is four paths, each path represented by a linked list. The four lists contain the following elements in their correct order:

- n1, n2, n4, n5, n6
- n1, n3, n2, n4, n6
- n1, n2, n4, n6
- n1, n3, n2, n4, n5, n6

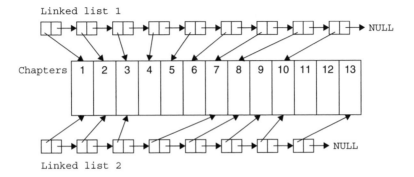

Figure 3.9 Linking chapters in a book

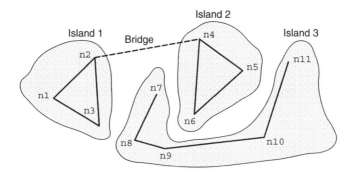

Figure 3.10 A road network

3.4.2 Graphs

There are a wide range of engineering tasks that involve reasoning about interconnected objects. Typically, such tasks involve finding paths between objects. A graph is an abstract data type that is useful for carrying out such tasks.

Example 3.1

Consider the road network shown in Figure 3.10. How does one determine whether any two given places, say n3 and n8, are connected? In simple cases this can be determined quickly by visual inspection of figures such as Figure 3.10. However, in complex networks, fast resolution by visual inspection is not possible. This explains the existence of puzzles involving mazes.

Example 3.2

Computers are connected as shown in Figure 3.11. A message needs to be sent from computer A to computer J. At any time, one or more links might become inoperative. How should the message be routed?

3.4.2.1 Mathematical definitions

A simple graph is a triple $G = (V, E, I)$, where V and E are discrete finite sets, and I is a relation between the sets V and E. V is called the set of vertices or nodes. E is

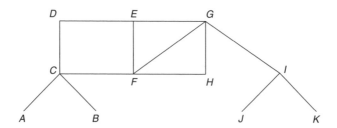

Figure 3.11 A network of computers

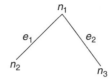

Figure 3.12   A simple graph

called the set of elements or edges. I is called the incidence relation or the connectivity relation. Consider the graph shown in Figure 3.12 in which, n_1, n_2 and n_3 are nodes, and e_1 and e_2 are edges. Hence $V = \{n_1, n_2, n_3\}$ and $E = \{e_1, e_2\}$.

There are two records in the connectivity relationship. The first one is the connectivity for e_1 and the second for e_2. The connectivity relationship may be expressed as $I = \{(e_1, n_1, n_2), (e_2, n_1, n_3)\}$. In general, the connectivity relationship is such that every element of E connects to exactly two distinct elements of V, and no two elements of E connect to the same pair of elements of V. Special types of graph are formed when these requirements do not hold.

The degree $d(v)$ of a vertex v is the number of edges that are connected to it. In Figure 3.12, n_1 is degree 2, and n_2 and n_3 are degree 1. Two vertices are adjacent if they are incident on a common edge. The set of neighbours $N(v)$ of a vertex v is the set of vertices that are adjacent to v. In the example, nodes n_1 and n_2 are neighbours. Nodes n_1 and n_3 are not neighbours since they are not connected by a common edge.

A walk is an alternating sequence of vertices and edges, with each edge being connected to the vertices immediately preceding and succeeding it in the sequence. A trail is a walk with no repeated edges. A path is a walk with no repeated vertices. A walk is closed if the initial vertex is also the terminal vertex. A cycle is a closed trail with at least one edge and with no repeated vertices except that the initial vertex is the terminal vertex. The sequence n_2, e_1, n_1, e_2, n_3 is a path but not a cycle. A non-null graph is connected if, for every pair of vertices, there is a walk whose ends are the given vertices.

Graph theory consists of a set of theorems that permit reasoning about properties of graphs. Many well-known problems have been solved using graph theory.

3.4.2.2   Types of graph

Graphs with special properties are categorized into the following types:

* directed;
* undirected;
* weighted;
* connected;
* disconnected;
* planar.

A graph is directed if each edge has a direction, otherwise it is undirected. A weighted graph has a weight associated with each edge. For example, road networks may be represented as weighted graphs in which the weights represent the lengths of the edges (road segments). In a connected graph there exists a path between every pair of nodes. A disconnected graph is one that is not connected. A planar graph can be drawn so that the edges do not cross over each other.

3.4.3 Trees

A tree is a graph that does not contain any cycles (Figure 3.13). Tree structures are often encountered in computing. They are often called hierarchies. Engineers deal with decomposition hierarchies, abstraction hierarchies (Chapter 4), classification hierarchies and dependency hierarchies. Trees are much easier to employ than graphs with cycles because there is a lower risk of reasoning loops (Chapter 4). Trees are also easier to maintain when information changes.

3.4.3.1 Binary search trees

Wherever tree representations are possible, efficient algorithms are usually available for processing the data contained in them. An example is the binary tree representation for sorted data. In this representation (Figure 3.14), all child nodes to the left of a node have data values less than or equal to that of the node. All child nodes to the right have data values greater than that of the node. During insertion, the data item is added to the left of a node if the value is less than that of the node. Consider a list that contains at first a single number, 56 (Figure 3.15(a)). A new number, 16, is to be added. Since 16 is less than 56, it is added to the left. When adding the number 89 to the tree, since it is greater

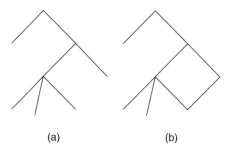

(a)   (b)

Figure 3.13   Trees are graphs that do not contain cycles: (a) a tree, (b) not a tree

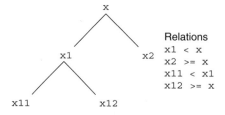

Figure 3.14   Binary tree representation of sorted data

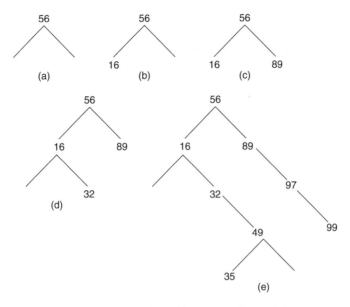

Figure 3.15   Creating a binary tree of sorted data

than 56, it is placed as the right child of the root. Next, adding the number 32, starting from the root of the tree, it is found that 32 is less than 56, so the left branch is chosen. Since 32 is greater than 16, the data item is added to the right of 16. The tree at this stage is shown in Figure 3.15(d). The process is repeated for each number that is added to the tree. Figure 3.15(e) shows the tree after the addition of the numbers 89, 49, 35, 97 and 99, in that order.

The ordering of nodes in the tree appears arbitrary. However, the tree represents a sorted list, and searching for an element in the tree is very efficient. Suppose we want to find out whether the number 91 exists in the tree. The search procedure is similar to the procedure used for adding elements to the tree. These are the steps:

1. Start from the root of the tree. Set this as the current node.
2. If the number that is searched for is equal to the data at the current node, the number is found. Hence stop the procedure.
3. If the number that is searched for is less than the data at the current node, set the current node as the left child. Otherwise set the current node as the right child.
4. If the current node is NULL, a leaf node of the tree has been reached. The number does not exist in the tree, so stop the procedure. Otherwise repeat from step 2.

Following the above steps, since the number 91 is greater than 56, set 89 as the current node. Since 91 is greater than 89, set 97 as the current node. Since 91 is less than 97, move left. Since there is no node to the left, the number 91 is not found and the procedure is terminated. In a list of 8 numbers only 3 comparisons were needed to conclude that the number is absent. By properly reordering the tree as insertions are made, it is possible to obtain $O(\log N)$ complexity in binary tree operations, where N is the total number of nodes.

3.4.3.2 Classification trees

Classification trees may be seen as extensions of binary trees. Instead of two children at every node, there are multiple children. Consider the classification tree shown in Figure 3.16. Through suitable criteria for classification, search may be restricted to a fraction of elements in the complete list of items. For example, if we are interested in prestressed bridges of medium span in Switzerland, we need to examine only the nodes under N10. The complete table of bridges is shown in Table 3.2. All the rows in the table need to be examined in the absence of a classification tree. In general, we need multiple classification trees to search for items according to different combinations of criteria.

3.4.3.3 Tree traversal

Tree traversal involves processing every node in the tree structure exactly once. In tree traversal we may have to pass through a node N several times, but we process the node N only once. Searching the binary tree in Section 3.4.3.1 is an example of tree traversal.

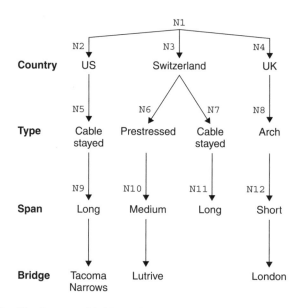

Figure 3.16 A classification tree of bridges. With proper classification, search is limited to a small fraction of elements in the complete list

Table 3.2 A flat list of bridges

Bridge	Country	Type	Span	Details
Lutrive	Switzerland	Prestressed	Medium	–
Tacoma Narrows	US	Cable-stayed	Long	
London	UK	Arch	Short	

In this example, processing of the node involves comparing the data at the node with the number that is searched. This example requires passing through the node only once. In general, there are three types of tree traversal:

- pre-order traversal;
- post-order traversal;
- in-order traversal.

In pre-order traversal, the node N is processed before processing the nodes in the subtrees at N. In post-order traversal, N is processed after processing the nodes in the subtrees at N. In in-order traversal, N is processed at some step during the processing of nodes in the subtrees at N. Here are some examples.

Pre-order traversal

Level measurements are taken during surveying for determining the elevation of points on a terrain. Measurements are started from a point whose elevation is known. Levelling equipment measures the difference in the elevation of a new point and a point where measurement has already been carried out. The elevations of all points are computed using the measured level differences through pre-order traversal.

The points where measurements are taken form a tree in which the point with the known elevation is the root node. Points whose level differences are measured are connected by the edges of the tree. To compute the elevation of all the nodes, follow a simple three-step procedure:

1. Start from the root of the tree. Set this as the current node N.
2. If N is not the root, compute the elevation of N by adding level difference to the elevation of the parent node of N.
3. Repeat for all the children of N: set the current node N as the next child and go to step 1.

In step 2 the elevation of N is computed before processing the child nodes of N, therefore this procedure is pre-order traversal.

Post-order traversal

The flow in a network of waste collection pipes is to be computed. The network forms a tree structure in which the root node is the destination to which all the waste is transported through the pipes. The inflow at each node other than the root is known. The flow in each pipe and the total outflow at the root node are computed using post-order traversal defined by the following steps:

1. Start from the root of the tree. Set this as the current node N.
2. Compute the outflow at each child node N_1 of N, by recursively repeating step 1 for the sub-tree at N_1.
3. Compute the outflow at N as the sum of the outflows of all child nodes of N.

Here computation of flow at the node is performed after the processing of child nodes, therefore this procedure is post-order traversal.

In-order traversal

Go back to the example of pre-order traversal. Suppose the tree contains a few intermediate points where elevations are known. Measurements are taken at these points in order to correct errors. Errors are computed at these points during tree traversal through calculating the difference between computed elevations and known values. These errors are then distributed to parent nodes and propagated to the root of the tree. Computing the elevations of nodes is no longer completed before processing of the subtrees. Tree traversal thus becomes in-order.

3.4.4 Stacks

The stack data structure is similar to stacks in real life. Consider a stack of books (Figure 3.17). We add books to the top of the stack. Without disturbing the stack, we can take out books only from the top. Stacks are also called LIFO (last-in first-out) data structures.

A stack is represented as a series of nodes, each linked to the previous element. In this sense, a stack is a linked list in which the directions of the links are reversed (Figure 3.18). A stack might also be implemented as an array (Figure 3.19). This form of implementation is very efficient and is used in many applications. New data added to the stack are stored at the end of the array. Data that are removed from the stack are taken out from the end of the array, so the last-in first-out order is maintained.

Figure 3.17 A stack of books. Without disturbing the stack, we can take out books only from the top

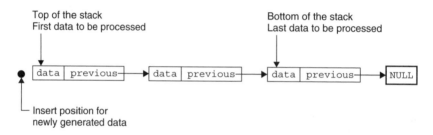

Figure 3.18 A Stack (LIFO). Data is added at the top and processed from the top

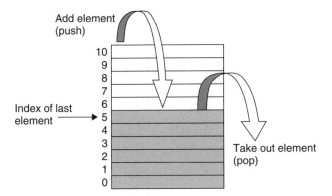

Figure 3.19 An array implementation of a stack. Elements are added and deleted by changing the index of the last element

The operations on a stack are push and pop:

- *Push* adds an element to the top of the stack.
- *Pop* takes out the element at the top of the stack.

In the linked list representation, the push operation is implemented by the following steps:

1. Create a new node.
2. Set the `previous` pointer of the new node to the one that is currently at the top of the stack.
3. Set the pointer to the top of the stack to the new node.

The pop operation is implemented by the following steps:

1. Set the node `nd` to be returned as the one at the top of the stack.
2. Set the top of the stack as the value of the `previous` pointer of the node `nd`.

The array implementation of stacks is also simple. The top of the stack is represented by the index of the last element in the array (Figure 3.19). The pop operation is simply decrementing the last index. In the beginning, the index of the last element is 0. When the first element is pushed on the stack, the index is incremented to 1. When the next element is added, the index becomes 2. Now, if an element is removed from the stack, the last index is decremented back to 1.

Stacks have a wide variety of applications. For example, stacks are used for recording and undoing changes during tasks that require backtracking. To understand how this works, consider a simple non-engineering application, a text editor. As the user types in characters, these are stored in an undo stack. The data stored in each node of the stack consist of the following attributes:

- operation: insert or delete;
- character: the character that is inserted or deleted;
- position: position of the character in the file.

	Operation	Character	Position
6			
5			
4	Delete	t	3
3	Insert	t	3
2	Insert	s	2
1	Insert	e	1
0	Insert	t	0

Top of the stack → 4

Figure 3.20   An undo stack for a word processing application

Consider a user who has typed in the word 'test' in a new file. The last character is then deleted. The stack contains the information shown in Figure 3.20.

For undoing, the operation at the top of the stack is reversed and popped from the stack. Thus, the character t is inserted back. The stack pointer is now at index $= 3$. For the next undo, the last operation 'insert t' is reversed. That is, the character t is deleted, and so on. The LIFO order of processing ensures the changes are done correctly.

3.4.4.1   Use of stacks: tree traversal

Binary trees can be searched efficiently in logarithmic time (Chapter 2 and Section 3.4.3.1). However, this assumes the selection of branches (left or right) at each node in the tree is correct and need not be reversed later on. There are many situations where the branches to be explored in a tree are not known a priori. In the absence of any information needed to make a choice, the first branch is chosen and the tree is traversed along that branch until it is clear solutions do not exist in that branch.

Consider the classification tree in Figure 3.16. Suppose we are interested in locating a short-span bridge situated in a corrosive environment. The attribute environment is not used in the classification. Hence bridges need to be selected and examined to determine whether they are situated in a corrosive environment. Starting from the root of the tree, the first branch with country=US is chosen. Moving down along this branch to the node N5, one realizes there is no bridge for the category span=short. Hence the search backtracks to the root and the next branch is chosen. This process is continued until a node is located where the span is short. The list of bridges in this category is then examined to check whether any bridge is situated in a corrosive environment.

This form of tree traversal is common in many engineering tasks and is called depth-first search with backtracking. In depth-first search, child nodes of a node N are processed before processing the node N itself. A recursive procedure for depth-first search of a binary tree is as follows:

```
Procedure depth-first (current-node)
     If current-node is not a leaf node {
          Step i. call procedure depth-first for the first child
             of current-node
          Step ii. call procedure depth-first for the second child
             of current-node
          Step iii. process current-node
     }
```

For example, consider the task of finding the sum of all the numbers in the binary tree in Figure 3.15(e). Here the processing of a node involves taking the sum and adding to it the value of data at the node. The procedure depth-first returns the sum of all numbers below a specified node. To start with, the procedure is called for the root node, 56. The procedure depth-first is called (first recursive call) for the first child, i.e. 16. The recursive call for node 16 results in calls for 32, 49 and 35. Since node 35 has no children, the recursive calls end and the function returns the value 35 (the value of the current node). For node 49, step (iii) results in adding 49 to 35, and so on, until all the nodes are processed and the resulting sum is returned.

The above procedure is pure depth-first search without backtracking. Now consider a slightly different task: locate a number x in the list such that $50 < x < 70$. Starting from the root, 56, the required number might exist on either the left branch or the right branch. Start with the left branch and move to the first child, 16. Since 16 is less than 50, we need to search only in the right branch of this node. Hence move to node 32, and so on, until the leaf node is reached. Since the number has not been located, backtrack all the way to the root and move to the right child, 89. Since 89 is greater than 70, try to move to the left branch of this node. Since the left branch is empty, it is determined that the required number does not exist. The following procedure might be used for performing depth-first search with backtracking:

```
Create an empty stack
Set current-node to be the root of the tree
Loop1: Repeat forever{
       if current-node is NULL{
             if the stack is empty then terminate
             Otherwise:
             set backtrack-node to be the node at the top of the stack
             set current-node to be the right child of backtrack-node
             start from the beginning of Loop1
       }
       If current-node satisfies the required criteria return
             current-node
       Add current-node to the stack
       Set current-node to be the left child of the current-node
}
```

Design that requires backtracking

Design is usually an iterative procedure that involves making decisions and reversing decisions when it is revealed that requirements are not met. One way to keep track of decisions involves the use of a stack. All design decisions are pushed on to the stack. When there is a conflict, the latest decision is undone by popping it from the stack and a new decision is made. More sophisticated procedures identify causes of conflicts and reverse decisions that have given rise to conflicts. Figure 3.21 illustrates the use of stacks for tracking decisions.

Unfortunately, tracking and updating decisions in this way has an exponential complexity with respect to the number of nodes that are traversed. Therefore such strategies need to be restricted to small subtasks when designing complex products.

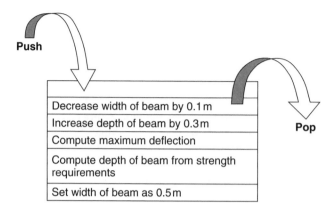

Figure 3.21   An undo stack for the design of a beam

3.4.5 Queues

Queues are used where data to be processed are generated while carrying out a task and need to be processed in the same order in which the data items arrive. The queue data structure simulates real-life queues such as the ones at cash registers and bus stops. In data queues, newly generated data are added at the tail, and data are taken out from the head of the queue (Figure 3.22). Queues are also called FIFO (first-in first-out) data structures.

As seen from Figure 3.22, queues might be implemented using linked lists. The queue data structure itself consists of two attributes, head and tail. The attribute head points to the first node in the linked list. The attribute tail points to the last element of the list. There are two important operations on queues, enqueue and dequeue. The enqueue operation adds a new element to the queue at the tail. The dequeue operation deletes the first element of the list.

In the previous section, stacks were used for depth-first search. Another procedure for searching trees is breadth-first search. In breadth-first search, nodes along the breadth are processed before traversing deeper. Queues are used for breadth-first search. Consider the tree shown in Figure 3.23. The order in which data are processed by the breadth-first search is n1, n2, n11, n18, n3, n4, n5, n9, n10, n12, n16, n17, n6, n7, n8, n13, n14, n15. The following procedure might be used for breadth-first search:

```
Add the root node of the tree to the queue
Repeat until the queue is empty {
        Set current node = the next element from the queue
        Process current node
        if the current node is not a leaf, add its children to the queue
        dequeue current node
}
```

Figure 3.24 illustrates the steps that are carried out when performing breadth-first search of the tree.

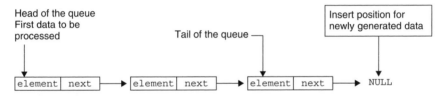

Figure 3.22   A queue. Data is added at the tail and processed from the head

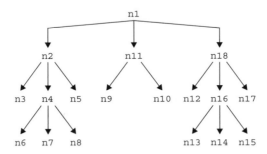

Figure 3.23   A tree

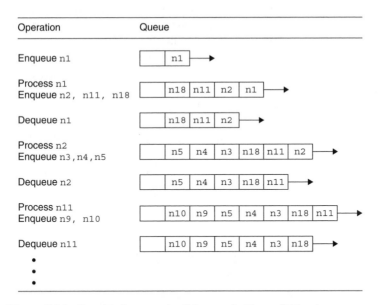

Figure 3.24   Breadth-first search of the tree in Figure 3.23 using a queue

3.4.5.1   Analysis of a simple determinate truss

Trusses are widely used in structural engineering. The 'method of nodes' is used to analyse simple trusses, such as the one in Figure 3.25, by applying the equations of static equilibrium to each node in turn. The nodes are processed such that there are at most two unknown forces at each node.

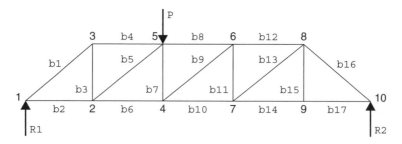

Figure 3.25 A simple determinate truss. The labels 1, 2, ..., 10 indicate the nodes and `b1`, `b2`, ..., `b17` indicate bar numbers

For example, if the reactions `R1` and `R2` are known, there are only two unknown forces at node 1, namely, the forces in the members that meet at this node (`b1` and `b2`). Since there are two equations of equilibrium (in the x and y directions), these forces are readily computed. Similarly, the forces in the members meeting at node 10 are also computed.

There are three members meeting at node 3 (`b1`, `b3` and `b4`), hence this node can be processed only after one of the forces is known. The force in the member `b1`, connecting nodes 1 and 3, is known after node 1 is processed, hence node 3 now has only two unknown forces and they are determined. After processing nodes 1 and 3, there are only two unknown forces at node 2, therefore this node can be processed. This procedure is repeated until all forces are known.

The above procedure is easily implemented using a queue. The next node to be processed is stored in the queue. As soon as the reactions `R1` and `R2` and computed, nodes 1 and 2 are added to the queue. At any point in time, the first node in the queue is taken for processing. The unknown forces in the members meeting at the node are computed. After computing the force in a member, the far node (the node at the other end of the member) is examined to see whether there are only two unknown forces left to determine. When this is true, it is added to the queue. The queue thus grows during the analysis. The growth of the queue is shown in Table 3.3.

Table 3.3 Queue for processing nodes of a truss

Node processed	Members solved	Queue $\longrightarrow$			
				10	1
1	b1, b2			3	10
10	b16, b17			9	3
3	b3, b4			2	9
9	b14, b15			8	2
2	b5, b6			5	8

3.5 CONCEPTUAL STRUCTURAL DESIGN OF BUILDINGS

Conceptual structural design of buildings involves selecting suitable options for subsystems such as the vertical support system and the floor systems. A simplified decomposition of a structural system is shown in Figure 3.26. For simplicity there are only two subsystems, the floor system and the vertical support system. The floor system can be beam and slab, waffle slab or flat slab. The vertical support system could consist of load-bearing walls or columns. The beam-and-slab system consists of two subsystems, namely, beams and the slab. Beams could be of concrete or steel. How many designs are possible? Design a procedure that generates all possible solutions.

Solution

All possible designs are shown in Table 3.4. The design solutions are generated using a procedure involving a queue and a stack (Figure 3.27). The queue is used for storing

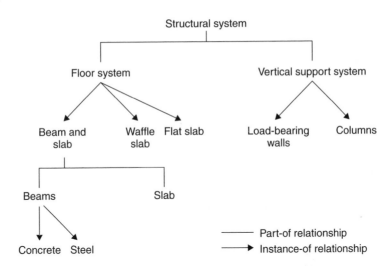

Figure 3.26 Simplified structural design of buildings

Table 3.4 Possible design solutions

	Floor system	Vertical support system	Beams
1	Beam and slab	Load-bearing walls	Concrete
2	Beam and slab	Load-bearing walls	Steel
3	Beam and slab	Columns	Concrete
4	Beam and slab	Columns	Steel
5	Waffle slab	Load-bearing walls	–
6	Waffle slab	Columns	–
7	Flat slab	Load-bearing walls	–
8	Flat slab	Columns	–

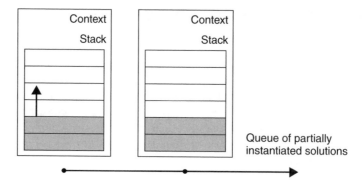

Figure 3.27   Use of queue and stack in conceptual structural design

partial solutions to be processed one by one. The stack is used to store the tasks that are yet to be completed. When a new task is identified it is pushed on the stack. The task at the top of the stack is taken for processing. In addition, the context representing the list of variables that have been instantiated for each solution is also maintained. Figure 3.28 shows stacks and queues at various stages during the generation procedure.

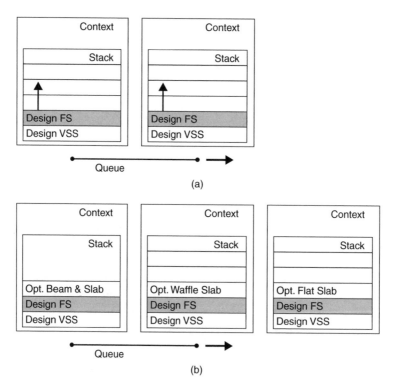

Figure 3.28   Illustration of the use of stacks and queues for the conceptual structural design of buildings. Shaded item in the stack indicates the element that is currently being processed. Abbreviations used: FS – floor system, VSS – Vertical Support System

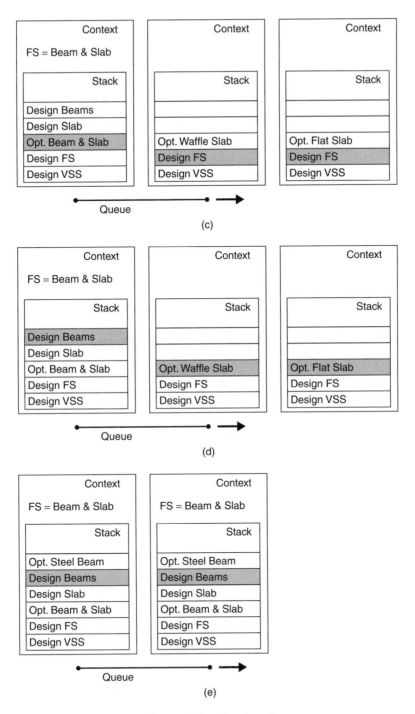

Figure 3.28 (*Continued*)

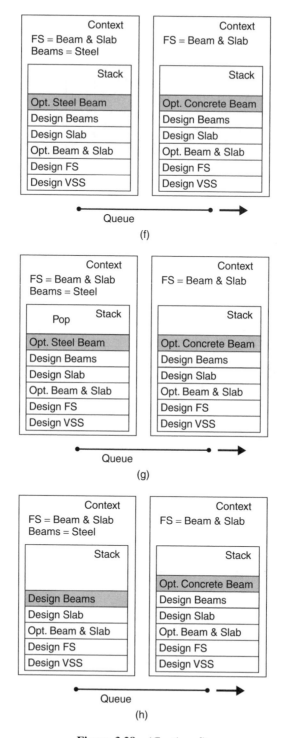

Figure 3.28 (*Continued*)

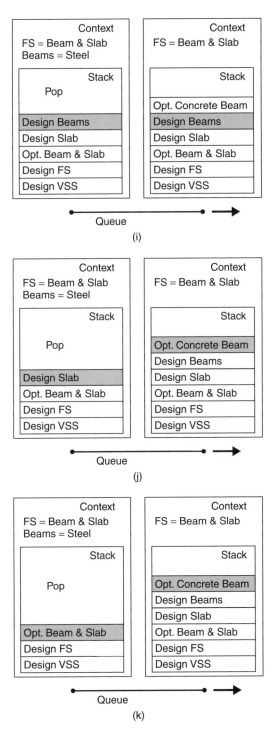

Figure 3.28 (*Continued*)

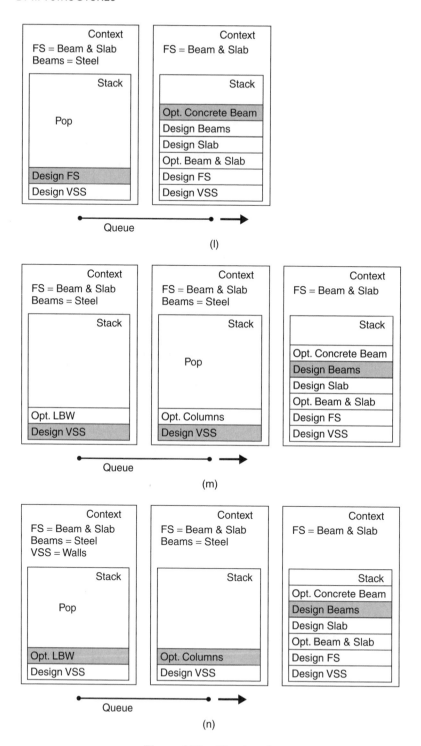

Figure 3.28 (*Continued*)

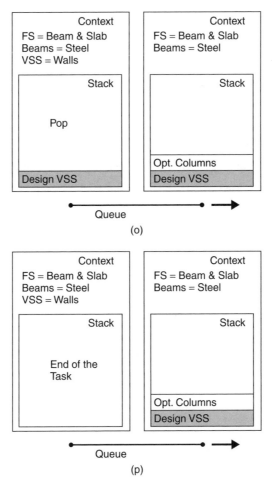

Figure 3.28 (*Continued*)

In practice the process is more complex because several compatibility constraints might be involved; for example, beam material must be the same as column material, and flat slabs can only be supported by columns. A simple method for accommodating such constraints is to reject solutions that violate constraints after they are generated. Better methods involve constraint-solving procedures (Chapter 7) or branch-and-bound methods (Chapter 8).

3.6 SUMMARY

- The organization of data determines performance characteristics as well as the level of difficulty associated with maintenance activities of software applications.

- The term 'data structure' refers to the organization of data within software applications.

- Derived data types are created by grouping primitive data types.

- Linked lists, stacks and queues are abstract data types that are commonly used to process information. The identification of appropriate data structures improves the efficiency of tasks.

- Linked lists are used to represent a collection of similar data when the order of elements in the list is important. It is easy to insert and delete elements using linked lists.

- Graphs are used where data items are linked together in a complex manner. They are classified into different types according to certain characteristics and these characteristics are useful for identifying appropriate algorithms.

- A tree is a special type of graph. Efficient algorithms exist for manipulating tree structures.

- Stacks are commonly used in tasks that require backtracking.

- Queues are used where the order in which subtasks of an activity are carried out is important and the order is discovered only during the process of carrying out the task.

FURTHER READING

Kruse, R. L., Leung, B. P. and Tondo C. L. 1991. *Data Structures and Program Design in C*. Englewood Cliffs NJ: Prentice Hall.
Liu, C. L. 1997. *Elements of Discrete Mathematics*. New York: McGraw-Hill.
Sage, A. P. and Palmer, J. D. 1990. *Software Systems Engineering*. New York: John Wiley & sons, Inc.

EXERCISES

3.1 The structural frame of a building consists of a rectangular grid of beams and columns (Figure 3.29). All columns and beams are rectangular in cross-section. All

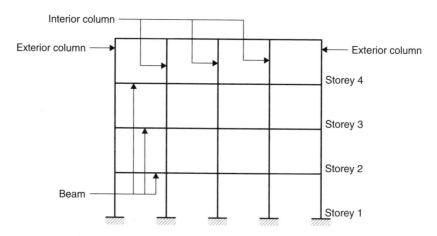

Figure 3.29   A structural frame consisting of beams and columns

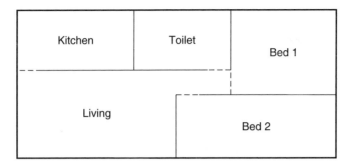

Figure 3.30   A house plan

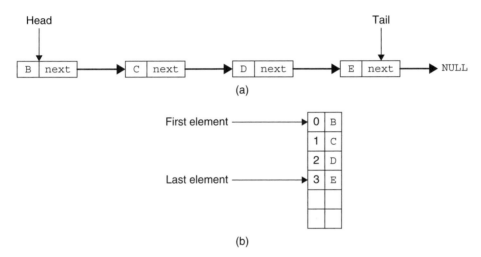

Figure 3.31   Alternate representations for the same data: (a) linked list, (b) array

exterior columns in each storey have the same dimensions, and all interior columns have the same dimensions. All beams in each storey also have the same dimensions. Design a data structure to represent this information.

3.2 A house plan is shown in Figure 3.30. Design a data structure to represent the connectivity of rooms. For example, it should be easy to find out whether `bedroom` is connected to `toilet`. Dotted lines indicate doors.

3.3 Consider the linked list and the array in Figure 3.31. Which representation is more efficient for the following operations?

(a) Inserting a new element A before the element B
(b) Inserting a new element A after the element E
(c) Deleting element B
(d) Deleting element E

3.4 What are the advantages of linked lists compared to arrays? What are the drawbacks?

3.5 Consider the graph in Figure 3.32.

  (a) Is the graph planar or non-planar?
  (b) Is the graph connected or disconnected?

3.6 Is the graph in Figure 3.33 planar or non-planar?

3.7 Figure 3.34 shows the relationship between variables in a design task. An arrow from a variable X to a variable Y indicates that the variable X depends on the value of

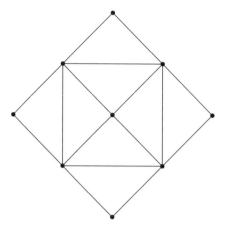

Figure 3.32 A graph. Nodes are indicated by dark dots and edges by straight lines

Figure 3.33 A graph. Nodes are indicated by dark dots and edges by straight lines

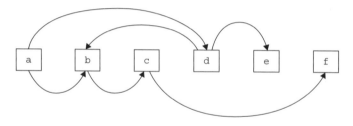

Figure 3.34 Relationships between variables in a design task

the variable Y. What are the independent variables if we are interested in computing the value of a? (Independent variables are those that do not depend on the value of any other variable.) If each arrow represents a linear relationship, does it require an interactive procedure to compute the value of f? Show the dependencies between variables in the form of a graph.

3.8 If buildings are classified as shown in Figure 3.35, how many buildings need to be examined to locate a building that was constructed in the year 1900. How many comparisons are needed to locate the group containing the building? In the absence of this classification tree, how many bridges need to be examined?

3.9 An engineer needs to choose between a circular column and a rectangular column for a building. Design decisions and calculations made by the engineer are showing in Stack A (Figure 3.36). How many push and pop operations are required to obtain the solution shown in Stack B?

3.10 Consider the graph in Figure 3.37. Is it a tree structure?

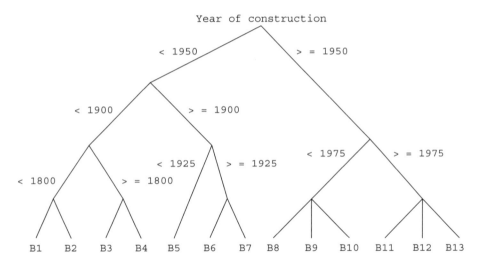

Figure 3.35 Classification of buildings based on year of construction. B1, B2, etc. represent the buildings

Cost = 20 000		Cost = 15 000
Beam dimensions = 200 × 200		Beam dimensions = 200 × 200
Beams = rectangular		Beams = rectangular
Radius = 200		Columns dimensions = 200 × 200
Columns = circular		Columns = rectangular
Stack A		Stack B

Figure 3.36 Backtracking design decisions using Stacks

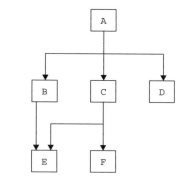

Figure 3.37   A graph

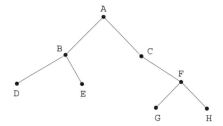

Figure 3.38   A graph

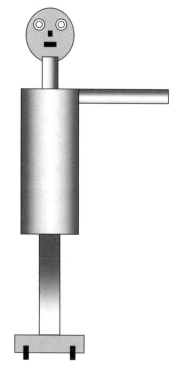

Figure 3.39   A robot made of cylinders and spheres

3.11 If the nodes in the graph in Figure 3.38 need to be examined in the order ABCDEFGH, which abstract data type should be used, stack or queue? If the nodes have to be examined in the order ABDECFGH, which abstract data type should be used?

3.12 A robot is created using spheres and cylinders connected by ball-and-socket joints (Figure 3.39). The coordinates of robot arms need to be computed from the position of the base for each move made by the robot. The rotation at each joint is known. Design a data structure to represent the robot.)

4

Object Representation and Reasoning

4.1 INTRODUCTION

Engineers design, build, use, monitor, repair and dismantle physical objects, therefore a representation that emulates physical objects is clearly attractive for applications in computer-aided engineering (CAE). In addition, object reasoning methods are a natural fit for many engineering tasks. Engineers are much more likely to use computer applications when they are able to make links to mental models that they have already formed of their tasks.

While it is relatively easy to build CAE applications that work for a few months, it is a very different task to create applications that are able to remain useful over many years and after repeated modifications. Engineering contexts are continually changing as materials, technologies and functional requirements evolve. In addition, environments where engineering products are expected to perform are increasingly uncertain. Under these circumstances, object representation schemas and reasoning methods often prove to be more robust than other approaches.

Engineering products have a high representational complexity. From the beginning of their training, engineers learn to place things into categories according to a range of criteria. One of the most widespread engineering strategies is to decompose complex products into parts that are more simply analysed. Indeed categorization and decomposition are effective strategies when faced with complex products; these two strategies are also central to object representation and reasoning in CAE.

This chapter describes the basic concepts of object representation and reasoning, using examples in engineering. Their special characteristics provide many advantages for knowledge representation and maintenance. Also, reasoning with objects may lead to reliable engineering support over many years. The chapter concludes with a brief explanation of message cycles – one of the risks of reasoning with objects.

4.2 GROUPING DATA AND METHODS

Chapter 3 emphasized the importance of grouping related data together. Data structures group related data so they are easy to manage and manipulate. But with such a

Fundamentals of Computer-Aided Engineering   B. Raphael and I. F. C. Smith
© 2003 John Wiley & Sons, Ltd   ISBNs: 0-471-48709-0 (HB); 0-471-48715-5 (PB)

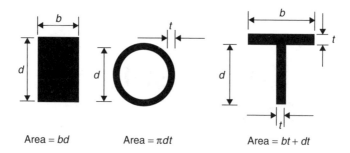

Area = *bd*   Area = *πdt*   Area = *bt* + *dt*

Figure 4.1   Beam sections with different cross sections

representation, data items and methods that manipulate the data are not closely linked together. Data items and methods that operate on them are defined independently. There is an implicit assumption that methods always operate on the right data.

Physical objects have closely coupled properties (or components) and methods (or processes) that manipulate the components. A car is started (a process associated with the car object) by turning its ignition key (a component of the car object). The bending behaviour of a beam (a process) is related to the properties of the beam. Processes that modify the state of an object are closely associated with the object.

Objects are a representational strategy for modelling physical entities. Their main difference with data structures is that objects contain data as well as methods that manipulate data; other differences are described in Section 4.4. For example, beam sections have different shapes, as shown in Figure 4.1. The method used to compute the cross-sectional area depends on the shape. Computing the area of a rectangular cross-section requires its width and depth, whereas computing the area of a circular section requires its diameter and thickness. The procedure that computes the area is linked to the properties of the section.

Storing data and methods within a single structure is known as encapsulation. Encapsulation makes it possible to develop self-contained entities that could be used in different situations. For example, a spreadsheet object might be embedded in a word-processing document or a drawing. All the methods that manipulate the data in the spreadsheet are reused in both situations.

4.3   DEFINITIONS AND BASIC CONCEPTS

4.3.1   Classes and Objects

A class is a generalization of an object. A class defines the attributes and methods that are part of every object belonging to the class. An object is created by instantiating a class. During the process of instantiation, attributes are assigned values.

Example 4.1

A class `SteelPlate` contains two attributes: `width` and `thickness` (Figure 4.2). It also contains methods `area()` and `momentOfInertia()`, which compute the

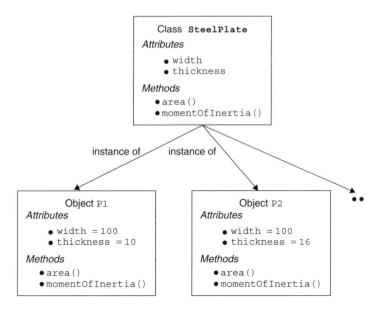

Figure 4.2   Instantiation of a SteelPlate

cross-sectional properties of the plate. Objects belonging to the class are instantiated by assigning values to all attributes. An object P1 belonging to this class has width = 100 and thickness = 10. Another object P2 has width = 100 and thickness = 16. Both objects contain the methods area() and momentOfInertia(), which are defined in the class.

A standard notation for accessing the attributes and methods of objects is the dot operator ".". According to this notation, P1.width refers to the value of the attribute width of the object P1.

4.3.2   Object-Oriented Programming

Object-oriented programming (OOP) refers to a style of programming in which an application consists of objects that interact with each other. Code is organized around classes rather than algorithmic modules such as in structured programming.

4.3.3   Messages

The external world interacts with an object by passing messages to it (Figure 4.3). A message consists of a message identifier and a set of arguments. In programming languages, a message is simply the name of a function along with its arguments. Objects respond to messages by invoking appropriate methods.

In the object-oriented notation, P1.area() refers to passing the message area to the object P1. The object responds to the message by executing the function area(), which is defined in the class to which the object belongs.

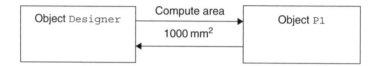

Figure 4.3 Objects communicate by sending messages. These messages result in the invocation of appropriate methods of the class

4.4 IMPORTANT CHARACTERISTICS OF OBJECTS

The term 'object' is used loosely by software vendors who claim that their products are object-oriented. Therefore, it is necessary to clarify essential features of objects. There are three defining characteristics of objects:

- encapsulation of data and methods;
- message passing;
- inheritance.

4.4.1 Encapsulation of Data and Methods

Many representations that claim to be object-oriented do not contain methods within objects. In the absence of methods, a data structure is more appropriately called a frame, as defined by Minsky (1975). A frame contains slots to store values. The values in a frame might be references to other frames, resulting in a decomposition hierarchy.

Objects contain more than a decomposition hierarchy. They contain methods (or procedures) which enable them to react to the outside world. Methods are necessary to model the behaviour of objects.

Encapsulation increases the modularity and maintainability of applications. Linking data and methods together reduces the risk of procedures operating on wrong data. In the object-oriented implementation of a stack, the method Push is implemented within the class Stack. It is impossible to apply this method on an object belonging to another class. When this class is used in an application, both data variables as well as methods are imported correctly into the application.

Encapsulation increases the simplicity of external interfaces. Since objects interact with the outside world using a well-defined message-passing mechanism, complex implementation details are hidden to the outside world. External objects need to examine only the methods that are exposed and they are not allowed to manipulate attributes that are internal to the object.

A weighing machine (Figure 4.4) contains a system of springs, dials and needles. If all these details are exposed to users, the machine becomes difficult to use. Users need to know only how to place an item on the machine and how to read the dial. The components of the machine and their operational behaviour are encapsulated inside the object to create a simple external interface.

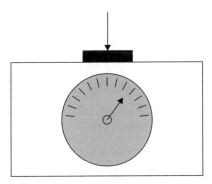

Figure 4.4   A weighing machine. The simplicity of the external interface is achieved by encapsulating complex operational details

4.4.2 Message-Passing Mechanism

Message passing is related to encapsulation. Since methods are stored inside objects, there needs to be a mechanism for invoking these methods. This is done through passing messages. Without the ability to pass messages, objects have no means of communication with the outside world. When it receives a message, an object might modify its internal state and send messages to other objects.

The message-passing architecture ensures that each object assumes the responsibility of maintaining its internal state without inconsistencies. Other objects do not modify the internals of an object directly and simply send messages to it to effect changes.

4.4.3 Abstraction Hierarchy

The most significant feature of object representation is the abstraction hierarchy. Classes are organized into a tree structure having abstract classes at the top and increasingly specialized classes down the tree. Abstraction involves a process of focusing on key aspects and leaving out details. Abstract classes have fewer details than specialized classes. In the implementation of object-oriented systems, specialized classes are created from abstract classes by adding more details. Generality is achieved by abstraction through the omission of details that distinguish more specialized classes. Therefore, abstract classes are also called general classes.

In computer science, the term 'derived class' is used instead of 'specialized class' since specialized classes are child nodes in the abstraction hierarchy and are created from parent classes. However, during knowledge formulation in engineering, abstract classes are often identified through an examination of specialized classes; the formulation of classes is from bottom to top instead of from top to bottom. Therefore the term 'derived class' is a misnomer and is not used in the rest of the book.

The properties and behaviour of abstract classes are made available to specialized classes by the mechanism of inheritance. During inheritance, a specialized class inherits all the attributes and methods of the parent class. This is the most common approach used in object-oriented languages, but there are exceptions to this rule. The specialized

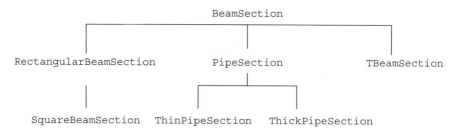

Figure 4.5   An abstraction hierarchy of beam sections

class might define new attributes and methods; it might also redefine the methods of the parent class.

Abstract classes might flag certain message-handling capabilities without implementing the methods used for responding to these messages. This allows applications to examine only the parent class to decide what messages might be sent to objects without examining each specialized class. Specialized classes implement the methods to respond to these methods. Only classes that implement all the methods are allowed to be instantiated.

Figure 4.5 shows an abstraction hierarchy of beam sections. `BeamSection` is an abstract class used to define all types of beam section. It contains no attributes and is used only as a common root to organize the specialized classes. `RectangularBeamSection`, `PipeSection` and `TBeamSection` are specialized classes of `BeamSection`. These classes contain definitions of attributes to store details of their cross-sections. The parent class only declares the messages that could be sent to objects belonging to its specialized class. Specialized classes implement methods to respond to these messages.

4.4.3.1   Reasoning using abstraction hierarchies

Abstraction hierarchy is an important part of domain knowledge. For example, knowing that water is a type of fluid permits application of the laws of fluid mechanics. We can infer that a cable cannot take bending stresses from the knowledge that a cable is a type of element that, along with string and rope, carries only tensile forces. Type-of relationships help to determine what knowledge should be applied.

Another advantage of abstraction hierarchies is that generic methods can be defined for abstract classes without having to define identical methods for each specialized class. For example, a method called `verifyDesign` that is defined in the abstract class `Beam-Section` involves the following steps:

- Compute the moment of inertia of the `BeamSection` object.
- Verify that the moment of inertia is more than is required for the design bending moment.

This method does not contain any reference to specific types of beam section. The method is applicable to all classes of beam section that are already defined and that might also be defined in the future. Each specialized class implements a separate method for calculating

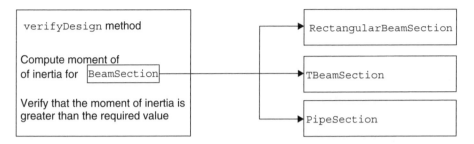

Figure 4.6   The mechanism of abstraction permits for a definition of generic methods that do not refer to specific types of objects. Methods contain references to abstract classes

the moment of inertia (Figure 4.6) and the method `verifyDesign` works without any modification.

For comparison, without abstraction hierarchies, these steps would have to be redefined as follows:

- If the beam section is rectangular, then compute the moment of inertia of the rectangular beam section.
- If the beam section is T-shaped, then compute the moment of inertia of the T-shaped beam section.
- If the beam section is a pipe, then compute the moment of inertia of the pipe section.
- Verify that the moment of inertia is more than what is required for the design bending moment.

When new beam sections are added, new 'if' conditions are added to the method to handle the new case. If there are many objects of different types, there are also many combinations of 'if' conditions. Using an abstraction hierarchy, the type of an object is determined at execution time and appropriate methods are invoked automatically. This avoids explicit checking of the object type.

Defining generic methods using abstract classes does introduce difficulties. The abstract classes have to be general enough to represent the behaviour of all specialized classes. Generic methods cannot refer to any property or behaviour that is absent in the abstract class. If an attribute, such as `width`, does not exist in the abstract class, the method `verifyDesign` cannot refer to this attribute even if it is present in all specialized classes. Parent classes have to be carefully designed to reasonably represent the behaviour of all specialized classes. In many practical object-oriented developments, new attributes are added to parent classes during the implementation of methods once the inadequacies of the class are realized.

The following rule is used to determine which methods should be applied to individual objects: If a method is defined to operate on a class `c1`,

- the method is feasible for all objects belonging to class `c1` or any of its specialized classes;
- the method cannot operate on an object belonging to a parent class of `c1`.

This is because it is assumed that all specialized classes inherit the features and behaviour of `c1`, whereas parent classes do not have all features of `c1`.

4.4.3.2   Two advantages of inheritance

- *Reuse of code*:   since code that is developed for parent classes is applicable for specialized classes, it is sufficient to code only what is different in the specialized classes. It permits better reuse of code than in structured programming.

- *Incremental application development*:   applications are incrementally enhanced by adding new classes without modifying existing code. Conventional structured programming requires addition of new code as well as modifications to existing code to integrate the new code.

4.4.4   Secondary Features of Object Representation

4.4.4.1   Data protection

Since methods are linked to objects, it is possible to enforce data protection by setting permissions on data items and methods. There are usually three types of attributes and methods depending on their access permissions: private, public and protected. Private attributes of a class can be accessed and modified only by methods belonging to the same class. That is, only objects belonging to the same class are allowed to modify these variables. Public attributes can be accessed and modified by methods belonging to all classes. Protected attributes can be accessed and modified only by methods belonging to the same class or any of the specialized classes. The same rules apply to methods. Only objects belonging to the same class can call private methods of a class. All objects can call public methods. Objects belonging to the same class or any specialized class can call protected methods.

The enforcement of data protection improves code reliability by disallowing incorrect modifications to data items by external objects. Usually there are hidden assumptions in code. Programmers assume that variables are always used in a certain manner. When other developers modify the code, they may not be aware of these assumptions and this causes undesirable side effects. Data protection is important if applications are continually modified during the life of the software. Only data and methods that are safe to be accessed by everyone are declared as public.

Example 4.2

A class `Room` represents a rectangular room in a building. The attributes of the class are `length`, `breadth`, `height` and `planArea`. The method `computeNumberOfTiles` calculates the number of tiles required for flooring by dividing the plan area by the area of the tile. It is assumed in this method that the variable `planArea` stores the value that is consistent with the `length` and `breadth` of the building. Therefore this variable is not recomputed each time the method `computeNumberOfTiles` is invoked. A designer realizes that the dimensions of a room are high and modifies the values of `length` and `breadth`. He is unaware of the requirement that `planArea` needs to be updated, therefore he does not modify this variable. The method `computeNumberOfTiles` returns an incorrect value after the modifications made by the designer.

To avoid such situations, the attributes of the class are declared to be private. Nobody is allowed to modify the values directly. In order to modify the dimensions of the room, a set of public methods are provided: `setLength` and `setBreadth`. Users call these methods for changing the `length` and `breadth` of the room. These methods modify dependent variables.

4.4.4.2   Polymorphism

Polymorphism refers to the behaviour that different objects respond differently to the same message. The use of a common language to communicate to different objects helps keep languages simple. An analogy is that we use the same verb to denote the multiplication of two numbers as well as two matrices, even though the procedures to perform these operations are different.

In object representation, polymorphism occurs due to a redefinition of methods in specialized classes. A specialized class responds differently to the same message `M1` because the method `M1` is redefined or because a method invoked by `M1` is redefined.

4.4.5   Decomposition versus Abstraction

Two hierarchies are encountered in object representations: decomposition (packaging) and abstraction. Decomposition hierarchies contain part-of relationships that specify what components are parts of an object. For example, a room consists of walls, windows, doors, etc. A window consists of a frame, glazed panels, etc. Such information is stored in the decomposition hierarchy.

Abstraction hierarchies contain type-of relationships that specify whether a class is a special case of another class. Figure 4.5 shows type-of relationships for beam sections.

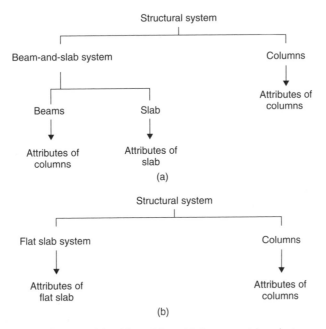

Figure 4.7   Variation of decomposition hierarchies with instance: (a) an instance where beams and slab are in the floor system, (b) an instance where a flat slab is in the floor system

An important difference between these two hierarchies is that abstraction hierarchies do not change if the class definitions are not changed, whereas decomposition hierarchies vary with the instance. They depend on classes that are used to instantiate attribute values of objects. Consider the structural design example in Section 3.5. In one instance the floor system might be beam and slab, resulting in the decomposition hierarchy of Figure 4.7(a). In another instance the floor system might be flat slab, resulting in the different decomposition hierarchy of Figure 4.7(b). Decomposition and abstraction hierarchies are important because engineering industries are defining standard product and process models that aim to define these hierarchies.

4.5   APPLICATIONS OUTSIDE PROGRAMMING

- *Knowledge representation*:   object-oriented concepts are used for knowledge representation (Chapter 9) for better maintainability. Knowledge (rules, facts, procedures) is organized around objects to create small and maintainable knowledge modules.

- *User interfaces*:   object-oriented user interfaces have improved human–computer interaction. Modern user interfaces contain easily identifiable objects through which users interact with the system. Users send messages to user interface objects through mouse clicks, drag and drop, etc., instead of typing in commands.

- *Off-the-shelf components*:   advances in object technology have made it possible to develop applications without any programming effort. Off-the-shelf components can be purchased and visually assembled using rapid application development (RAD) tools to create applications. A general-purpose designer class from company X might be combined with a beam class from company Y to create an application that supports the design of beams.

4.6   AN OBJECT-ORIENTED DESIGN METHODOLOGY

Object-oriented design involves several aspects. Engineers need to decide on the classes, their attributes and methods, how the classes are organized into abstraction hierarchies, which attributes and methods are private and which are public, etc. There is no single correct design for any non-trivial task. Several assumptions are usually involved and engineers might create different hierarchies.

There are many methodologies that have been proposed for object-oriented analysis and design. This is a specialized area of software engineering and is not covered here. The following subsections discuss selected issues in object-oriented design.

4.6.1   Single versus Multiple Inheritance

In single inheritance each class is derived from a single parent class. In multiple inheritance a class might have multiple parent classes. In reality it is difficult to find clearly defined hierarchies. For example, a steel plate is both a bending member and an axial force-carrying member. It has to inherit properties of both bending members and axial force-carrying members. An employee of a company might be a structural engineer and a manager at the same time. Situations are frequently encountered where it is difficult to identify a single parent class. Multiple inheritance is used in some object systems to accommodate such circumstances.

However, multiple inheritance introduces several complexities. The same attribute might exist in multiple parents that have different meanings. There is ambiguity related to the meaning of the attribute in the specialized class since it inherits the same attribute from multiple parents. Similarly, the same method might exist in different parents and therefore it is not clear which method should be called in a particular instance.

Many object-oriented systems avoid the use of multiple inheritance to eliminate these problems. Where multiple inheritance is not supported, a common strategy is to manually encapsulate the required properties and behaviour in the new class. For example, the class `SteelPlate` could contain two additional attributes: (a) `beamBending-Behaviour` belonging to class `BeamBendingMember` and (b) `axialForceMember` belonging to the class `AxialForceCarryingMember`. Thus, instead of inheriting the two behaviours through multiple inheritance, the two behaviours are encapsulated within the class. Of course, standard reasoning mechanisms using abstraction hierarchies are no longer applicable because the new class `SteelPlate` is not a type of `BeamBending-Member` or an `AxialForceCarryingMember`.

4.6.2   *Message-Passing Architecture*

C. L. Dym has written that 'Message passing in OOP is like having one or more fireworks in a box of fireworks start exploding, igniting other fireworks in the box and finally burning out, without any apparent control' (Dym, 1991: 148).

Message-passing architectures in object-oriented systems have to be carefully designed. Even though objects are meant to be self-contained modular units, application designers need to examine the total system, including all interacting objects. Classes can never be designed independently of each other. Only during implementation might classes be developed in isolation.

Without careful design, message-passing architectures may contain infinite loops similar to those caused by recursive function calls in structured programming. Consider three objects A, B and C (Figure 4.8). A sends a message to B to perform a task without a detailed knowledge of how B performs this task. Object B in turn delegates this task to C and C to A. This results in cycles that repeat forever. This is a simplified scenario and is easy to detect. In systems containing hundreds of objects that interact with each other in a complex manner, these loops may be harder to spot.

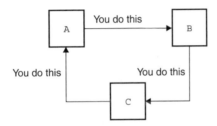

Figure 4.8   Infinite loops with message passing

4.7 SUMMARY

- Objects are useful for representing complex information.

- Objects have characteristics such as encapsulation of data and methods, message passing, and abstraction hierarchies. Other features, such as data protection and polymorphism, are useful in code maintenance.

- Object-oriented analysis and design are tasks that require special attention.

- Concepts in object representation have found a wide range of applications outside programming. For example, they are used in knowledge representation, rapid application development and user interfaces.

REFERENCES

Dym, C. L. and Levitt, R. E. 1991. *Knowledge-Based Systems in Engineering*. New York: McGraw-Hill.
Minsky, M. 1975. A framework for representing knowledge. In *The Psychology of Computer Vision*. P. Winston (ed.). New York: McGraw-Hill.

FURTHER READING

Booch, G. 1994. *Object Oriented Analysis and Design with Applications*. Redwood City CA: Benjamin Cummings.
Budd, T. 1991. *An Introduction to Object-Oriented Programming*. Reading MA: Addison-Wesley.
Campione, M. and Walrath, K. 1986. *The Java Tutorial: Object-Oriented Programming for the Internet*. Reading MA: Addison-Wesley.

EXERCISES

4.1 Different types of load acting on a simply supported beam are shown in Figure 4.9. To find out the reactions of the beam, it is necessary to compute the resultant load

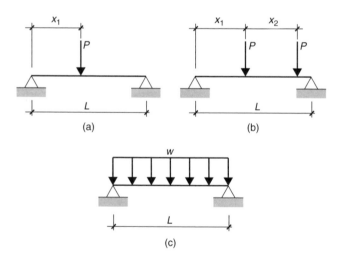

Figure 4.9   Loads acting on a beam: (a) point load, (b) 2-point load, (c) uniformly distributed load

and its point of application. Define classes to represent different types of load. Enumerate the attributes and methods of each class.

4.2 An electronic circuit consists of a single voltage source and a number of resistors connected in series and parallel, as shown in Figure 4.10(a). There is no internal loop in the circuit, as in Figure 4.10(b). It is necessary to compute the current through each resistor. Design an object representation for the circuit.

4.3 A storm water drainage system is shown as a network in Figure 4.11. At each node in the network there is inflow and outflow. The net outflow at each node is equal to the net inflow. It is necessary to compute the outflow at any specified node. Design an object representation for the drainage system.

4.4 A road network is shown in Figure 4.12. Junctions are denoted by dots and roads by lines. Each junction is represented by the following class:

```
Class Junction {
        Attributes:
                junctionNumber          : integer
                numberOfRoads           : integer
                roads                   : array of class road
```

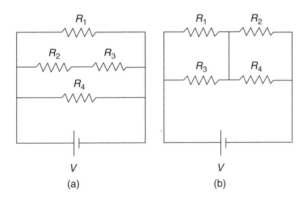

Figure 4.10   Electronic circuits: (a) a simple circuit, (b) a circuit with inner loops

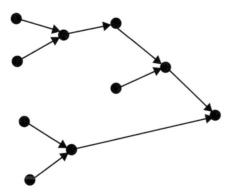

Figure 4.11   A storm water drainage network. Arrows represent direction of flow in pipes that connect nodes

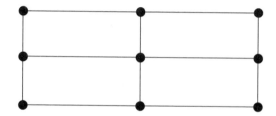

Figure 4.12   A simple road network

```
Methods:
  checkPath (Junction junctionB)
      : checks if there exists a path from this junction to
        junctionB
      : returns true if a path exists
}
```

The following class represents each road:

```
Class Road {
    Attributes:
        junction1 : Class Junction
        junction2 : Class Junction
    Methods:
        connectedTo (Junction aJunction)
          : checks if this road is directly connected to
            aJunction. Returns true if aJunction is the
            same as junction1 or junction2

}
```

Consider the following algorithm for the method `checkPath`:

```
Method checkPath (Junction junctionB)
    Send the message connectedTo(junctionB) to each element of the
    array roads of this junction. If any element returns true,
    then return true

    Send the message checkPath(junctionB) to junction1 and junction2
    of each road in the array roads. If any element returns true,
    then return true

    Return false
}
```

What is wrong with this method?

4.5 Tensile bars are made of composite material in the construction of a truss (Figure 4.13). The following combinations of material are available:

- wood + steel;
- concrete + steel;
- wood + aluminium.

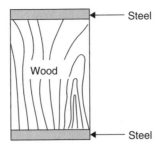

Figure 4.13   Cross-section of a bar made of composite material

The elongation of the bar is computed as

$$dl = LP/EA$$

where L is the length of the bar, P is the tensile force, A is the total cross-sectional area and E is the effective Young's modulus, which is computed using the formula

$$E = \frac{E_1 A_1 + E_2 A_2}{A_1 + A_2}$$

where E_1, E_2 are the Young's moduli of each material and A_1, A_2 are the areas of each material. In a non-object-oriented representation, the following data structure is used:

```
structure CompositeBar {
        material1    : any material, wood, steel, concrete, aluminum, etc.
        material2    : any material
        width        : number representing the width of the cross-section
        depth1       : number representing the total depth of material1
        depth2       : number representing the total depth of material2
}
```

All material properties are stored in an array. Write a procedure without object representation to compute the elongation of the bar. The inputs for the procedure are P, L, and the structure CompositeBar. How many comparisons (if statements) are needed in the procedure?

Design an object representation for the bars. How many comparisons (if statements) are required in the method to compute the elongation of the bar. Discuss the advantages in terms of code reuse and adding new combinations of materials.

4.6 Consider this implementation of an array that grows dynamically (Figure 4.14):

```
Class DynamicArray{
  Attributes
        numElements: integer representing actual number of elements
            currently present in the array
        elements : an array of integers containing all the elements
        dimension : dimension of the array elements (memory allocated
            for the array). This is always greater than or equal to
            numElements
```

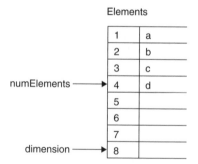

Figure 4.14   Implementation of an array whose size grows dynamically

```
Methods
      setElementAt (position, element)
             : the method to store an element at the specified position
             : it allocates more memory to the array elements if
                position is greater than dimension
      }
```

Which attributes and methods should be made private in the class `DynamicArray`?

4.7 Consider the following relationships. If multiple inheritance is not allowed, how can they be represented?

(a) A hospital is a type of building.
(b) An office building is a type of building.
(c) A residential building is a type of building.
(d) A multi-storey building is a type of building.
(e) A single-storey building is a type of building.
(f) Hospital X is a hospital.
(g) Hospital X is a multi-storey building.

4.8 A certain library for developing graphical user interfaces (GUIs) contains the class `GridPanel` for arranging user interface elements such as text boxes and images on a regular grid. All columns in the grid are of constant size but the row height may vary. The class `GridPanel` has the following attributes:

```
numRows         : number of rows
numColums       : number of columns
GUIElements     : an array of GUI elements arranged on the uniform grid
```

Each GUI element on the grid could be a text box (editable), label (non-editable), a button or even a `GridPanel` object. Draw the decomposition hierarchy for the screen in Figure 4.15.

4.9 Consider the abstraction hierarchy in Figure 4.16. Consider the following instances:

```
A    StructuralEngineer
B    GeotechnicalEngineer
C    TransportationEngineer
D    MechanicalEngineer
E    ElectricalEngineer
```

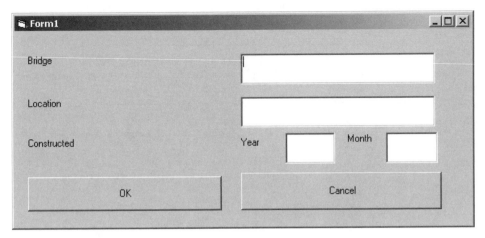

Figure 4.15   Arrangement of GUI elements in a decomposition hierarchy

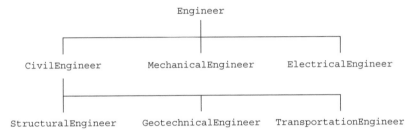

Figure 4.16   An abstraction hierarchy of professionals

Let x be a variable denoting any `CivilEngineer` and y be a variable denoting any `StructuralEngineer`. Which of the following assignments are valid?

```
x = A
x = D
x = y
y = x
```

4.10 Consider the abstraction hierarchy in Exercise 4.9. Now consider the additional abstraction hierarchy in Figure 4.17. An abstract method `performTask` is defined in the class `Engineer` in order to simulate the performance of a task by an engineer:

```
performTask (EngineeringTask t1)
```

This method is redefined (method overriding) for each subclass. The method argument t1 belongs to the class `EngineeringTask`. In addition, the class `StructuralEngineer` contains another method

```
doDesign (DesignBeamTask t1)
```

The method argument t1 belongs to the class `DesignBeamTask`.

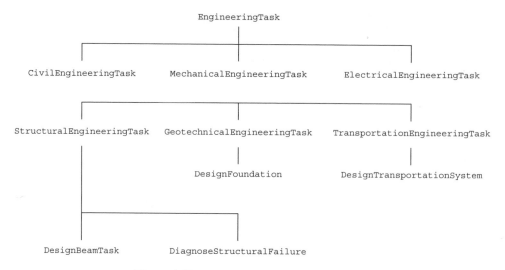

Figure 4.17   An abstraction hierarchy of tasks

Which of the following message passings are correct if db is an instance of Design-BeamTask and df is an instance of the task DesignFoundation?

```
A.doDesign(db)
x.doDesign(db)
x.performTask(db)
A.performTask(df)
```

5

Database Concepts

5.1 INTRODUCTION

There are few practical computer applications in engineering that do not use databases. The amount of digital information in engineering is increasing exponentially, and this trend is not expected to slow in the foreseeable future. Some experts are even concerned that we will soon be 'drowned' in data to the point where our inability to manage information adequately may create situations where we would be better not using it at all.

Regardless of whether such events will occur or not, engineers will be increasingly expected to ensure that engineering data are organized so that access and retrieval are easy, reliable and robust. An equally important requirement is to create databases that are easy to update and change. In the past, failure to satisfy this requirement has led to CAE applications that did not outlive the presence of their developers. New people on the job find it easier to start again from scratch rather than modify bad database designs. The total cost of such redevelopment is surely very high, especially considering the number of consulting firms and engineering industries that maintain in-house databases.

Here are some examples of information that is contained in typical engineering database applications:

- design calculations;
- simulation data;
- drawings;
- measurement data;
- experimental results;
- geographical information;
- weather data;
- cost data;
- product models;
- material properties;
- loading data;
- performance criteria;
- non-destructive testing data.

The term 'information' is used to denote both data and knowledge as defined in Chapter 9.

Fundamentals of Computer-Aided Engineering   B. Raphael and I. F. C. Smith
© 2003 John Wiley & Sons, Ltd   ISBNs: 0-471-48709-0 (HB); 0-471-48715-5 (PB)

Engineering data are rarely independent of other data. Indeed, when engineers use the term 'complex tasks', they are usually referring to the interdependence of data rather than computational complexity (Chapter 2). Such strong interdependence creates challenges to those who design databases for engineering applications.

This chapter begins with a short introduction to database technology and an explanation of important terminology. Relational database systems are described in detail since they are the predominant type. A key part of this chapter deals with good database design. This discussion builds on a description of functional dependencies and normal forms. Later parts of the chapter include sections on transaction processing, distributed databases, object-oriented databases, multimedia database systems and geographic databases. All of these subjects contribute to the increasing scope of possibilities for database applications in computer-aided engineering (CAE).

5.2 BASIC CONCEPTS

5.2.1 Initial Definitions

A *database* is a collection of persistent and structured data. The word *persistent* in this definition implies that data are stored on a secondary storage device and remains available after a session on the computer is terminated. Examples of non-persistent data are values of variables in a program which are stored in the primary RAM memory and which vanish when the program terminates. The word *structured* means that data are stored in a form that is easily separable into logical parts. This is different from the idea of structure used in Chapter 1. According to the definition, a word-processing document is not a database since the information contained in it is not structured. Some textbooks classify persistent and unstructured data as a type of database. This definition is not used here.

A *database management system* is a software component that manages databases. Database management systems (DBMS) provide controlled access to data such that multiple users and processes are able to retrieve and modify data without causing data corruption. A *database application* is a program, along with its data, that employs the services of a database management system for carrying out its tasks. In this chapter the term 'database application' is often shortened to 'application'.

5.2.2 Evolution of Different Types of Database

Before the advent of databases, all data were stored in flat files. A difficulty with flat files is that the structure of data is not explicitly stored. Although users are able to examine and manually modify data parts using tools such as text editors, automating modifications is difficult due to a lack of knowledge about the structure of data. Many software products store data in their own internal format (usually proprietary). While these products are able to read and modify their own data, other software is not often able to do so because the data format is unknown.

Database management systems were first created in the 1960s to allow sharing of data between multiple users and applications. One of the early database management systems is DB2, which is a hierarchical DBMS. As its name implies, a hierarchical database contains hierarchically organized data, similar to the structure of a directory tree. Hierarchical databases were an improvement over completely unstructured flat files. However, the field of databases lacked firm mathematical basis until E. F. Codd published a paper on the relational model in 1970. With the emergence of standards such as SQL, relational databases are now employed within the majority of industrial and commercial applications.

Since the 1980s object-oriented programming (OOP) has become a popular paradigm, and software vendors have strived to propose object-oriented products. The field of databases was not unaffected by this trend. Although several object-oriented database management systems have appeared, their use in commercial applications is still limited. This is mainly because their ability to manipulate large volumes of data has not been sufficiently demonstrated. Another reason is the lack of standards. The development of an object query language (OQL) is a significant step towards rectifying this drawback.

Several other database types exist, such as multimedia and geographic databases. These are used in specialized areas such as in entertainment and geographic information systems (GIS).

5.2.3   The Three-Level Architecture

Data may be viewed at three different levels (Figure 5.1). At the application level, data are organized into high-level categories that have meaning for specific applications. At the conceptual level, the application-oriented categories are mapped to representations that are unique to the type of database. At the level of internal representation, data are physically stored in files in proprietary formats; these formats are of interest only to the developers of a particular DBMS. Engineers who develop database applications need to concentrate on mappings between application-level and conceptual-level representations.

For example, consider a business application that processes orders from customers. The application-level representation consists of data structures for customers and orders. At this level, operations such as 'place an order' and 'delete an order' are defined. If a relational DBMS is used for this application, the conceptual view consists of tables in which these data are stored. Operations such as 'insert a record' and 'delete a record' are defined at this level. Internally, all these data might be stored in one or many files in formats proprietary to the DBMS. Low-level read and write operations are defined at this level. Engineers dealing with applications need not be concerned with this level.

5.3   RELATIONAL DATABASE SYSTEMS

Relational databases are based on the relational model presented by Codd (1970). The main theme of Codd's model is a conceptual representation scheme that protects users from having to know how the data are organized in files (i.e. the internal representation described in Section 5.2.3). This representation scheme has firm mathematical foundations with roots in set theory.

The principle behind the relational model is to organize data in the form of two-dimensional tables (called relations). Each table consists of a fixed number of columns

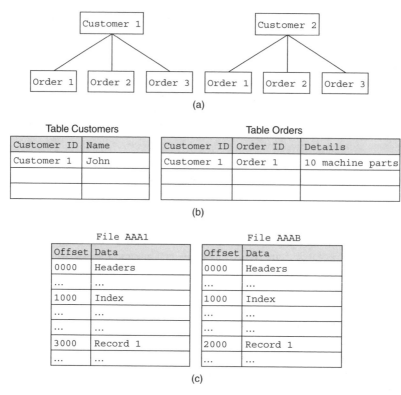

Figure 5.1   Viewing data in an order-processing application: (a) application-level view, (b) conceptual-level view, (c) internal representation

(attributes) and a variable number of rows (records). A standard set of operations is defined on tables so that data can be modified in an implementation- and application-independent manner (i.e. at the conceptual level described in Section 5.2.3).

Relational databases are popular for the following reason:

- Commercial applications contain large amounts of structured data that are easily organized into tables.
- Tables are a natural way of organizing many types of data; the simplicity of table representation is appealing.
- Standard table operations such as selecting, inserting, updating and deleting of records are efficiently implemented, thus accommodating large volumes of data.

There are many examples of data organized into tables within commercial applications. Here are some common examples:

- sales and purchase records;
- address lists;
- personnel files.

And here are some engineering examples:

- material costs;
- product properties and dimensions;
- measurement data;
- load data;
- data on past projects;
- topological data.

Since the relational model is the mathematical basis for relational databases, it is necessary to understand it in detail. This is the next topic.

5.3.1   The Relational Model

Consider the sets A_1 and A_2 in Figure 5.2. From set theory, the cross product $A_1 \times A_2$, also known as the Cartesian product, is the set of all ordered pairs obtained by selecting one element from A_1 and the other from A_2. Extending this operation, the cross product of n sets can be defined as the set of all ordered n-tuples containing one element from each set (Figure 5.3). This set contains all possible combinations of elements contained in the constituent sets. A subset of this set might be defined such that it contains only combinations that are valid according to a certain relationship. Such a subset is called a relation.

Formal definition   *An n-ary relation among sets, $A_1, A_2, \ldots, A_n$ is a subset of $((A_1 \times A_2) \times \ldots) \times A_n$. The sets $A_1, A_2, \ldots$ are called the domains. The variable n is called the degree of the relation.*

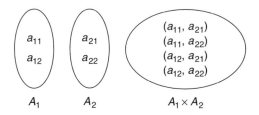

Figure 5.2   Cross product of two sets

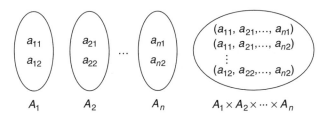

Figure 5.3   Cross product of 'n' sets

Example 5.1

Consider the set of symbols denoting available steel plate sections, {P10, P12, P16}. Also consider the set of available plate thicknesses, {10,12,16}. The cross product of these sets contains all combinations of elements from the two sets. However, the relation Steel Plate Sections is defined as the set consisting of all legal combinations, for example {(P10, 10), (P12, 12), (P16, 16)}. The elements contained in the relation might vary over time, but they always compose a subset of the cross product of the two sets.

For all practical purposes, a relation may be considered to be a table. Domains are columns or attributes of the table. The degree of the relation is the number of columns. Each n-tuple (or simply tuple when the degree n of the relation is known), is a row or record in the table. Table 5.1 represents a relation of degree 4 with 4 elements.

Here are three key properties of relations:

- The order of attributes (columns) is immaterial.
- The order of tuples (rows) is immaterial.
- There are no duplicate tuples (rows).

These properties are essential to ensure that the result of all relational operations remains a relation.

5.3.1.1 Further definitions

A domain of a table is called a *primary key* if its value in a record uniquely identifies the record in the table. The attribute Section-ID in Table 5.1 uniquely identifies records in the table Steel Plate Sections. Hence it is the primary key in that table. The significance of the primary key is that it is a reliable mechanism for referring to a particular record in a table. This is because records in a table are unordered. Suppose we need to delete the third row of the table of steel plate sections shown in Table 5.1, the only way to express this requirement is 'delete the record in the table Steel Plate Sections where Section-ID is P16'.

A *composite primary key* is the Cartesian product of two or more domains such that its value in a record uniquely identifies the record in the table. In many practical situations it is not possible to find a single attribute that uniquely identifies a record within a table. However, combinations of attributes might uniquely identify records. Consider the shipments of steel sections shown in Table 5.2. This table contains the number of

Table 5.1   Illustration of a relation

Steel Plate Sections

Section-ID	Thickness	Width	Area
P10	10	100	1000
P12	12	100	1200
P16	16	100	1600
P20	20	120	2400

Table 5.2 A relation with a composite primary key

Shipments		
Supplier-ID	Section-ID	Number
S1	P10	12
S1	P12	10
S2	P10	20

items supplied by each supplier. The attribute Supplier-ID cannot be the primary key because the same supplier supplies multiple plate sections. Similarly, Section-ID cannot be the primary key since multiple suppliers provide the same plate section. But the combination of Supplier-ID and Section-ID uniquely identifies records in the table, hence this combination is a composite primary key.

A domain of a table is called a *foreign key* if it refers to the primary key of another table. Consider the attribute Section-ID in the table Shipments. This attribute refers to the primary key of the table Steel Plate Sections. This attribute is analogous to a pointer in a programming language. It contains a reference to another record, although it is not a memory address. A value for Section-ID in the table Shipments cannot exist without a corresponding value in the table Steel Plate Sections. This condition is called the referential integrity constraint and is enforced by the relational database management system (RDBMS). RDBMS do not allow users to insert records in tables if foreign key attribute values do not have matching values in the tables to which they refer.

In theory it is possible to have more than one set of attributes that uniquely identify a record in a table. In practice only one is chosen as the primary key in a table. Other sets are known as alternate keys. The term *candidate key* is used to denote both the primary key and alternate keys.

5.3.1.2 Operations on relations

A *select* or *restrict* operation on a relation R returns another relation consisting of all rows of R that satisfy a specific condition. The select operation returns a table containing a subset of rows in the original table. For example, a single record is selected from the table Steel Plate Sections if the condition is specified as Thickness less than 12.

A *projection* of a relation R is an m-ary relation, $m \leq n$, obtained from R by deleting $n - m$ of the components in each ordered n-tuple in R. It is an abstraction of the original table. A projection is simply a table obtained by deleting columns from another table. Table 5.3 is a projection of Table 5.1 obtained by removing the columns Width and Area.

The operation *join* combines two tables into one. Here is the formal definition. Let {X1, X2, ..., Xm, Y1, Y2, ..., Yn} be the columns of a table A, and {Y1, Y2, ..., Yn, Z1, Z2, ..., Zp} be the columns of a table B, where columns {Y1, Y2, ..., Yn} are common to both tables. The join of A and B is a table C containing the columns {X1, X2, ..., Xm, Y1, Y2, ..., Yn, Z1, Z2, ..., Zp} such that for every

Table 5.3   Projection of the table `Steel Plate Sections` (Table 5.1)

Steel Plate Section thickness	
Section-ID	Thickness
P10	10
P12	12
P16	16
P20	20

Table 5.4   Join of `Steel Plate Sections` and `Shipments`

Shipment details				
Supplier	Section-ID	Number	Area	Width
S1	P10	12	1000	100
S1	P12	10	1200	100
S2	P10	20	1000	100

pair of rows in A and B that have common values for {Y1, Y2, ..., Yn} there exists a row in C whose values of columns are the same as those in corresponding rows. This operation is called equi-join; there are more complex joins but they are not considered in this chapter.

The join operation takes rows from tables that contain related data and combines them into a single table. This permits a unified view of data and thus avoids retrieving information from several tables. For example, the table `Shipments` does not contain details of the sections supplied by each supplier. This information is obtained from the table `Steel Plate Sections`. The two kinds of information can be combined into a single table by performing a join of the two tables as shown in Table 5.4.

5.3.2   Limitations of Relational Databases

The use of relational databases requires that all data be represented as tables. Each table has a fixed number of columns, and each column contains atomic values of fixed size. The term 'atomic' means indivisible. That is, values cannot be separated further into meaningful pieces of data. Numbers (real and integer) and fixed-sized strings are atomic. Lists, arrays and other abstract data types discussed in Chapter 3 are not atomic. They are compound data types which can be separated further into meaningful components. Such data types cannot be stored as values in tables. This limitation is usually overcome through storing variable-length elements in separate tables. The next example illustrates this approach.

Example 5.2

Leaf springs are fabricated by welding together multiple steel plates as shown in Figure 5.4. The number of plates varies and so does with their thickness. The width of each plate is constant. The following details for each leaf spring need to be stored:

Figure 5.4   Leaf springs

- total weight;
- position, length and thickness of each plate used.

Perform a table design so that all required details are stored in a relational database.

Solution

The data might be stored in two relational tables: (a) leaf springs (Table 5.5) and (b) steel plates used in all leaf springs (Table 5.6). We cannot store all details in a single table because the number of plates used in each leaf spring varies. It is not possible to have a variable list of columns or a variable list of elements within a single column. Therefore the variable list of elements (steel plate details) is stored in a separate table. Rows in this table are linked to the table of leaf springs by the attribute `Spring ID`, which is a foreign key. To obtain the list of all steel plates used in a particular leaf spring, it is enough to select rows from the second table using the condition that the value of the attribute `Spring ID` is equal to the ID of the spring we are interested in.

Discussion   *This example illustrates the process of converting data to the relational form. It is necessary to follow a process of decomposition to convert data to tables such that each column contains only atomic values. This process is particularly challenging when the data structure involves complex decomposition hierarchies. Chapter 3 contains a more detailed discussion of decomposition hierarchies.*

Table 5.5   Leaf spring table

Spring ID	Weight
S1	100
S2	200

Table 5.6   Steel plates used in leaf springs

Sl No.	Spring ID	Thickness	Position	Length
1	S1	24	0.0	10.0
2	S1	36	10.0	30.0
3	S1	24	30.0	10.0
4	S2	24	0.0	15.0
⋮	⋮	⋮	⋮	⋮

5.3.3 *Accessing Data in Relational Databases*

Relational databases allow us to define data manipulation operations at the conceptual level. But in practical applications we need to have a common language that is independent of database management systems and vendors. This was made possible by the introduction of SQL, Structured Query Language. SQL was introduced by IBM in the early 1970s and later adopted as an international standard.

5.3.3.1 Structured query language

SQL defines the syntax for performing standard operations on databases such as

- creating tables;
- inserting rows;
- selecting rows;
- updating rows;
- deleting rows;
- joining tables;
- projecting tables.

SQL statements are grouped into two categories: data definition operations and data manipulation operations. Table creation is an example of a data definition operation (the structure of a table is defined). Inserting and deleting rows are examples of data manipulation operations.

The complete specification of SQL is voluminous and beyond the scope of this book, but here are a few examples to illustrate its use.

Example 5.3

```
INSERT INTO steel_plates (Section-ID, Thickness, Width, Area)
   VALUES ('I-100', 12, 100, 1200)
```

This statement inserts a row into the table `steel_plates`. The values of attributes are given within the brackets following the keyword `VALUES`. The values are given in the same order as the attribute names listed in brackets following the name of the table.

Example 5.4

```
CREATE TABLE emp_details (
        first_name char(15) not null,
        last_name char(15) not null,
        comment text(50),
        dept char(20),
        emp_id int,
        PRIMARY KEY (emp_id)
      )
```

This statement creates a new table called `emp_details`. The attributes of the table are `first_name`, `last_name`, `comment`, `dept`, and `emp_id`. The data types of each attribute are also specified in the statement. The last line before the bracket specifies that the primary key for the table is the attribute emp_id.

Example 5.5

```
DROP TABLE table_name
```

This statement deletes a table along with all rows in it.

Example 5.6

```
SELECT first_name, last_name FROM emp_details
       WHERE dept = 'civil'
       ORDER BY last_name, first_name
```

This statement is used to retrieve a set of rows from the table emp_details. All rows which have the value of the attribute dept as 'civil' are returned. The rows are ordered (sorted) according to the attributes last_name and first_name.

Example 5.7

```
DELETE FROM emp_details WHERE emp_id = 12345
```

This statement deletes the row in the table emp_details in which the value of the attribute emp_id is 12345.

Example 5.8

```
UPDATE emp_details SET salary = 50 000 WHERE emp_id = 1234
```

This statement updates a row in the table emp_details. The row where attribute emp_id has value 1234 is selected and the field salary is updated to 50 000.

5.4   RELATIONAL DATABASE DESIGN

Databases need to be carefully designed. Good database designs produce applications that have less redundant information and fewer difficulties associated with changes. A notation has been proposed to help avoid such difficulties. This notation categorizes tables into forms (known as normal forms) that have special characteristics. There are primarily five normal forms: 1NF, 2NF, 3NF, 4NF and 5NF. They are defined such that higher forms include the definition for lower forms. For example, if a table is in 3NF, it is also in 2NF and 1NF. There is also a special case of 3NF called the Boyce–Codd normal form.

Normal forms are important concepts in good database design, so we will look at them in detail. For simplicity, informal definitions are used wherever possible instead of rigorous mathematical definitions. Only the first three normal forms are discussed, but this is enough to illustrate normalization.

5.4.1   First Normal Form

A relation is said to be in first normal form (1NF) if it contains only atomic (scalar) values. That is, all attribute values are simple data types such as numbers and strings. Since the assumption of atomic values for all attributes is fundamental to the relational model, all relational tables are automatically in first normal form. In other words, only relations in first normal form can be stored in a relational database. Table 5.7 is not in first normal form and consequently cannot be stored in a relational database.

Since all relational tables are in first normal form, the process of normalization refers to converting them into higher normal forms. A prerequisite for a relation to be in a higher normal form is that it belongs to lower normal forms. It also needs to satisfy other criteria.

The concept of functional dependency is used when defining higher normal forms. A functional dependency (FD) is a relationship from one set of attributes to another within a given relation. That is, there is a correspondence between a set of attributes Xi and another set of attribute Yj in a relation A (Figure 5.5).

Functional dependencies have semantic foundations. They are formulated according to the meaning of data and the way parts of the data are related to each other in an application. Knowledge about relationships between attributes is not stored in a relational database. Although database tables are designed using knowledge of relationships between attributes, the only form of knowledge that is explicitly stored in a database is that all attributes in a relation are related to the primary key (by the definition of a primary key). The process of normalization is aimed at expressing all functional dependencies (semantic relationships) in terms of primary key definitions so that DBMS can enforce these relationships. Whether a relation is in a higher normal form is only determined by a semantic analysis of relationships between attributes at the application level.

5.4.2   Second Normal Form

A relation is said to be in second normal form (2NF) if it is in 1NF and every non-key attribute is irreducibly dependent on the primary key. The term 'irreducible' means that when the primary key is composite, a non-key attribute depends on the entire primary

Table 5.7   A table of leaf springs that is not in first normal form (1NF). A leaf spring consists of a variable number of plates having different thickness. The last column of the table does not contain atomic values, hence the table is not in 1NF. This table may be converted to 1NF by splitting it into two tables as shown in Table 5.5 and Table 5.6

Sl No.	Spring ID	Thickness of plates used
1	S1	24, 36, 24
2	S2	24, 30
:	:	:

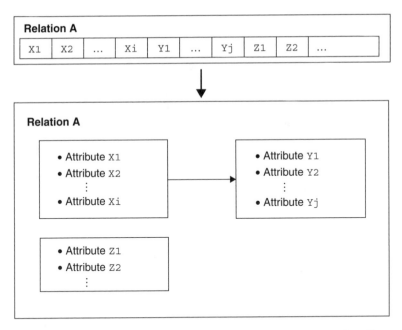

Figure 5.5   A Functional dependency (FD) is a relationship between a set of attributes {Xi} and another set of attribute {Yj} within a relation

key and not on a subset of the attributes that form the primary key. Figure 5.6 shows two relations that are in 2NF and one relation that is not in 2NF.

Example 5.9   A bridge database

A bridge database contains a list of bridges in a country. A bridge is identified by a name and a location where it exists, perhaps the name of a city. Since bridges with the same name exist at different locations in the same country, only the combination of the name and location uniquely determines the bridge. Details of the bridge as well as the environment are stored in the table. Table 5.8 shows a simplified table.

Since the combination of Location and Name uniquely identifies each row in the table, the primary key is the combination of the two attributes. However, the environment is a function of Location only, not the combination. The functional dependencies are shown in Figure 5.7.

The table can be converted to second normal form by splitting it into two tables, a table of environment state (Table 5.9) and a table of bridge details (Table 5.10). The attribute Location is the primary key in the first table, and the combination of Location and Name is the primary key in the second table. The attribute Location in the second table is a foreign key that refers to the attribute with the same name in the first table. Now in both tables non-key attributes depend on the whole primary key, hence both tables are in 2NF.

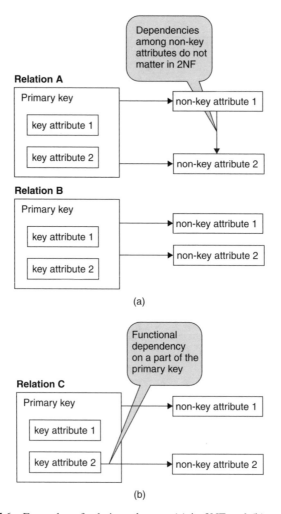

Figure 5.6 Examples of relations that are (a) in 2NF and (b) not in 2NF

Table 5.8 Bridge details

Location	Name	Year of construction	Environment
London	Tower Bridge	1894	Corrosive
London	London Bridge	1973	Corrosive
⋮	⋮	⋮	⋮

5.4.2.1 Update anomalies

If a table is not in second normal form, several update anomalies and redundancies might occur. The bridge database offers an illustration. In the following discussion, the term 'fact' will be used to denote a piece of information about an object or concept.

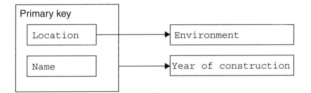

Figure 5.7 Functional dependencies in the bridge table. The primary key is the combination of location and name which uniquely identifies the bridge. Although the year of construction is a function of the complete primary key, the environment is a function of the location alone. Hence, this table is not in 2NF

Table 5.9 Environment state

Location	Environment
London	Corrosive
⋮	⋮

Table 5.10 Bridge details

Location	Name	Year of construction
London	Tower Bridge	1894
London	London Bridge	1973
⋮	⋮	⋮

- *Redundancy*: values of attributes that depend on a part of the primary key might be repeated several times in the table, causing redundancy and extra memory requirements. In Table 5.8 the fact that London is in a corrosive environment is repeated twice.

- *Insert*: each row contains more than one fact. A fact cannot be inserted unless other facts in the row are known. In Table 5.8 the fact that Glasgow is in a non-corrosive environment cannot be inserted into the database unless there is a bridge at this location to be inserted into the database.

- *Update*: since there are redundant and repeated data, facts need to be updated at multiple locations. If due to unknown factors (global climate change or redefinition of corrosion thresholds) London turns out to be a non-corrosive environment, this fact needs to be updated in multiple rows.

- *Delete*: information is lost when rows are deleted since each row contains more than one fact. If there is only a single bridge in London, the fact that London is in a corrosive environment is lost when that row is deleted.

5.4.3 Third Normal Form

A relation is said to be in third normal form (3NF) if it is in 2NF and every non-key attribute is mutually independent. The definition of mutual independence is as follows:

two or more attributes are mutually independent if none of them is functionally dependent on any combination of the others. Relation B in Figure 5.6(a) is in 3NF since there are no dependencies between non-key attributes. Although Relation A is in 2NF, it is not in 3NF (Figure 5.8).

Consider the table of bridge details shown in Table 5.11. The column `Age of the bridge` has been added. This attribute is functionally dependent on the attribute `Year of construction`, hence the table is not in 3NF. However, it is possible to convert the relation into 3NF by removing the last column and putting this information into another table, as shown in Table 5.12.

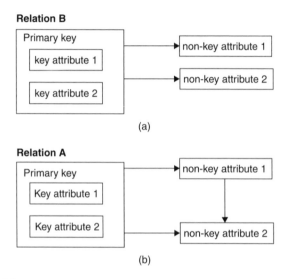

Figure 5.8 Examples of relations that are (a) in 3NF and (b) not in 3NF

Table 5.11 Bridge details (modified)

Location	Name	Year of construction	Age of the bridge
London	Tower bridge	1894	Old
London	London bridge	1973	Recent
⋮	⋮	⋮	⋮

Table 5.12 Classification of the age of the bridge

Year of construction	Age of the bridge
1894	old
1973	recent
⋮	⋮

5.4.3.1 Update anomalies related to 3NF

If a table is not in the third normal form, several update anomalies and redundancies might result, similar to Section 5.4.2.2. Some can be illustrated using Table 5.11.

- *Redundancy*: values of attributes that depend on a non-key attribute might be repeated several times in the table, causing redundancy. The fact that bridges built in 1894 are old would be repeated several times if there were several bridges built in that year.

- *Insert*: each row contains more than one piece of information, or fact. A fact cannot be inserted unless other facts in the row are known. The fact that bridges built in 1894 are old cannot be inserted unless there is at least one bridge built in that year.

- *Update*: since there are redundant and repeated data, facts need to be updated at multiple locations.

- *Delete*: information is lost when rows are deleted since each row contains more than one fact. If there is only a single bridge built in 1894, the fact that bridges built in 1894 are old is lost when that row is deleted.

5.4.4 Boyce–Codd and Higher Normal Forms

Boyce–Codd Normal Form (BCNF) is an extension of 3NF to account for situations where there are several candidate keys that are composite. Higher normal forms (4NF and 5NF) use a new type of dependency called multivalued dependency (MVD), an extension of functional dependency. 4NF and 5NF are rarely used in practice, so they are not discussed here.

5.4.5 Importance of Database Design

An important objective of all design activities in software engineering is to improve maintenance reliability. The importance of good object-oriented design with respect to maintenance reliability was emphasized in Chapter 4. In database design, the process of normalization results in tables that are easier to maintain. Bad database designs result in several types of update anomalies when tables are modified and this reduces the useful life of applications. The significance of update anomalies goes beyond databases. Similar ideas are found in Chapters 7, 9, 11, 12 and 13.

5.5 TRANSACTION PROCESSING

Databases are typically employed in multi-user and multi-process environments. Several users and processes might attempt to modify the same data at the same time, and this could cause inconsistencies.

Example 5.10 A Steel Inventory

Consider an application that manages inventory of available steel plates in a fabrication plant. Two operators use the application at the same time (Figure 5.9). They both request

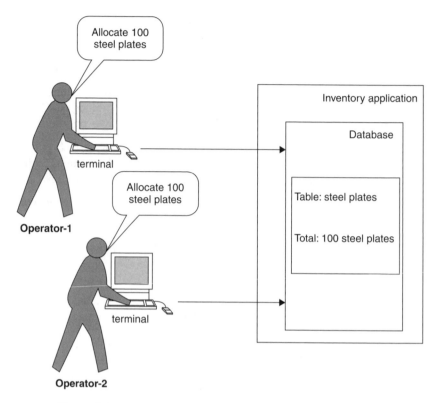

Figure 5.9 Two users modifying the same data at the same time

100 steel plates to be allocated for the fabrication of two different components. Only 100 steel plates are currently available in the inventory.

The inventory application checks the remaining number of steel plates before allowing users to allocate them for fabrication. If the application services only a single client at a time, either Operator-1 or Operator-2 is able to allocate the available steel plates, since after the first client is serviced, the remaining number of steel plates is zero. Modern DBMS service requests from several clients simultaneously in order to avoid delays. Assume that a novice programmer who is unaware of transaction processing requirements developed the application. The function to allocate resources was written with three steps:

1. Check current balance (select query).
2. If balance is okay, allow resource allocation.
3. Update new balance (update query).

The select and update queries are sent as two separate requests. Under normal circumstances the procedure works well. However, inconsistencies might result if two clients operate at the same time. Assume that the select query from Operator-2 reaches the DBMS immediately after step 2 of the procedure has been completed for Operator-1. The old balance (100) is returned even though 100 steel plates have already been allocated. The update (step 3) for Operator-1 is performed only after step 1 is completed for Operator-2.

In this situation, both operators are able to allocate 100 steel plates for their activities, even though the inventory contained only a total of 100 steel plates.

5.5.1 Definition of Transaction

The situation described in the previous example arose because queries were sent as independent requests, not as part of a single unit. A single logical unit consisting of multiple related requests is called a *transaction*. A transaction is sometimes called a logical unit of work (LUW). Either all requests in a transaction go through successfully or all of them fail. It is not possible for some requests to be carried out and some to fail. If any request fails, all effects of previous requests from the transaction are undone.

5.5.2 Implementing Transactions

Modern databases provide support for implementing transactions. Two essential requirements for transaction processing are

- data locks;
- ability to undo changes without loss of consistency.

These techniques are widely used in business applications to avoid problems due to simultaneous access and modification of data.

5.5.2.1 Data locks

There are two types of locks. Exclusive locks (write locks) and shared locks (read locks). Exclusive locks are acquired when applications modify data. Only one application holds an exclusive lock to a data item at any time. Other applications that require the lock must wait until the existing lock is released. The application releases the lock when all updates are complete.

Shared locks are acquired by applications that do not need to modify data but need to ensure that data do not change until a set of operations are complete. Multiple applications may acquire shared lock simultaneously. If any application has acquired a shared lock for a data item, no other application is granted an exclusive lock until all shared locks are released. This ensures that data are not modified during this period.

In the example of resource allocation, the right sequence of operations is as follows:

1. Acquire an exclusive lock for the data item, remaining number of steel plates.
2. Check the remaining number of steel plates (select query).
3. If the remaining number of steel plates is okay, allow resource allocation.
4. Update the remaining number of steel plates (update query).
5. Release the lock.

All five steps are part of a single transaction. The lock is acquired at the beginning of the transaction and released at the end of the transaction.

5.5.2.2   Undoing changes

Database servers permit users to define transactions consisting of a sequence of operations that need to be completed in their entirety. The DBMS ensures that, for each transaction, either all operations are completed or no operation is completed. This is normally done by implicitly acquiring locks and keeping a record of all changes until the end of the transaction. If any of the operations fail, all changes are undone until the beginning of the transaction. The process of undoing is termed rolling back. The process of confirming all changes is called commit.

Example 5.11   Bridge inspections

To understand the significance of transactions, consider a non-DBMS solution to maintain rows of bridge inspections. Assume that all bridge inspection details are stored in a simple text file on a file server. Each bridge inspector updates this file when they have finished inspecting a bridge. Suppose two inspectors complete inspections at around the same time and open the file from two different computers. The first inspector adds the result of his inspection and saves the file. Then the second inspector adds his results to the document, which he opened before the update of the first inspector. When the second inspector saves the file, the update made by the first inspector is lost.

   File locks are provided by certain word-processing applications to prevent lost updates. DBMS extend this idea and provide locks at the row level (instead of complete files). In fact, the process is more complex than simply locking rows because a DBMS needs to recover automatically from errors.

5.5.2.3   Deadlocks

Transactions need to be carefully designed to avoid deadlocks. A typical scenario is when two applications attempt to acquire locks for the same two resources (Figure 5.10). Application 1 has acquired the lock for resource 1 and is waiting to acquire the lock for resource 2. Resource 2 is locked by application 2, which is waiting to acquire the lock for resource 1. Application 2 will not release the lock it has acquired for resource 2 until it completes the transaction, and for this it needs to acquire the lock for resource 1. Similarly, application 1 will not release the lock for resource 1 unless it has acquired the lock for resource 2. Both applications are in a state of deadlock; without intervention, they wait forever.

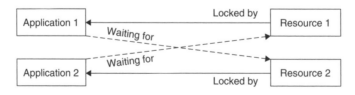

Figure 5.10   A typical deadlock scenario

Deadlocks are difficult to detect when there are multiple resources and multiple applications that are competing to acquire locks, hence deadlock detection is not attempted by many systems. It is easier to avoid deadlocks by careful design with a simple method that properly orders the acquisition of locks. For example, if all applications first attempt to acquire the lock for resource 1 and only then proceed to acquire the lock for resource 2, deadlock will not occur. Application 2 will not be able to lock resource 2 until it has acquired the lock for resource 1. It is able to lock resource 1 only when application 1 has released the lock.

5.5.3   Properties of Transactions

All transactions satisfy four important characteristics known as ACID properties. The acronym comes from taking the initial letter of each property. Modern databases support transactions satisfying ACID properties. However, users need to analyse applications carefully and identify operations that should be implemented as transactions.

- *Atomicity*:   this term implies that transactions form a single unit which has to be completed in its entirety.

- *Consistency*:   if a transaction cannot achieve a correct state, it must return to its initial state.

- *Isolation*:   there should not be any interference between concurrent transactions; that is, changes made by a transaction are visible to another transaction only when the first transaction commits.

- *Durability*:   after a transaction commits, the changes are permanent; there should be no lost updates.

5.6   OTHER TYPES OF DATABASE

5.6.1   Object-Oriented Databases

The example of a leaf spring was discussed in Section 5.3.2 to illustrate converting data into tables for storage in a relational database. In engineering, this type of situation is common where data structures are complex, and attributes are not simple data types such as numbers and strings. Decomposition hierarchies might be dynamic, and the size of the decomposition tree may change according to values of key attributes. Converting information into two-dimensional tables may be difficult. Furthermore, and most importantly, the representation that results is often abstract and difficult to understand.

Many computer-aided design (CAD) systems used in engineering employ object representations and Object-oriented programming languages are increasingly used (Chapter 4). A tighter integration is desired between the data structures in the programming language and the persistent data model. Object-oriented database systems have been developed to satisfy these requirements. The kernel entity used in these systems is an object having a variable number of attributes as well as attribute types that may vary depending on the instance.

Database systems have also been developed to store objects that are created during the execution of programs written in object-oriented languages. The complete state of an object is saved in a database such that an identical object can be created on a different machine or the same machine at a later time.

5.6.2 Geographic Databases

Data models in a standard database environment have been recognized to be inefficient for handling geographic information. For example, geographic objects might be continuous fields with indeterminate boundaries. Objects frequently overlap, and the object to be retrieved at a specific point depends on the level of resolution. Due to the inadequacies of conventional representations such as relational tables, special methodologies and concepts have been developed for storing geographic information.

Geographic databases contain conventional map information as well as a wide variety of other geographic information such as natural features of the earth's surface, including topography, climate, soil and vegetation. The database is assembled from simple objects such as points and lines. Lines are linked together to form complex hydrologic or transportation networks. Points and lines are used to represent areas and surfaces. Natural and man-made objects such as lakes, forests and districts are represented as areas. Rainfall, pressure, temperature and population density are examples of entities represented as continuous surfaces. Attributes are associated with points, lines, networks, areas and surfaces in order to represent different types of geographic object.

Geographic databases are increasingly used in communication, transportation, logistics and many other fields. There is active research into improving the interoperability of geographic database systems and combining them with other types of database.

5.6.3 Multimedia Database Systems

Consider a geographic information system in which buildings, bridges and other parts of civil infrastructure are linked to maps of cities and countries. Explanations of entities might also be stored as audio data. This creates a need to integrate different types of data such as voice, text, video and imagery. Multimedia database systems are meant to manage such data types. A multimedia database is a database that contains multimedia data. Multimedia data may include structured data as well as semi-structured and unstructured data, such as voice, video, text and images. A common approach is to store multimedia data in files and meta-data (information about them) in a relational (or object) database.

A multimedia DBMS provides support for storing, manipulating and retrieving multimedia data. Apart from typical DBMS functions such as query processing, transaction management, security and integrity, different types of data such as voice and video often have to be synchronized for display, so real-time processing is important in multimedia DBMS.

Multimedia databases are increasingly used in applications such as computer-aided design (CAD), computer-aided manufacture (CAM), air traffic control, and especially in entertainment. Standardization in the areas of data representation and query languages will further improve the use of multimedia databases. Two areas of research are representing relationships between parts of multimedia objects, and synchronization.

5.6.4   *Distributed Databases*

Storing all data on a single computer creates performance and scalability problems. Consider a big engineering corporation that has several branches worldwide. Some operations in each branch might be independent, so these data may be stored in local databases. But there could also be a need to access and modify data in other branches. Storing all data in a single central database increases the time required to access the data and requires the use of powerful servers. Splitting the processing among multiple machines might be a better option than increasing the server power.

Here are some important functions of distributed databases:

- distributed query management for sending database queries to a single system even when data may be physically distributed;
- distributed transaction processing to ensure data concurrency when transactions span multiple machines;
- distributed meta-data management for locating specific pieces of data on multiple machines;
- enforcing security and integrity across multiple database management systems.

To understand the issues in distributed databases, consider a table in which rows are distributed on multiple machines. If all databases were independent, inserting a row would require checking for duplicate keys only in the local database. But if all databases were to act as a single distributed database, it would require that keys were not duplicated in any remote database. If this data consistency requirement needed to be enforced for every operation, all databases would need to be consulted and this would defeat the advantages of distributing the data. Therefore distributed databases lead to different mechanisms for data consistency and concurrency control.

5.7   SUMMARY

- Data management requirements exist everywhere.

- Data should be organized so they are easily modifiable. Improper organization leads to inconsistencies during modifications.

- DBMS allow systematic organization and manipulation of data. They permit users to ignore low-level details related to physical storage and retrieval.

- The most widely used database type is the relational database. Object-oriented databases are also used in engineering for modelling complex products and processes.

- In relational databases, data are stored in two-dimensional tables. They are based on the relational model. Understanding the relational model is essential for the proper use of relational database technology.

- SQL was developed to standardize operations on relational databases. Use of SQL ensures portability across different DBMS.

- Good database design requires a sound knowledge of the subject area and functional dependencies among data items.

- In relational database design, normalization procedures are used to avoid problems such as update anomalies.

- Concurrency control is of crucial importance in the use of databases in multi-user environments. Transactions ensure concurrency. A transaction is defined as a set of operations that need to be completed as a single unit. Databases provide mechanisms for implementing transactions.

- Special types of database have been developed for use in situations where data may not be easily organized into tables.

REFERENCE

Codd, E. F. 1970. A relational model of data for large shared data banks. *Communications of the ACM* , **13**(6), 377–387.

FURTHER READING

Date, C. J. 1995. *An Introduction to Database Management Systems*. Reading MA: Addison Wesley.
Thuraisingham, B. M. 1997. *Data Management Systems*. Boca Raton FL: CRC Press.
Ullman, J. D. and Widom, J. 1997. *A First Course in Database Systems*. Englewood Cliffs NJ: Prentice Hall.

EXERCISES

5.1 Why are databases important in engineering applications?

5.2 Give two examples of persistent and non-persistent data?

5.3 What is the difference between a database and a database management system?

5.4 What are the advantages of using a database management system instead of storing data in flat files? Are there any disadvantages?

5.5 Consider a database application for maintaining information about bridges in a country. List two operations that are defined at the application level. List two operations that are defined at the conceptual level.

5.6 What is not true about a table in a relational database?

    (a) A table contains variable number of rows.
    (b) A table contains variable number of columns.
    (c) A table may contain references to other tables.
    (d) A column in a table may not store an array of numbers.

5.7 Give two examples of data that are organized into tables and used in engineering design?

5.8 What is meant by the degree of a relation?

5.9 Identify the primary key in Table 5.13. Justify your conclusion.

5.10 Identify the primary key in Table 5.14.

Table 5.13 Stress–strain relationship of steel

Stress $(N m^2)$	Strain
0	0
100	4.76×10^{-4}
150	7.14×10^{-4}
150	1.42×10^{-3}
250	0.08

Table 5.14 Reinforcement bars used in a concrete slab shown in
Figure 5.11

Diameter (mm)	Position from left end (mm)	Length (mm)	Number
10	0.01	6	2
12	1	4	2
10	1	4	2
16	2	2	1

5.11 What possible errors might you encounter while performing the following operators
in a relational database table?

(a) insert a record
(b) delete a record

5.12 What is the relational operator which when applied to Table 5.15 produces
Table 5.16?

Figure 5.11 Reinforcement bars used in a concrete slab

Table 5.15 Rooms in an apartment

Room	Length (m)	Width (m)	Area
Kitchen	3	2	6
Bedroom	4	4	16
Living room	4	3	12

5.13 Join Table 5.17 and Table 5.18 on the attribute `Year of construction`.

5.14 Join Table 5.19 and Table 5.20 on the attribute `Firm`.

5.15 How will you store the information in Table 5.21 using a relational database?

Table 5.16 Area of rooms in an apartment

Room	Area (m^2)
Kitchen	6
Bedroom	16
Living room	12

Table 5.17 Year of construction of buildings

Building	Year of construction
Building 1	1992
Building 2	1994

Table 5.18 Unit cost of concrete

Year of construction	Unit cost
1991	1
1992	1.1
1993	1.2
1994	1.3

Table 5.19 Bolt manufacturers

Firm	Location
X	London
Y	Chicago

Table 5.20 Bolt sizes manufactured by firms

Size	Firm
6	X
8	X
8	Y
10	Y

Table 5.21 Elements connected
to each node in the finite element
mesh shown in Figure 5.12

Node	Elements
1	e1,e2
2	e1,e3,e4,e5
3	e2,e3,e6
4	e4,e7,e9
5	e5,e6,e7,e8
6	e8,e9

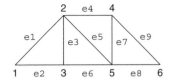

Figure 5.12   A finite element mesh

5.16 An authority managing bridges in a country maintains records of bridge inspections.
Here are the important functional dependencies in the system:

```
bridge identifier (ID) → Location
ID → Year of construction
(ID, Date of inspection) → Bridge inspector
```

Consider Table 5.22 and treat Date of inspection as an atomic quantity.
Answer these two questions:

(a) Which normal form does the table belong to?
(b) What are the primary keys in the table?
      Now consider Tables 5.23 and 5.24. Answer these two questions:
(c) Which normal form does this design belong to?
(d) What are the primary keys in Table 5.24?

Suppose there is only a single bridge inspector in a given city at any time; that is,
the following additional functional dependency is valid:

```
(Location, Year of inspection) → Bridge inspector
```

Decompose Table 5.22 into third normal form.

5.17 What type of lock might be required for the data items X and Y in order to implement
the following transaction?

```
RETRIEVE X
RETRIEVE Y
If X > 10 THEN INCREMENT Y
UPDATE Y
```

Table 5.22 Bridge inspections

Id	Location	Year of construction	Date of inspection	Bridge inspector
1	City 1	1980	June/1990	X
1	City 1	1980	July/1995	Y
2	City 2	1990	June/1996	Y

Table 5.23 Bridges

Id	Location	Year of construction
1	City 1	1980
2	City 2	1990

Table 5.24 Bridge inspections

Id	Year of inspection	Bridge inspector
1	June/1990	X
1	July/1995	Y
2	June/1996	Y

5.18. Will the following transactions ever deadlock?

Transaction A

```
LOCK X
LOCK Y
RETRIEVE X
INCREMENT X
INCREMENT Y
SAVE X
RELEASE LOCK ON X
RELEASE LOCK ON Y
```

Transaction B

```
LOCK Y
RETRIEVE Y
SAVE Y
RELEASE Y
LOCK X
RETRIEVE X
INCREMENT X
RELEASE LOCK ON X
```

6

Computational Mechanics

6.1 INTRODUCTION

Computational mechanics is one of the earliest applications of computer-aided engineering (CAE). The importance of the topic is implicitly reflected by the observation that many engineers are still unaware of the potential for the use of computers outside computational mechanics, apart from office tasks such as electronic messaging, drafting, web communication and word processing. The objective of this chapter is not to provide a detailed discussion of this topic as many other textbooks do this very well. Instead, computational mechanics is described in terms of the general context of computer-aided engineering.

Computational mechanics involves the application of mechanics, mathematics and numerical methods in engineering. Mathematical models are used to represent physical phenomena that occur in practical engineering systems. Such representation helps simulate the behaviour of engineering artefacts. Simulation is used for tasks such as design verification and performance optimization. For example, crashworthiness of automobile bodies might be examined using simulation without performing tests on physical models.

Areas covered by computational mechanics are broadly classified into solid mechanics and fluid mechanics. In general, the aim is to analyse the combined effects on matter of thermal, chemical and mechanical phenomena. Depending on the variation of effects with respect to time, simulation might be static (time independent), pseudostatic (approximating long-term effects) or dynamic. It requires engineering judgement to decide which physical phenomena to include in the model and to choose the most appropriate simulations.

The most widely used method in computational mechanics is the finite element method (FEM). It has been successfully applied to stress analysis, fluid flow, heat transfer and many other phenomena. Other methods include the boundary element method, finite differences, finite volume and element-free Galerkin.

The term 'computational mechanics' has also been used in a more narrow sense to denote a method for discovering and describing patterns using tools from statistical mechanics. This chapter adopts the more general definition. The following paragraphs give a sample list of topics that are considered to be part of computational mechanics.

Simulation is a common aspect that links together many subjects in computational mechanics. Traditional computational mechanics aims to simulate the behaviour of engineering systems under the influence of known (or estimated) environmental conditions

Fundamentals of Computer-Aided Engineering B. Raphael and I. F. C. Smith
© 2003 John Wiley & Sons, Ltd ISBNs: 0-471-48709-0 (HB); 0-471-48715-5 (PB)

such as load and temperature. In general, simulation involves modelling the behaviour of systems under the action of multiple events that might be random.

Discrete event simulation is an area of computational mechanics that deals with analysing the behaviour of systems under sequences of random events at specific points in time. Continuous simulation refers to analysis of situations where changes happen continuously. In discrete event simulation, systems are decomposed into a set of logically distinct processes (LPs) autonomously progressing through time. Each event takes place on a specific process at a specific time (sometimes assigned randomly). As a result of this event, other events are generated that act on the same process or other processes. The principal restriction placed on discrete event simulation is that an event cannot affect the outcome of a prior event; in other words, time cannot run backwards. The resulting state of the total system at any time is evaluated using the laws of physics.

In continuous simulation, events do not occur at discrete points in time. They occur continuously. An example is the change in the water level of a reservoir. A method to perform continuous simulation is to discretize time into finite steps and lump the effects of changes at discrete points in time.

6.1.1 Challenges of Computational Mechanics

Simulation is a deductive task (Chapter 1) and might be performed more reliably than other types of task. But simulation requires accurate mathematical models to provide results that reflect reality. Accurate mathematical models involve parameters whose values are not known precisely in real systems. Simplifying assumptions are used to construct reasonable models for practical systems. Even with simplifications, exact solutions to mathematical models are available for trivial cases only.

Since accurate mathematical models are difficult to analyse, numerical models are created. This usually involves discretization of space and/or time. Most popular methods follow this decomposition approach. In the finite element method, objects are discretized into a mesh consisting of nodes and elements. In the boundary element method, only the boundary is discretized.

Objects having complex shapes present a challenge for discretization. Many elements are needed to represent complex shapes. A large amount of computer memory might be required to store the properties of the elements. Also, a large amount of central processor (CPU) time is required for processing information. Even with exponential increases in the power of computers, finite element applications have always demanded more resources than are available. When the required accuracy is not possible with available computational resources, engineers proceed with approximate analyses and make provisions for approximation errors in the analysis.

6.2 FROM PHYSICAL PRINCIPLES TO PRACTICAL SYSTEMS

Physical principles are often formulated in terms of partial differential equations. Solutions to partial differential equations depend on the boundary conditions; direct solutions exist only for simple geometrical shapes, so numerical solutions are sought in engineering. The following examples illustrate mathematical models that are relevant to engineering.

Example 6.1   Fluid Flow

The flow of incompressible fluids is described by the continuity equation

$$\frac{\partial u}{\partial x} + \frac{\partial v}{\partial y} + \frac{\partial w}{\partial z} = 0 \tag{6.1}$$

and the Navier–Stokes equation (momentum equation) for constant viscosity

$$\rho \left[\frac{\partial u}{\partial t} + u \frac{\partial u}{\partial x} + v \frac{\partial u}{\partial y} + w \frac{\partial u}{\partial z} \right] = \rho g_x - \frac{\partial P}{\partial x} + \mu \left[\frac{\partial^2 u}{\partial x^2} + \frac{\partial^2 u}{\partial y^2} + \frac{\partial^2 u}{\partial z^2} \right]$$

$$\rho \left[\frac{\partial v}{\partial t} + u \frac{\partial v}{\partial x} + v \frac{\partial v}{\partial y} + w \frac{\partial v}{\partial z} \right] = \rho g_y - \frac{\partial P}{\partial y} + \mu \left[\frac{\partial^2 v}{\partial x^2} + \frac{\partial^2 v}{\partial y^2} + \frac{\partial^2 v}{\partial z^2} \right]$$

$$\rho \left[\frac{\partial w}{\partial t} + u \frac{\partial w}{\partial x} + v \frac{\partial w}{\partial y} + w \frac{\partial w}{\partial z} \right] = \rho g_z - \frac{\partial P}{\partial z} + \mu \left[\frac{\partial^2 w}{\partial x^2} + \frac{\partial^2 w}{\partial y^2} + \frac{\partial^2 w}{\partial z^2} \right] \tag{6.2}$$

where u, v and w are components of velocity in the x, y and z directions; ρ is the density; g_x, g_y and g_z are components of gravity in their respective directions; P is the pressure; and μ is the viscosity.

The solution to these equations involves finding the velocity at all points within the fluid for a given set of boundary conditions. Boundary conditions specify the velocity along the boundaries of the domain, which are usually known. Closed-form solutions that satisfy the partial differential equations exist only in idealized situations. Figure 6.1 illustrates the solution for flow through an idealized infinite medium over a cylinder. Streamlines indicate the direction of velocity. The direction of flow is parallel to the x-axis far away from the cylinder and the flow changes direction due to the presence of the cylinder in its path.

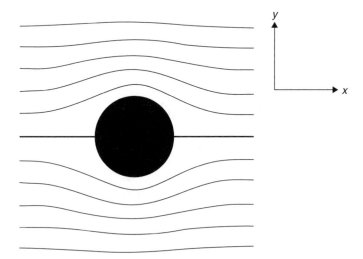

Figure 6.1   Fluid flow over a cylinder. Streamlines indicate the direction of velocity

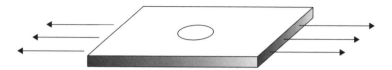

Figure 6.2   A plate under axial force

Example 6.2   Stress Distribution

Internal stresses occur in objects under the action of external forces. A well-known case is a plate under axial load (Figure 6.2). The objective of stress analysis is to determine the magnitude and direction of stresses within the object.

Assuming linear elastic behaviour and plane stress conditions (no stresses perpendicular to the plane of the plate) and in the absence of body forces (distributed or concentrated forces within the body), the governing partial differential equation for two-dimensional stress analysis is

$$\frac{\partial^4 \Phi}{\partial x^4} + \frac{\partial^4 \Phi}{\partial x^2 \partial y^2} + \frac{\partial^4 \Phi}{\partial y^4} = 0$$

where Φ is the Airy stress function and is related to the normal and shear stresses by the following equations:

$$\text{normal stress in the } x\text{-direction, } \sigma_{xx} = \frac{\partial^2 \Phi}{\partial y^2}$$

$$\text{normal stress in the } y\text{-direction, } \sigma_{yy} = \frac{\partial^2 \Phi}{\partial x^2}$$

$$\text{shear stress in the } xy\text{-direction, } \sigma_{xy} = -\frac{\partial^2 \Phi}{\partial x \partial y}$$

Boundary conditions are specified through the knowledge that stresses are zero along the boundary where there are no external forces. Principal stresses are calculated by solving the equations numerically.

6.3   METHODS FOR FINDING SOLUTIONS

The classical method for solving partial differential equations is the finite difference method. In the finite difference method, the partial derivative $\partial F / \partial x$ is approximated as

$$\frac{\Delta F}{\Delta x} = \frac{F_{i+1} - F_i}{x_{i+1} - x_i}$$

where ΔF is the change in the value of the function F between the points i and $i + 1$. The governing partial differential equations are written in the finite difference form using this approximation and then the values of the function F_i are solved for all discrete points i. A drawback of the finite difference method is that discretization is difficult for complex shapes.

The most popular method used in engineering is the finite element method (FEM), a special case of the Galerkin method, so the next section explains the Galerkin method.

6.3.1   Galerkin Method

In many branches of engineering, we are interested in solving partial differential equations of the form

$$Au = f$$

where A is a matrix consisting of differential operators, and the elements of the vectors **u** and **f** are functions of the spatial coordinates. The aim is to find the function **u** such that the above equation is satisfied at every point in the domain for a known function **f**. If we multiply both sides of the equation by a set of test functions **v** and integrate over the entire domain Ω, we obtain

$$\int A\mathbf{u}\mathbf{v}\,d\Omega = \int \mathbf{f}\mathbf{v}\,d\Omega \tag{6.3}$$

This form of the equation is known as the weak form or the variational form. (The term 'strong form' refers to the original partial differential equations.) The Galerkin method uses an approximation where the function $u(x)$ is a linear combination of a finite number of trial functions $\psi_1(x)$, $\psi_2(x)$, $\psi_3(x)$, …, also known as basis functions or shape functions:

$$u(x) = \sum a_i \psi_i(x)$$

After substituting the above approximation in the weak form (6.3) and expanding the integral, the unknown coefficients a_i are obtained by applying the condition that (6.3) is satisfied for every test function that belongs to a chosen set. In the Bubnov–Galerkin method, the set of test functions is the same as the set of trial functions, $\psi_i(x)$.

In the finite element method, the domain is discretized into a finite number of non-overlapping elements that cover the entire domain, and the trial functions are defined with respect to individual elements. As an illustration, Figure 6.3 shows a one-dimensional bar discretized into three elements. The trial functions ψ_i are defined such that each function takes a value of one at node i and zero at all other nodes. The deflection u at any point in the bar is a linear combination of the shape functions given by

$$u(x) = a_1\psi_1 + a_2\psi_2 + a_3\psi_3 + a_4\psi_4$$

The unknown coefficients a_1, a_2, a_3, a_4 are the deflections at the nodal points. This is a consequence of choosing shape functions with the forms shown in Figure 6.3. The deflection at any point within the bar is interpolated from the nodes using the shape functions. The governing differential equation for a bar under the action of distributed axial forces within the bar is

$$EA\frac{d^2u}{dx^2} = -f$$

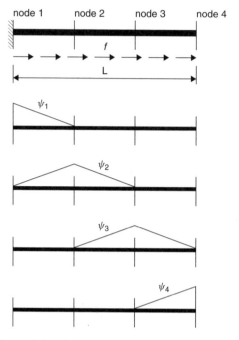

Figure 6.3   A finite element formulation of a bar under axial load

where f is the uniformly distributed body force in the bar. The test functions are chosen to be the same as the shape functions. Integrating using equation (6.3) and applying the boundary condition that the deflection at node 1 is equal to zero, results in the following set of simultaneous equations. (A detailed discussion of this procedure can be found in Zienkiewicz and Taylor, 2000: 39–53 or Bathe, 1982: 124–129):

$$\frac{3EA}{L}\begin{bmatrix} 2 & -1 & 0 \\ -1 & 2 & -1 \\ 0 & -1 & 1 \end{bmatrix}\begin{bmatrix} a_2 \\ a_3 \\ a_4 \end{bmatrix} = \begin{bmatrix} fL/3 \\ fL/3 \\ fL/6 \end{bmatrix}$$

Solving the simultaneous equations, the values of nodal deflections are obtained as follows:

$$\begin{bmatrix} a_2 \\ a_3 \\ a_4 \end{bmatrix} = \frac{fL^2}{9EA}\begin{bmatrix} 5 \\ 8 \\ 9 \end{bmatrix}$$

6.3.2   Remarks

In elastic stress analysis, the left-hand side of (6.3) is the change in strain energy due to a virtual displacement (defined by the test function) that is applied to the structure. The right-hand side is the virtual work done by external forces. The resulting matrix equations obtained by evaluating the integral equate internal forces to external forces. This is usually of the form

$$\mathbf{K}\mathbf{a} = \mathbf{F}$$

where **a** is the vector of nodal displacements, K is the stiffness matrix and **F** is the force vector. The stiffness matrix is evaluated for each element then assembled into a global stiffness matrix. Similarly, the force vector is evaluated for each element then assembled into the global force vector. The resulting set of linear simultaneous equations is solved using Gaussian elimination or other techniques.

Different types of finite element are created by choosing appropriate shape functions, substituting in the weak form of the governing differential equations, and integrating over the volume of the element. Shape functions might be linear or higher-order polynomials. The geometric shape of elements is usually triangular or quadrilateral.

Shape functions are chosen such that displacements are continuous across the boundaries of elements, but usually their derivatives (stresses) are not continuous across element boundaries. Therefore it is common to have stress jumps along element boundaries. The amount of jump in the stresses provides an indication of the discretization error in the analysis. Errors are reduced by decreasing the element size, but this increases the size of the stiffness matrix and requires more computation time to solve the simultaneous equations.

6.4   ISSUES IN COMPUTER-AIDED ENGINEERING

Even though computational mechanics has been successfully used for a variety of engineering analyses, there are several challenges. These are discussed in the following subsections.

6.4.1   Accuracy

Results of computational mechanics simulations involve errors that are introduced at three stages (Figure 6.4):

1. Creating mathematical models of real structures, error e_1
2. Representing mathematical models using numerical models, error e_2
3. Simulating numerical models on computers, error e_3

Improving the accuracy of stage 1 is an engineering challenge, whereas improving the accuracies of stages 2 and 3 is mostly a computational challenge.

Creation of numerical models often involves discretization of space and time. In the finite element method, discretization errors are reduced by reducing element sizes and

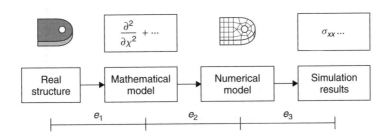

Figure 6.4   Errors in computational mechanics simulations

through the use of more accurate elements involving higher-order polynomial shape functions. But both options increase the amount of memory required for the simulation. One solution is to decrease the mesh size only in regions that contain high error levels. This requires the estimation of discretization errors and is a specialized topic in finite element analysis. Modern FEM packages provide results of finite element analysis as well as approximate estimates of errors involved. Adaptive finite element analysis is a method that automatically refines finite element meshes in regions containing high errors until error estimates are within acceptable limits.

Simulation of numerical models on computers (stage 3) involves further errors (e_3). There are two sources of error at this stage. The first is the propagation of round-off errors caused by the binary representation of real numbers. When real numbers are represented with 32 bits on a computer, there might be errors starting from the seventh significant decimal place. After many floating-point operations, errors propagate and the precision of the results decreases. Round-off errors are reduced by having 64-bit (double-precision) representations of real numbers. Be aware of rounding effects when interpreting the results of simulations.

The second source of error in stage 3 is due to uncertainties in model parameters and boundary conditions. In real structural systems, material properties and environmental conditions change with time and are not known precisely. Idealized boundary conditions such as pinned rollers and rigid connections do not exist in practice, therefore simulation results often do not match expectations and observations. Choosing appropriate models requires expertise and often models have to be iteratively refined to conform to expected results. Research is carried out into providing adequate levels of support for creating models that closely match observations and measurements.

When mathematical modelling of real structures is not reliable, excessive sophistication during stages 2 and 3 cannot be justified. Conversely, when the errors introduced during stages 2 and 3 are more than those introduced during stage 1, it is justified to use more approximate mathematical models of engineering systems. In both situations, seemingly accurate mathematical models might contain more parameters, and errors due to uncertainties in the values of these parameters offset the potential increase in accuracy offered by the models.

6.4.2 Speed

Even though many computational mechanics algorithms have polynomial complexity, simulations of practical systems require large amounts of CPU time. Reducing the time required for simulations has always been a challenge.

In static finite element analysis, most of the computation time is taken for the solution of simultaneous equations. This task is $O(n^3)$ in the worst case (Chapter 2), where n is the number of degrees of freedom and is related to the number of nodes in the finite element mesh. When the mesh size is decreased, the number of nodes increases according to a polynomial of degree 3 for three-dimensional objects, therefore the execution time increases by a polynomial of degree 9. Such a high-order polynomial is the reason why simulations take a long time. For example, if the mesh size is reduced by half, the time required for analysis should increase by more than a billion times if the complexity is $O(n^9)$. In practice the complexity is less than $O(n^9)$ because of the banded nature of the stiffness matrix.

Dynamic and non-linear simulations further increase complexity. Many methods of dynamic and non-linear simulations repeat static simulations for different geometry and load conditions until convergence is achieved. Research in computational mechanics aims at developing better algorithms that reduce the computation time. Considerable effort has been spent in the development of parallel algorithms and the use of distributed computing (Chapter 13).

6.4.3 User Interaction

Finite element analyses require large amounts of input data and they usually generate much output data. Challenges in user interaction are related to preparing the input and post-processing the output.

Creating good numerical models requires experience and skill. Decision-support systems have been developed for assisting engineers in this task. Tasks that require much time when performed manually, such as mesh generation, have been automated. With minimum user input, automatic mesh generators are able to treat complex shapes and generate data required for simulation.

A final challenge of computational mechanics involves the interpretation of results. Good presentation is essential for appropriate interpretation. Post-processing tasks aim to convert the results into forms that are easy to understand. Converting output from simulations into meaningful information that is useful to engineers requires the application of modern techniques in human–computer interaction and visualization (Chapter 12).

6.5 SUMMARY

- Computational mechanics is an area of computer-aided engineering that aims to simulate the behaviour of engineering systems under the influence of environmental conditions such as loading and temperature.

- Many physical phenomena are described by partial differential equations. Solutions to these equations are required to simulate the behaviour of engineering artefacts. Computational mechanics provides tools for solving these equations for complex shapes and boundary conditions.

- FEM is a popular method for solving partial differential equations. It is a special case of the Galerkin method, in which the solution is approximated using a linear combination of selected trial functions.

REFERENCES

Bathe, K. 1982. *Finite Element Procedures*. Englewood Cliffs NJ: Prentice Hall.
Zienkiewicz, O. C. and Taylor, R. L. 2000. *Finite Element Method*, Vol. 1, *The Basis*. London: Butterworth Heinemann.

FURTHER READING

Reddy, J. N. 1993. *An Introduction to the Finite Element Method*. New York: McGraw-Hill.

7
Constraint-Based Reasoning

7.1 INTRODUCTION

All of us know about constraints. We drive according to speed limits; there are maximum loads for elevators; there are minimum parking charges; there are noise limits around airports; pollution levels have maximum values for health purposes; and there are minimum grades required for university entrance. Indeed our life is filled with constraints. In spite of affirmations from people who favour alternative lifestyles, we simply cannot live without them.

In engineering, constraints are very useful. For example, they help focus on good solutions during important tasks. Often, good solutions are found when constraints are exactly met. Varying constraints and observing the effects helps engineers to understand important characteristics of the task. When there are too many constraints, they may also create situations where no solution is feasible. Given such importance, it follows that for computer-aided engineering (CAE), explicitly defined constraints enable engineers to express, modify and change them in the most transparent manner. The field of constraint-based reasoning focuses on the use of explicitly defined constraints.

Engineers recognized the potential of constraint-based reasoning many years ago. Initial proposals can be traced back to exploratory graphics systems in the 1960s. These early systems contained features that demonstrate valuable advantages of using constraints. For example, attractive aspects of constraint-based reasoning that were proposed early on include the opportunity to perform declarative engineering task modelling, mechanisms for propagating decisions and support for solution search.

Declarative engineering task modelling involves modelling using standard engineering language to describe aspects of the knowledge required for performing a task without direct consideration of *how that knowledge will be used*. For example, when determining dimensions for a steel bar under tension, engineers could declare independent constraints related to maximum stress and maximum elongation without considering which constraint would be relevant for which application. Much engineering knowledge is already in the form of constraints. Here are some examples:

- Design requirements for structural safety: effect of actions $\leq$ provided resistance.
- Workers can perform only one task at a time.
- Part A is compatible with assembly B.

Fundamentals of Computer-Aided Engineering   B. Raphael and I. F. C. Smith
© 2003 John Wiley & Sons, Ltd   ISBNs: 0-471-48709-0 (HB); 0-471-48715-5 (PB)

Constraints provide a natural language of discourse for many engineering tasks. Indeed such knowledge is directly employed by constraint software. Declarative modelling provides advantages throughout the life cycle of a CAE application. During design and development, information is easily modelled, and later modifications to information can also be carried out in a straightforward manner.

Propagation of decisions is carried out mainly to provide feedback related to the consequences of fixing values of variables and making modifications to the set of constraints under consideration. Propagation is often used to filter out variable values that are no longer feasible. Such activity may identify whole variable sets that are infeasible. For example, when all constraints are considered for design of a product, it may be concluded that certain materials cannot be used for its manufacture. Other applications are common in planning and scheduling as well as in user interfaces when, for example, pull-down menu options are deactivated (greyed) under certain conditions.

Constraint-based reasoning is particularly helpful during solution search. Since engineers often wish to consider several solutions in detail among a very large number of possible solutions, such help is especially advantageous for computer-aided engineering. Addition of constraints may reduce the computational complexity of solution enumeration. For example, when value propagation results in just one possible value for a variable, the complexity of the task drops because a variable becomes a constant. This could reduce the complexity of a task from, say, $O(n^3)$ to $O(n^2)$, i.e. polynomial 3 to polynomial 2 (Chapter 2). But it is also possible that the addition of constraints increases the complexity of the problem, as in the brick wall example (pages 24–28).

Constraints often describe the boundaries of solution spaces. For example, a constraint limiting the stress in a bar excludes those solutions that exceed a particular maximum allowed stress. There is, however, no guarantee that all solutions with stresses lower than this maximum stress are good solutions; other constraints may disqualify some of them. Although constraints define what may be possible, a reliable definition of what is possible can only be provided when all constraints are known. This is rare in engineering, so it is often clearer to think of constraints as defining, through their complement, what is not acceptable (Figure 7.1).

Another example taken from engineering is the addition of a constraint requiring that stresses in an element must be *below* a certain value; the more reliable message is that no solution having stresses *above* this value is acceptable. This does not mean that engineers should never consider regions where stresses are unacceptable; good solutions are

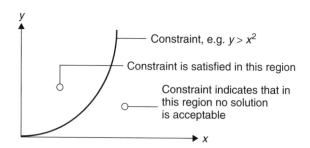

Figure 7.1 The more reliable message is that no solution exists below this line since above this line one cannot say for sure that there is a solution. Other constraints may preclude feasibility

sometimes found when certain constraints are violated in the intermediate stages of tasks. In this example an engineer who is designing an element may subsequently devise a way to reduce the loads, thereby satisfying the constraint at a later stage.

The next section introduces some terminology. Several constraint-solving methods are then described in terms of necessary input information and the type of solution required. Many successful applications have been implemented for discrete variables, so the following section describes some of the important ones. Of greatest importance to engineering is the last section, on continuous variables; the ideas are explained using an example from collaborative engineering.

7.2 TERMINOLOGY

Since computer scientists, who are more inclined to mathematics than practical engineering, carry out most theoretical work on constraint satisfaction, the terminology and much of the methodology are mathematical in nature. For example, constraint satisfaction is often described as a *constraint satisfaction problem* (CSP) that has the following components:

- A set of variables $X = \{x_1, x_2, x_3, \ldots, x_n\}$. For example, the set X describing an elevator might include parameters such as elevator dimensions, maximum capacity, number of floors covered and speed.

- A set of domains $D = \{d_1, d_2, d_3, \ldots, d_n\}$. Each domain is itself a set of possible values for the corresponding variable. For example, an elevator company may produce elevators that have only three speeds. The set d_{speed} would include the values for the three speeds that the variable x_{speed} could take on.

- A set of constraints $C = C_1(x_1, x_2, x_3, \ldots, x_n), C_2, C_3, \ldots, C_m$. Each constraint includes information related to *constraining* the values for one or more variables. For example, elevators that cover more than ten floors may not be available in the slowest speed.

- A task that requires identification of at least one solution that satisfies the constraints. For example, given a required minimum capacity and number of floors, the task may be to generate all elevator dimensions and speeds that are supplied by a particular company.

When considering the number of variables used to construct a constraint, constraints may be categorized into the following types:

- *Unary constraints*: $E = 207\,\text{GPa}$; part A must be galvanized; minimum clear span is 20 m.
- *Binary constraints*: the value of x_1 cannot be the same as x_2; worker A must work with worker B; length must be greater than width.
- *Ternary constraints*: force = mass × acceleration; workers A, B and C must work together; clear area > width × length.
- *N-ary constraints*: $x_1 > f(x_2, x_3, x_4, \ldots, x_n)$.

Tasks related to satisfaction of constraints may have several goals; here are some typical ones:

- Find one consistent solution.
- Prune inconsistent solutions from domains of variables.
- Find all solutions that satisfy constraints.

The last two goals have most relevance to complex engineering tasks. As discussed in Chapter 1, complex engineering tasks cannot be modelled completely, therefore engineers are usually not interested in single solutions since they may not be the best ones when aspects that are not modelled are considered. Engineers like to have choices, especially when a computer is doing the suggesting.

A solution is *consistent* when variable values satisfy all relevant constraints. Local consistency refers to satisfaction of constraints that are directly related to variable values. Global consistency refers to satisfaction of all constraints affecting all variable values. Other types of consistency are discussed in the next section.

7.3   CONSTRAINT-SOLVING METHODS

The method that is most appropriate depends on the available information and the task. The following four methods are used:

- value propagation;
- value relaxation;
- label propagation;
- constraint propagation.

Value propagation is used when some variables have values, and the task is to find values for other variables that satisfy the constraints. The method involves beginning with the domain of values for variables and iteratively refining values for each variable through sequential and repeated application of relevant constraints. Weaknesses of this method are that there is often more than one set of values for variables and that solutions are often generated arbitrarily. Also, solution searches may diverge or go into cycles when a feasible solution exists.

Value relaxation is used when all variables have values and some are not consistent with constraints. The task here is to identify consistent values for all variables, but finding good values is not guaranteed; it is also possible to get divergence or cycling.

Label propagation is used when each variable has a domain of possible values. A label is a set of values for a variable. Initially, the labels for variables are their domains. The task is to find labels in the domain that are consistent with all constraints. Since engineers cannot model all aspects of their tasks, this method is the closest to their needs. Label propagation allows them to identify possible solutions for consideration with criteria that are not modelled. For overall (global) consistency and large domains, this method may be exponentially complex in terms of the number of variables. Avoiding exponential complexity may involve lowering consistency requirements. These requirements are described next.

7.3.1 Levels of Consistency for Label Propagation

Here are some examples of consistency levels for sets of binary and unary constraints:

- *Node consistency*: all values of labels satisfy all unary constraints; this is a trivial exercise that has linear complexity with respect to the number of variables.

- *Arc consistency*: values of node-consistent labels for pairs of variables satisfy the constraints that include the variables.

- *Path consistency*: for each pair of admissible values for two variables and for each path that connects them in a constraint network, there are admissible values for all variables on the path such that all relevant constraints are satisfied.

To illustrate the last two terms, consider this simple example in task allocation. Two workers have to do three tasks. The constraint associated with this example is that a worker can do only one task at a time. Two cases having different start and end times are examined (Figure 7.2). The three variables W_{task1}, W_{task2} and W_{task3} represent the workers assigned to the respective tasks. Possible values of these variables are `worker1` and `worker2`. Therefore, the domain of the variables W_{task1}, W_{task2} and W_{task3} is the set {`worker1, worker2`}.

In the graph representation, variables are represented as nodes, and the constraints that connect the variables are represented as links between the nodes. In case A, since task 1 overlaps with task 2 and task 3, and since a worker can perform only a single task at a time, the constraints are expressed as

```
Wtask1 NOT EQUAL TO Wtask2
Wtask1 NOT EQUAL TO Wtask3
```

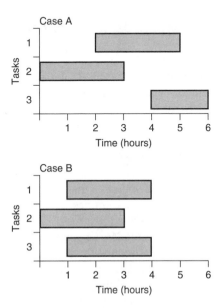

Figure 7.2 Two cases of task allocation

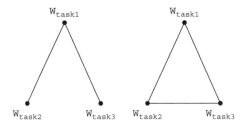

Figure 7.3 Graphs of the two cases. Links indicate where task allocations (workers) cannot be the same

Similarly, constraints for case B are expressed as

```
Wtask1 NOT EQUAL TO Wtask2
Wtask2 NOT EQUAL TO Wtask3
Wtask1 NOT EQUAL TO Wtask3
```

These constraints are shown in Figure 7.3. Links represent task allocations that cannot be the same.

Figure 7.3 demonstrates that case A can be modelled as a tree graph whereas case B cannot. Case B is not feasible. Nevertheless, arc consistency for both cases can be obtained since arc consistency considers one link at a time. Path consistency, being more restrictive, cannot be obtained for case B since two workers cannot do three tasks at the same time and this is detected through considering a path of dependencies. Achieving path consistency thus requires constraining pairs of values instead of just restraining variable domains. This is constraint propagation in its restricted sense; see Section 7.3.3.

7.3.2 Global Consistency in Label Propagation

Global consistency means that among all values of all labels there is at least one combination that leads to a feasible solution. Each feasible solution can be obtained by sequential instantiation of variables without backtracking. This usually means that finding a feasible solution from a globally consistent set of labels does not have an exponential complexity in terms of the number of variables. Labels of variables have to be revised once values are assigned to other variables, and this may require some computation.

Nevertheless, achieving globally consistent labels is an attractive practical goal when using constraint-based reasoning strategies. Once global consistency is achieved, engineers are able to view the space of feasible solutions that are defined by the constraints. This provides a platform to consider many possibilities and combine such information with criteria and information that is not modelled *prior to* fixing actual values to variables.

This platform provides support for modern engineering task strategies such as least-commitment decision making. In least-commitment decision making, engineers delay committing to values of variables until the last moment. The goal is to minimize costs associated with changes and backtracking through decisions when conditions change. For example, clients may change requirements, or new information may reveal that previous commitments for values of variables are not feasible.

Globally consistent labels are also useful in collaborative engineering where several people – engineers, suppliers, tradesmen, etc. – work toward completing a common project. When partners combine constraints that are important for achieving their goals, labels are generated that reduce requirements for negotiation. An example of constraint-based collaboration is given at the end of this chapter.

Unfortunately, globally consistent labelling is difficult to obtain for many complex tasks. Over the last thirty years much research has focused on the conditions when global consistency can be obtained. An important factor is convexity. This parameter describes the shape of the feasible region. A region is convex if a straight line between any two points within the region lies entirely in the feasible region. Arc consistency is equivalent to global consistency when the constraint network is a tree graph. Path consistency is equivalent to global consistency when the feasible region is convex and the constraint network is binary.

7.3.3 Constraint Propagation

Although the term 'constraint propagation' is often employed for all types of propagation, it is also used in a more restricted sense. Constraint propagation is the incremental determination of implicit constraints on variables that result from the combination and resulting composition of constraints of a CSP. The procedure terminates when one large composite constraint is determined. This constraint describes all globally consistent values. From an engineering viewpoint, there are few practical cases where constraint propagation would terminate since feasible solution spaces are too complex to be described using one constraint. This type of propagation is useful for small CSPs.

7.4 REASONING WITH CONSTRAINTS ON DISCRETE VARIABLES

Many engineering applications of constraint-based reasoning involve discrete variables. Discrete variables have domains that can be described using sets of discrete values. For example, the task allocation example in Figure 7.2 illustrates tasks as variables whose domains are two workers each. When variables are not discrete, they are continuous. Continuous variables have domains that cannot be described using sets of discrete values. For example, dimensions, stresses and deformations are often continuous variables since their domains may be expressed as ranges of real values. Reasoning with continuous constraints is discussed in Section 7.5.

Scheduling, task allocation and simple configuration tasks are the most active engineering applications of reasoning with constraints on discrete variables. For example, configuration tools are used commercially for providing clients with cost estimates of products such as personal computers, new cars and elevators. Some applications have reduced the time required for cost estimates from hours and days down to minutes. Estimates for some products are now provided to clients over the phone.

Example 7.1   An Example of Reasoning with Discrete Variables

Task *Find consistent types of material for use in the production of an industrial component.*

Given   *The component has three parts: X1, X2, X3. Each part can be made of carbon steel (cs), stainless steel (ss), aluminium (al) or copper (cu). Fabrication and functional requirements state that only certain combinations of material are feasible. Feasible combinations are expressed in terms of constraints as follows: x2*

C1 (X1, X2) : (cs, ss) (cs, al) (al, cu)
C2 (X1, X3) : (cs, ss) (ss, cu) (al, cu)
C3 (X2, X3) : (cs, ss) (cs, al) (cu, cu)

Solution   *The variables are the part names: X1, X2 and X3. Labels for these variables are denoted as L1, L2 and L3. Each variable has the same domain (cs, ss, al, cu). Begin label propagation employing arc consistency:*

1. Start with C1 to determine initial labels for X1 (L1) and X2 (L2)
   C1 requires that L1 = (cs, al) and L2 = (ss, al, cu)

2. Apply C2 to refine label for X1 and determine initial label for X3 (L3)
   C2 requires that L1 = (cs, al) and L3 = (ss, cu)

3. Apply C3 to refine labels for X2 and X3
   C3 requires that L2 = cu and L3 = cu
   (since only the last combination in C3 is feasible for L2)

4. Reapply C1 with the current label of X2 (L2)
   C1 now requires that L1 = al

5. Checking with C2 confirms the feasibility of the labels L1 and L3

Label propagation terminates with a unique solution:

X1 is aluminium
X2 is copper
X3 is copper

Although an initial inspection of the constraints would indicate that cs and ss should be part of the solution, label propagation reveals that the feasible solution excludes them. It is easy to imagine that a system involving such a procedure would easily adapt to changes in feasible combinations due to modifications in fabrication methods, etc. Only the constraints (input) would need to be changed. For example, if C3 is changed to

C3 (X2, X3) : (cs, ss) (al, ss) (cs, cu)

the outcome is as follows:

• Application of C3 now requires that L2 = al and L3 = ss
  (since only the second combination in C3 is feasible for L2)

• Application of C1 now requires that L1 is cs

• Checking with C2 confirms the feasibility of labels L1 and L3

Label propagation terminates with a new unique solution:

X1 is carbon steel
X2 is aluminium
X3 is stainless steel

7.4.1   CSP Complexity for Discrete Variables

The upper-bound complexity for finding all solutions of any form of a CSP in discrete variables is exponential in terms of the number of variables. For unary constraints, complexity is even linear in the number of variables since only node consistency is required. Arc consistency leads to a solution in polynomial time when there are only binary constraints and when they can be arranged in a tree graph. There are other conditions that lead to resolution of CSPs in polynomial time. However, the restrictions on them mean that most practical engineering tasks fall outside their range of validity. Nevertheless, many constraint-reasoning systems of this type are used successfully in practical situations where it can be assured that constraints always have particular forms.

7.5   REASONING WITH CONSTRAINTS ON CONTINUOUS VARIABLES

Continuous variables are unavoidable in engineering. Often their values govern decision making. For example, values of continuous variables dominate evaluations of factors such as project cost, duration and many aspects of engineering quality. While it is sometimes possible to discretize the range of values that continuous variables can have into finite numbers of fixed values, this is often not desirable. For example, when values of continuous variables are used to determine other variables in sequences of calculations, large errors accumulate when values are approximated through discretization.

Tasks involving continuous variables are supported by methods that have been developed in the fields of operations research and optimization. Methods for reasoning with continuous variables are available when these more traditional methods cannot be applied. In this way, constraint-based reasoning has widened the possibilities for supporting engineering tasks. This field is undergoing many developments and a comprehensive treatment is outside the scope of this book. An example in the area of computer-supported collaborative work is treated in the next section to illustrate important aspects.

7.5.1   Constraint-Based Support

Engineering tasks such as design and diagnosis can be supported by constraint representation and reasoning. These tasks are rarely performed alone. The effectiveness of collaboration between partners during such tasks often has an important influence on project success. Negotiation is an important part of this collaboration. An application of how constraints are used to improve decision making during negotiation reveals several key features of constraint-based reasoning with continuous variables.

Example 7.2 Computer building

A client wishes to construct a building for a large number of high-performance computers. This building is located in an area where there are height restrictions on construction. To provide adequate ventilation, a design solution is adopted involving steel beams with holes cut out of the webs. The task in this example is to determine the size and spacing of the holes.

Four groups of people – engineers, architects, ventilation suppliers and steel fabricators – must collaborate to obtain an acceptable solution. Engineers are concerned with ensuring that strength and deflection behaviour of the beams are adequate. Architects favour aesthetically pleasing solutions. Ventilation suppliers need enough space for the ventilation ducts. Finally, steel fabricators need to ensure the holes can be fabricated accurately and reliably without interfering with the beam-to-column connection. These considerations mean that the four groups need to agree on values for the continuous variables in Figure 7.4.

Since engineers want small holes that are spaced far apart and ventilation suppliers would prefer to have large holes that are closely spaced, negotiation is unavoidable. Since steel fabricators have to ensure that distances between holes are sufficient for fabrication needs and that the hole closest to the column does not weaken the connection, this process is further complicated. Finally architects need to ensure that the size and spacing are adequate from an aesthetic viewpoint.

Table 7.1 shows the evolution of values for these variables. This collaboration was carried out using traditional methods. No computer support for collaboration was employed. Table 7.1 indicates that the four groups are not close to agreement. During a real case that inspired this example, the steel fabricator could not wait any longer for agreement as the construction schedule would not allow it. Fabrication went ahead for beams having a depth, h, of 730 mm. The fabricator was not aware that building height restrictions meant these beams would cause the structure to exceed the limits set out in the local building requirements. The architect was forced to refuse these elements, causing considerable additional expense to the fabricator.

In reality there are many solutions that would have satisfied all partners. The difficulty is that in traditional collaborative exercises, partners propose 'point solutions' without communicating the requirements that actually inspired them to assign values to variables.

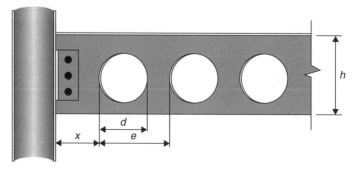

Figure 7.4 Values of four continuous variables need to satisfy constraints by engineers, architects, ventilation suppliers and steel fabricators

Table 7.1 Evolution of the values of variables during traditional negotiation. Values in bold indicate changes initiated
by the group named at the beginning of the row

Partner	d	e	x	h
Architect	550	650	500	650
Steel fabricator	550	**900**	**1100**	650
Engineer	**200**	900	1100	650
Architect	200	900	**1000**	650
Ventilation supplier	**450**	**800**	**600**	650
Engineer	**400**	**900**	**700**	**730**
Steel fabricator	400	900	**800**	730

Table 7.2 Simplified constraints for holes in beams having
a constant beam depth of 700 mm

Partner	Constraint
Architect	x
	$d \geq 300$
	$600 \leq e \leq 1200$
Engineer	$d \leq 4h/7$
	$e \geq 900$
Steel fabricator	$x \geq 2d$
	$e \geq d + 50$
Ventilation subcontractor	$d \geq 250$
	e as small as possible
	(maximize number of holes)

When variables are continuous constraints, such requirements can often be expressed explicitly in the form of inequalities. Simplified constraints for $h = 700$ mm are illustrated in Table 7.2.

More scientific constraints (have a look at a textbook on steel design, for example) are more complicated than the unary and binary constraints in Table 7.2. Nevertheless, even this representation could have led to more productive collaboration between partners, thereby reducing the chances of fabricating the wrong beams. For example, if the collaborating partners had the solution space shown in Figure 7.5, negotiation would have converged more effectively on an acceptable solution.

7.5.1.1 Collaboration using solution spaces defined by constraints

Engineers have found that when important aspects of a task can be described using constraints, the following advantages are possible:

- Negotiation cycles between partners are reduced.
- Artificial conflicts (such as those causing the iterations in our example) are reduced.
- The responsibility for changes in values stays with the initiator of the change.

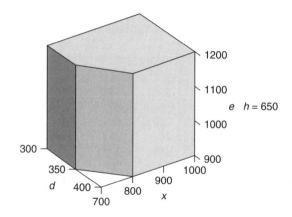

Figure 7.5   The solution space for the simplified constraints described in Table 7.2

- Negotiation, when necessary, is guided more effectively.
- Search and optimization tasks are bounded more accurately.
- Modifications to requirements (constraints) are managed better due to their explicit representation.

With reference to changes in values staying with the initiator, practical use of many computer-supported collaboration tools results in a 'responsibility shift' to the receiver of the change. When many changes are made, these partners can become overloaded to the point where changes are not checked for conformity with all requirements. Responsibility shifts can completely negate the advantages of the tool.

For simple constraints it is useful to try mathematical approaches, particularly from operations research. But constraints that are relevant to engineering tasks often have the following characteristics:

- Constraints have non-linear expressions that contain real numbers for exponents.
- Key constraints are inequalities.
- Variable dependency cannot be described using a tree graph.

These characteristics create conditions where traditional operations research methodology is not adequate for defining solution spaces. Creation of solvers for continuous constraints is an active area of research in computer science. Software is emerging for specific types of continuous constraints. Engineers are able to visualize solution spaces using constraints. This is leading to modifications in the way computer-supported collaborative work is carried out.

For example, consider the more general task of designing and building a large structure. Many CAE tools currently reflect the assumption that the information flow should follow the schema in Figure 7.6. Indeed worldwide initiatives that are supported by large industries and the International Organization for Standardization (ISO) are founded in this area. These initiatives exist to define the important attributes of a database for structural elements. Unfortunately, such efforts include the assumption that engineers will continue to work with single (point) solutions since no support for constraints and solution spaces has been envisaged.

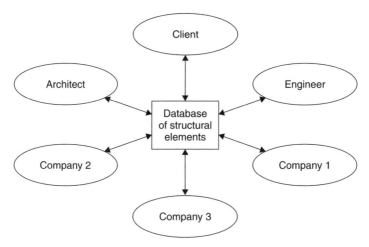

Figure 7.6 An example of information flow for point solutions using a central data base

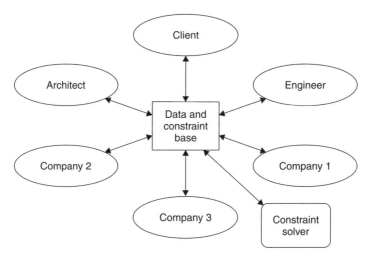

Figure 7.7 An example of information flow for solutions spaces and point solutions

An alternative information schema involves representing structural elements using data and constraints so that solution spaces, as well as the current point solution, can be consulted and modified by collaborating partners. Figure 7.7 shows an example of a schema.

7.6 SUMMARY

- Important aspects of many engineering tasks can be expressed in terms of constraints.
- Since constraints are close to traditional ways of representing engineering knowledge, modifying and updating knowledge are easier than with other representations.

- Constraints are categorized in terms of the number of variables they include. For example, a constraint may be unary, binary, ternary or n-ary.

- Since most engineering tasks cannot be modelled completely, engineers are not interested in single solutions to constraint sets. Engineers use constraints to prune feasible values for variables and to define solution spaces.

- There are four constraint-solving methods: value propagation, value relaxation, label propagation and constraint propagation.

- Techniques for reasoning with constraints on discrete variables are better established than techniques for reasoning with constraints on continuous variables.

- Constraint solvers improve the usefulness of collaboration-support systems and can assist least-commitment decision-making strategies.

REFERENCE

Tsang, E. 1993. *Foundations of Constraint Satisfaction*. New York: Academic Press.

8

Optimization and Search

8.1 INTRODUCTION

Optimization is a field of mathematics. In mathematics, problems are typically defined through an initial definition of a closed world. Accordingly, optimization methods are most appropriate for closed worlds where all objectives and constraints can be defined mathematically and where there are algorithms that lead to complete identification of solutions. These conditions correspond to the definition for well-structured tasks given in Chapter 1.

Since there are often many tens, and sometimes thousands, of good solutions to engineering tasks, engineers are interested in finding the best solutions among them. However, engineering tasks are rarely well defined. Usually, tasks cannot be described completely, functions do not reflect all requirements, and algorithms do not lead to complete identification of solutions.

In order to perform tasks, engineers often choose mathematical representations that correspond best to the task at hand. These representations (models), being incomplete, have a limited scope and are usually the result of subjective decisions of the modeller. When the model is approximate, engineers cannot reliably optimize since critical information may not be included in the model. These tasks are poorly defined (Chapter 1). Therefore, the term 'optimal solution' should be used with caution. A solution is optimal only with respect to the model that is used.

When exact mathematical methods cannot be applied due to the complexity of models, engineers perform what is known as exploration. During exploration, solutions are generated and tested according to criteria that are relevant to the task. While explicit criteria can be tested automatically, implicit (or non-modelled) criteria must be evaluated interactively. Generate-and-test procedures have traditionally been used in computer science in situations where solutions need to be systematically evaluated (Figure 8.1). Methods that employ generate-and-test procedures without checking mathematical characteristics of the evaluation function are called direct search techniques or simply search techniques. They depend on the generation of good solutions usually using information from evaluations of solutions generated previously.

The usefulness of optimization methods for engineering tasks depends on the interdependency between the parameters that are modelled and the parameters that are not included in the model chosen by the engineer. For example, if the surface roughness of a product has no influence on the functional objectives that were identified to be relevant,

Fundamentals of Computer-Aided Engineering   B. Raphael and I. F. C. Smith
© 2003 John Wiley & Sons, Ltd   ISBNs: 0-471-48709-0 (HB); 0-471-48715-5 (PB)

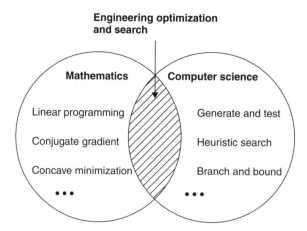

Figure 8.1   Optimization has traditionally been an area of mathematics. Search is an area of computer science. A combination of the two areas is useful for engineering tasks

it does not matter whether or not surface roughness is modelled. Therefore, in some situations, optimization methods can be useful for engineering tasks. Furthermore, optimization methods are sometimes employed to simplify subsequent search efforts through the identification of sets of good possibilities.

This chapter begins with a description of several types of optimization method. At its simplest level, optimization is reduced to the solution of equations. At higher levels of difficulty, optimization methods become more akin to search methods. Several modern search methods are compared and evaluated for their appropriateness to particular engineering tasks. For simplicity this chapter concentrates on searching for minimum values.

8.2   BASIC CONCEPTS

Here is an optimization problem in one variable. Find the minimum of the function

$$f(x) = (x-1)^3(x+3)(x+5)(x-5)(x-7) \tag{8.1}$$

within the range $-10 < x < 10$. The solution to the problem can be obtained by setting the first derivative to zero and ensuring that the second derivative is positive. This is a necessary condition but not a sufficient condition for a global minimum. The first derivative is zero at all local maxima and minima, as well as at saddle points. A saddle point is a point where both the first and second derivatives are zero and is neither a minimum nor a maximum (Figure 8.2). The global minimum will be the minimum of all the local minima. Setting the derivative of a function to zero might require solving a non-linear equation. Although this can be done analytically for certain simple cases, it requires numerical techniques for some equations. There are efficient methods, such as the Newton–Raphson method, for solving non-linear equations in a single variable.

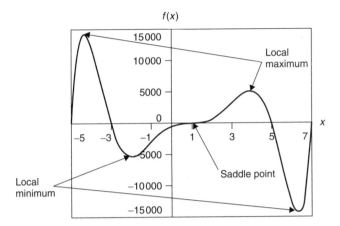

Figure 8.2   A plot of a function (equation 8.2a) with multiple local optima. Derivatives are zero at maxima, minima and saddle points

Optimizing a function of *multiple variables* is a more difficult problem. Consider this problem of two variables: Find the minimum of the function $x^2 - y^2 + 2xy$ in the range $[-1, 1]$ for both x and y. Setting the partial derivatives to zero results in the following system of equations:

$$x - y = 0$$
$$x + y = 0$$

The solution to these equations is $x = y = 0$, but this is not a minimum point. In fact, it is a saddle point. The real minima are found along the boundaries at $x = 1$, $y = -1$ and $x = -1$, $y = 1$. Therefore, finding the minima of even simple functions of multiple variables requires more sophisticated approaches than differentiation.

Definition   *The general global optimization problem is mathematically defined as follows:*

Given a set D (domain) and a function f(x) defined over D, minimize f(x) subject to the constraint x ∈ D.   (8.2)

The function $f(x)$ is called the objective function. The variable x represents an n-dimensional vector of unknown values.

8.2.1   Types of Optimization Problem

Optimization problems may be classified according to several characteristics (Table 8.1). Variables are described as continuous, discrete or mixed. The size and extent of the domain are characterized as finite or infinite and bounded or unbounded. Objective functions are classified as linear, non-linear, continuous and discontinuous. Not all methods are suitable for all types of problem. In Section 8.3 we will examine the suitability of methods for different cases.

Table 8.1 Classification of optimization problems

Characteristic	Classification
Type of variable	Continuous
	Discrete
	Mixed
Size of domain	Finite
	Infinite
Extent of domain	Bounded
	Unbounded
Shape of objective function and constraints	Linear
	Non-linear
	Continuous
	Discontinuous

Minimum weight design of a rectangular beam is an example of a continuous, constrained, non-linear optimization problem; it is described in Section 8.2.5.1. An example of discrete optimization is the travelling salesman problem (TSP) described in Section 8.2.5.2. An example of a linear optimization problem is considered in Section 8.4.1.2.

8.2.1.1 Minimization, maximization and decision problems

The classical optimization problem involves minimizing or maximizing a function. That is, the objective is to find the values for a set of variables such that the value of the function is a minimum or a maximum. A modified version of the formulation is encountered in many situations. In this version we are not interested in finding the minimum or maximum but in proving whether a solution exists that satisfies certain conditions. These formulations are known as decision problems. The answer to a decision problem is either yes or no (i.e. whether or not a solution exists), whereas in a minimization or maximization problem the result involves finding optimal values of variables. Here are some examples of decision problems:

- Is it possible to design a rectangular beam such that the total weight is less than a specified value?
- Is it possible to have a pipe network connecting locations such that none of the pipes intersect?
- Is it possible to complete a set of tasks within a specified time?

A method for solving decision problems is to identify at least one solution that satisfies the required conditions. This can be done by converting the decision problem into a minimization problem. For example, to find out whether there exists a beam design having a weight less than a specified value, it is sufficient to find the design having the minimum weight and check whether its weight is less than the specified value. However, this procedure is usually not efficient. Optimization problems are usually more complex than decision problems. Some decision problems are solvable in polynomial time, whereas the corresponding minimization problems are exponentially complex. That is, it is possible to find out whether solutions exist in polynomial time, but exact solutions may only be found in exponential time.

8.2.2   Formulating Optimization Tasks

Engineering tasks may be formulated in different ways depending on what criteria are considered to be important. Consider the design of a bridge. The task may be formulated as the minimization of the use of materials. This requires the use of formulas for computing the volume of concrete and weight of steel. Although solutions that use minimum material may be identified using this approach, these solutions may not correspond to minimum costs. Another formulation may involve additional formulas for the cost of materials, labour and equipment in order to minimize cost. However, this might not correspond to minimal life-cycle costs. A third formulation may involve additional formulas for material deterioration, periodic maintenance and dismantling that lead to values for life-cycle costs. But even this formulation may not provide solutions that are close to good compromises between factors such as low life-cycle costs, good aesthetics, low environmental impact and widespread societal acceptance. Thus, models become increasingly complex as more and more factors are considered. In addition, approximations and assumptions increase, hence the optimization becomes less reliable. Nevertheless, optimization tasks require mathematical models in order to be carried out on computers. These models involve methods to compute the objective function (Section 8.2) so that solutions can be evaluated and good solutions identified.

If a single criterion is used to evaluate solutions, the objective function is easily formulated. But in the presence of multiple criteria, the objective function becomes more complex. Two commonly used approaches are

- combining objectives using weights;
- Pareto filtering.

Consider two functions $f_1(x)$ and $f_2(x)$ to be minimized simultaneously. They may be combined into a single objective function as follows:

$$F(x) = w_1 f_1(x) + w_2 f_2(x) \tag{8.3}$$

where w_1 and w_2 are weight factors that reflect the relative importance of the functions f_1 and f_2. These factors are fixed arbitrarily so that the optimization might be carried out.

Pareto filtering uses a different approach for accommodating multiple criteria. A solution x_0 is said to be Pareto-optimal if there exists no other feasible solution that is better than x_0 under all criteria. Thus the Pareto methodology may be used to filter out sub-optimal solutions. The solutions in Table 8.2 have been evaluated using three different criteria.

Solutions 1, 2 and 4 are the best under criteria 1, 2 and 3, respectively, hence they belong to the Pareto set. There are solutions better than solution 3 under some criteria but not all of them at the same time. For instance, solution 2 is better than solution 3 under criteria 2 and 3. However, solutions 2 and 3 are equal under criterion 1. So solution 3 also belongs to the Pareto set. The only solution in the table that does not belong to the Pareto set is solution 5. Solution 1 is better than solution 5 under all criteria.

Table 8.2 Pareto filtering with three criteria

Solutions	Criterion 1	Criterion 2	Criterion 3
1	3	5	8
2	8	4	6
3	8	6	9
4	4	5	3
5	4	7	9

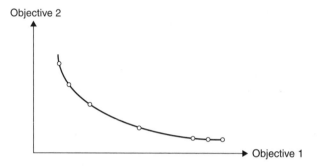

Figure 8.3 An example of a Pareto surface

Points belonging to the Pareto set form an n-dimensional surface where each criterion is represented on a different axis. Such a surface is known as the Pareto-optimal surface, or simply the Pareto surface (Figure 8.3). Pareto surfaces are useful in determining how trade-offs might be made among different criteria.

8.2.3 Representing Search Spaces

Search spaces of problems with continuous variables are often represented using bounds on the values of variables. For discrete variables it is often useful to represent solution spaces as trees. In search trees, solutions are represented by one of the following (Figure 8.4):

- each node in the tree;
- leaf nodes only;
- complete paths from the root to leaf nodes.

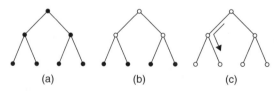

(a)   (b)   (c)

Figure 8.4 Representation of solution spaces as trees with solutions as (a) nodes, (b) leaf nodes, (c) paths from root to leaf node

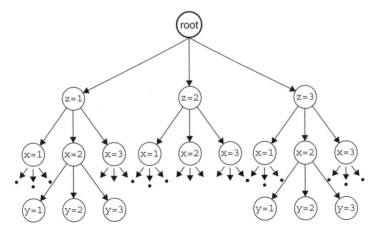

Figure 8.5   Search Tree for the integer programming problem. In this case, solutions are complete paths from the root to leaf nodes

Consider the following integer programming problem. Find all integer values of x, y and z satisfying the equation

$$x^2 + y^2 = z^2 \tag{8.4}$$

in the interval [1, 3]. Possible solutions to this problem are represented in the form of a search tree (Figure 8.5). A path from the root to a leaf node is a potential solution in this representation. At each node in the tree, a value is assigned to a variable. Subtrees at each node represent smaller search spaces with fewer variables since other variables are assigned values in their parent nodes. Each subtree may be called a subdomain (a subset of the original domain).

Search trees provide a mechanism for visualizing and representing solution spaces, but complete trees are rarely generated in their entirety during most search processes. Solution spaces grow exponentially with the number of variables, making it impossible to enumerate all possibilities in most practical engineering situations.

8.2.4   Representing Constraints

Constraints are continuous or discrete depending on the nature of the variables. An expression of the form $x > y$ is an example of a continuous constraint, where x and y are continuous variables. The zero-one integer programming problem (ZOIP) from Chapter 2 contains discrete constraints, since each variable takes only discrete values (0 and 1). Discrete constraints are treated in Chapter 7.

Continuous constraints have linear and non-linear forms. Manipulating non-linear constraints is an extremely difficult task. Non-linear constraints often make the domain shapes extremely complex. It may not be possible to find closed-form expressions representing boundaries of domains, hence finding a point on the boundary involves solving a system of non-linear equations. Since non-linear constraints are difficult to manipulate, many methods accommodate them indirectly. Common approaches include

- generate and test;
- penalty functions;
- Lagrangian methods.

These approaches are described briefly in the following paragraphs.

Most search algorithms that use the generate-and-test method for constraint handling simply discard solutions that violate constraints. They do not use the information related to constraint violation for the generation of future points, hence they tend to be inefficient.

Penalty functions are a means of discouraging search in regions of constraint violation. If constraints are violated, a penalty is added to the objective function. The value of the penalty function is normally much higher than the range of values of the objective function, thus search algorithms are led away from regions where constraints are violated.

Lagrangian methods manipulate constraints mathematically through a set of variables known as Lagrange multipliers. Suppose the objective is to minimize a function $f(x)$ subject to a set of constraint equations of the form $Ax = B$ (referred to as the original problem). A modified function L is defined as

$$L(x, \lambda) = f(x) + \lambda(Ax - B) \tag{8.5}$$

where λ is called the Lagrange multiplier and $L(x, \lambda)$ is called the Lagrangian function. According to a theorem (the saddle-point theorem), x^* is a solution to the original problem if there exists a λ^* such that (x^*, λ^*) constitutes a saddle point of $L(x, \lambda)$. Hence, by searching for saddle points of the Lagrangian function, it is possible to identify optimal values satisfying the constraints.

8.2.5 Some Optimization Problems

Example 8.1 Minimum weight design of a rectangular beam

Consider a simply supported wooden beam of rectangular cross-section subject to a concentrated load at midspan (Figure 8.6). The beam needs to be designed so that stresses do not exceed a permissible limit (strength constraint) and the deflection at the midspan is less than a specified value (serviceability constraint). The optimization task is to determine the values of width (b) and depth (d) of the beam such that the weight of the beam is a minimum. The following relations might be used:

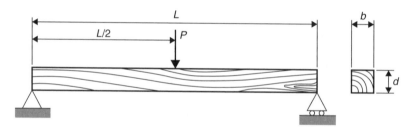

Figure 8.6 A rectangular beam loaded at midspan

- maximum moment, $M = \dfrac{PL}{4}$

- maximum stress, $\sigma(b, d) = \dfrac{6M}{bd^2}$

- maximum deflection, $\delta(b, d) = \dfrac{PL^3}{4Ebd^3}$

- weight of the beam, $W(b, d) = Lbd\rho$

E is the Young's modulus of the material and ρ is the density of the material; both are constant. The maximum stress and the maximum deflection are usually determined by material and context; they are constant for a given design. The above relations are valid only if d is small compared to L. This is an assumption used in the formulation of the equation. It is therefore stipulated that d should be less than $L/10$.

The design task can be formulated as an optimization problem:

Minimize $W(b, d)$ such that

$\sigma(b, d) \leq \sigma_{max}$	(strength constraint)
$\delta(b, d) \leq \delta_{max}$	(serviceability constraint)
$d < L/10$	(modelling constraint)

b, d are positive real numbers

σ_{max} and δ_{max} are usually determined by material and context

The objective function $W(b, d)$ is linear with respect to b and d. The first two constraints are non-linear. The last constraint specifies bounds on the variable d. Hence this is an instance of a continuous, constrained, non-linear optimization problem.

Example 8.2   Travelling salesman problem

The travelling salesman problem (TSP) creates one of the most well-known optimization problems. It has practical applications in areas of engineering such as the design of networks, planning, and programming of robots. A travelling salesman needs to visit n cities such that (a) he visits each city exactly once and (b) he returns to the starting point at the end of the tour. Distances between each pair of cities are given. The objective is to find the optimum tour such that the total distance travelled is the minimum.

It is possible to determine the total number of possible tours as follows. Assuming that the starting point is fixed, there are $n - 1$ options to select the second city, $n - 2$ to select the third city, and so on. Thus the total number of tours is $(n - 1)!$. In symmetric TSP the distance from city i to city j is the same as the distance from city j to city i. Since for each path there exists another path containing cities in the reverse order, exactly half the tours are equivalent. Thus, in the symmetric version, the number of possible tours is $\frac{1}{2}(n - 1)!$. For the apparently simple set of cities shown in Figure 8.7, there are 2520 possible tours. There are more than a billion possible tours for 15 cities.

The travelling salesman problem can be posed as a discrete optimization problem. Let each city be represented by a unique number from 1 to n (node number). Let $D[i, j]$ be the distance between city i and city j. Let P be a sequence of n numbers representing

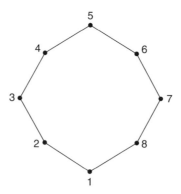

Figure 8.7   An instance of the traveling salesman problem with 8 cities. Cities are marked with solid dots. The optimal tour is shown as solid lines

the node number of each city in a given path. That is, $P(k)$ is the node number of the kth city in a given path P. Let $L(P)$ be the length of the path P given by

$$L(P) = \sum_{k=1}^{n-1} D[P(k), P(k+1)]$$

that is, the sum of distances between adjacent nodes in the path. Find $P(k)$, $k = 2$ to n, such that $L(P)$ is a minimum, subject to $P(i) \neq P(j)$ if $i \neq j$; that is, node numbers should not be repeated in a sequence P.

There are $n - 1$ optimization variables: $P(2), P(3), \ldots, P(n)$. These variables take discrete values between 1 and n (node numbers), therefore this is a discrete optimization problem.

8.3   CLASSIFICATION OF METHODS

Search methods are considered as local or global, depending on the type of solutions identified by them. Local search methods identify only local optima. Global search methods aim to identify the global optimum. Although every global search method has some means of avoiding convergence to a local optimum, the global optimum may not always be attained. The success of a global method in a specific situation depends on how effectively it is able to avoid local optima. A method is said to be trapped in local optima when it is unable to come out of a region containing a local optimum (Figure 8.8).

There are two classes of methods for global optimization: deterministic and stochastic. Deterministic methods result in the same solution every time for the same problem (Figure 8.9). Stochastic methods use random numbers and might produce different results if the sequence of random numbers generated is different (this depends on the starting seed value of the random number generation algorithm). Examples of deterministic methods include the simplex, branch-and-bound and cutting-plane methods. Stochastic

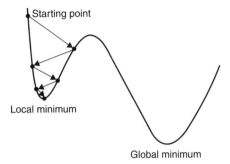

Figure 8.8   An example of an algorithm becoming "trapped" in a local optimum. There is nothing in the algorithm that enables it to come out of the region containing the local optimum

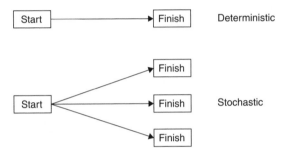

Figure 8.9   Deterministic methods result in the same solution all the time. Stochastic methods might result in different solutions depending on the sequence of random numbers used

methods include local optimization with random starts, genetic algorithms and simulated annealing (Section 8.5). A classification of search techniques is shown in Figure 8.10.

8.4   DETERMINISTIC OPTIMIZATION AND SEARCH

For engineering tasks, deterministic methods usually require many simplifying assumptions related to the objective function and the relevant constraints. In spite of such assumptions, there are several situations where they provide useful engineering support. Examples of mathematical problems that can be effectively treated through deterministic methods include the concave minimization problem, the concave complementarity problem and the quadratic programming problem. These are special cases of global optimization problems. As special cases, they are simpler than most others. To illustrate the simplifications in these special cases, some are considered in the following sections.

8.4.1   Special Cases

8.4.1.1   Concave minimization

This is a special case when $f(x)$ is a concave function and D is a convex set in equation (8.1). These conditions can be stated mathematically as follows. For arbitrary

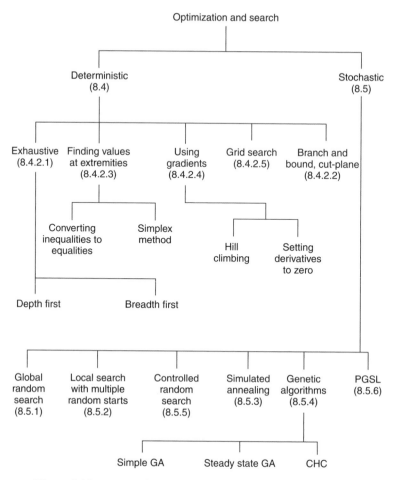

Figure 8.10   A classification of optimization and search methods

$x_1 \in D$ and $x_2 \in D$, and $0 \le \lambda \le 1$,

$\lambda x_1 + (1 - \lambda)x_2 \in D$ (condition for a convex set)

$f(\lambda x_1 + (1 - \lambda)x_2) \ge \lambda f(x_1) + (1 - \lambda)f(x_2)$ (condition for a concave function)

$$(8.6)$$

A convex set implies that if two points belong to the set, then every point on a straight line joining the two points also belongs to the set. Examples of convex and non-convex sets are shown in Figure 8.11. A concave function implies that the value of the function at any point on a straight line joining two interior points is equal to or greater than a linear interpolation between the function values at the two points (Figure 8.12).

For the concave minimization problem, the global minimum is always located at an extreme point of D. However, locating the minimum along the boundaries of D might involve an exponentially complex algorithm. For example, even when D is a polyhedron it might be necessary to evaluate the function at every vertex. The complexity of this

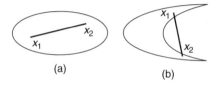

Figure 8.11 Examples of (a) convex and (b) non-convex sets. Part of a line joining two points in a non-convex set might lie outside the set

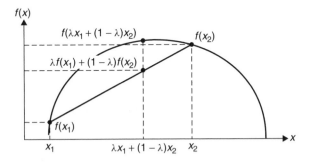

Figure 8.12 Example of a concave function

evaluation is $O(2^n)$, since there are 2^n vertices for a polyhedron representing a space consisting of n variables.

8.4.1.2 The linear programming problem

The linear programming (LP) problem is stated as follows:

Given an $m \times n$ vector A, an m-vector $\mathbf{b}$, and an n-vector $\mathbf{c}$, find an n-vector

$$\mathbf{x} \geq 0, \text{ which minimizes } f(\mathbf{x}) = \mathbf{c}^T \mathbf{x} \text{ such that } A\mathbf{x} = \mathbf{b} \tag{8.7}$$

The above formulation is known as the standard form in linear programming. There are many practical problems that can be formulated as LP problems. Linear programming is widely used in engineering areas such as transportation, planning, and network analysis.

Here is a simple example. The cost (C) of a construction project consists of three parts:

(a) The cost of designing $=$ unit cost of engineer's time (c_d) multiplied by the time required for design (t_d).
(b) The cost of construction $=$ the unit cost of worker's time for construction (c_c) multiplied by the time required for construction (t_c).
(c) The cost of materials and equipments (m).

That is,

$$C = c_d t_d + c_c t_c + m \tag{8.8}$$

The quantity of material required for construction decreases linearly with the time spent on design due to increases in design quality. It is observed that there is a reduction of 0.2 units of material for each month spent on design. It is not possible to complete the construction in less than 3 months, and it is not possible to complete the project (design + construction) in less than 6 months. The total time for design and construction should not exceed 12 months. The minimum time for design is taken as zero since it is possible to use an existing design.

This example can be expressed mathematically as follows. Minimize $C = c_d t_d + c_c t_c + m$ such that

$$m = m_0 - 0.2t_d \tag{8.9}$$

$$t_d + t_c \geq 6 \tag{8.10}$$

$$t_d + t_c < 12 \tag{8.11}$$

$$t_c > 3 \tag{8.12}$$

where m_0 is a constant representing the minimum material cost. For simplicity m_0 is taken as zero here. The variable m can be eliminated from the objective function by substituting (8.9) in (8.8). To express these relations in the form given in (8.7) it is necessary to convert inequalities to equalities. This can be done by using slack variables, sometimes called dummy variables. For example, the inequality $t_d + t_c \geq 6$ is written as $t_d + t_c - s_1 = 6$, where s_1 is a slack variable; s_1 may assume any value greater than zero such that the original inequality is satisfied. Similarly, the inequality $t_d + t_c < 12$ is written as $t_d + t_c + s_2 = 12$. The last inequality is written as $t_c + s_3 = 3$. The problem is therefore expressed in standard form as

$$\text{Minimize} \begin{bmatrix} (c_d - 0.2) & c_c & 0 & 0 & 0 \end{bmatrix} \begin{bmatrix} t_d \\ t_c \\ s_1 \\ s_2 \\ s_3 \end{bmatrix}$$

such that

$$\begin{bmatrix} 1 & 1 & -1 & 0 & 0 \\ 1 & 1 & 0 & 1 & 0 \\ 0 & 1 & 0 & 0 & 1 \end{bmatrix} \begin{bmatrix} t_d \\ t_c \\ s_1 \\ s_2 \\ s_3 \end{bmatrix} = \begin{bmatrix} 6 \\ 12 \\ 3 \end{bmatrix}$$

The task of cost minimization is thus expressed in the standard form of linear programming. Although all linear programs can be transformed into the standard form, in practice it may not be necessary. For example, the standard form requires all variables to be non-negative. However, most implementations allow bounds to be specified for the variables, thereby avoiding the use of slack variables.

The solution to the LP problem is found at a vertex of the polyhedron representing the domain. The oldest and the most widely used algorithm for solving the LP problem is the simplex method proposed by Dantzig (1951). It consists of moving from vertex to vertex in a downhill direction. This procedure is formulated mathematically as a sequence of matrix operations. Details can be found in textbooks on linear programming.

Since our construction project example involves only two variables, t_d and t_c, ignoring slack variables, the solution might easily be found by plotting the constraints in two dimensions (Figure 8.13). The tinted region represents the feasible region where constraints are satisfied. The minimum value of the objective function is located at a vertex of this polygon. Values of the objective function at all vertices for different values of c_d and c_c are tabulated in Table 8.3. The location of the minimum depends on the relative values of c_d and c_c.

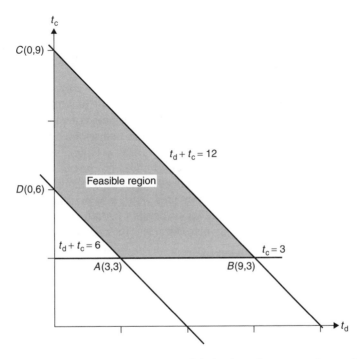

Figure 8.13   Solution space for cost minimization of a construction project

Table 8.3   Values of the objective function at vertices of the polygon representing the feasible region

Vertex	t_d	t_c	Cost	Minimum?
		$c_c = c_d = 1$		
A	3	3	5.4	yes
B	6	3	7.8	
C	0	9	9	
D	0	6	6	
		$c_c = 1, c_d = 2$		
A	3	3	8.4	
B	6	3	13.8	
C	0	9	9	
D	0	6	6	yes

Although the simplex method is extremely simple and solutions involving several thousands of variables are easily found, it is exponentially complex in the worst case. A particular condition called degeneracy is encountered in rare situations when the same vertices are repeated over and over. This happens when the algorithm reaches a point where improvements in the objective function cannot be made by moving along edges incident at the point. Other methods exist that have polynomial complexity, such as the ellipsoid method and the interior-point algorithm. However, for many engineering tasks, the simplex method is the most efficient.

8.4.2 Deterministic Methods

8.4.2.1 Exhaustive search

Exhaustive search requires the systematic evaluation of all possible solutions until the required objectives are met. Classical methods for performing complete enumeration of all possibilities employ either breadth-first search or depth-first search. In breadth-first search, all nodes at a given level in the search tree (siblings) are processed before traversing deeper to child nodes. In depth-first search, child nodes are processed completely before processing the next sibling. Solutions obtained by both methods are the same if the objective is to select the best solution, provided there is only one best solution. If the objective is to select a satisfactory solution (satisfying certain criteria), the results might be different. These two methods might also differ in efficiency depending on the order of nodes in the search tree.

8.4.2.2 Branch-and-bound methods

The branch-and-bound method avoids exhaustive search by eliminating certain branches of the search tree by deriving conditions which indicate that no solutions exist in such branches. Branch and bound is a deterministic method that is used to find the exact solution for certain classes of problem. The method works by recursively dividing the domain into smaller and smaller subsets and solving the problem over each subdomain, as illustrated in Figure 8.5. When it is discovered that no solution exists in a particular subdomain, that branch is eliminated altogether. Conditions for eliminating branches are established for different classes of problem, such as integer programming. A frequently adopted strategy involves solving a relaxed problem in the subdomain (which may be solved easily). If a solution does not exist, it is concluded that the solution to the original problem does not exist in the subdomain.

For example, assume that we are interested in finding integer values of x, y and z satisfying the following constraint in a certain interval:

$$x^2 + y^2 = z^2 \tag{8.13}$$

A relaxed version of this problem is to find real number solutions of the equation. If real solutions do not exist in an interval, it can be concluded that integer solutions do not exist either.

To illustrate the branch-and-bound method, consider the solution to the above problem in the interval [1, 3] for all three variables. The search tree is shown in Figure 8.5. In the absence of any knowledge about the constraint, it is necessary to evaluate 27 solution points (each leaf node of the tree) to ascertain the non-existence of a solution. However, with the branch-and-bound method, it is possible to avoid certain branches by evaluating certain criteria at intermediate nodes. Consider the node $z = 1$. The lower bound for $x^2 + y^2 - z^2$ is 1, hence no solution exists for the relaxed problem. Therefore the entire branch of the search tree can be eliminated. At the nodes $z = 2$ and $z = 3$, the corresponding lower bounds are -2 and -7. Hence these branches have to be further expanded. Further expanding the node $z = 2$ at the child nodes $x = 2$ and $x = 3$, the lower bounds are 1 and 6, hence they can be eliminated. Thus, by deriving appropriate conditions, it is possible to avoid an exhaustive search and still achieve exact results.

The suitability of the branch-and-bound technique for solving practical problems depends on the availability of criteria for dividing and pruning. Furthermore, the method is exponentially complex in its general form with respect to the number of variables. However, it has been successful in establishing the existence or non-existence of solutions to many mathematical problems. This has led to simplification of engineering tasks such as resource allocation and scheduling.

8.4.2.3   Locating the optimum along boundaries

The optimum for a concave minimization problem is located at a point on the boundary of the domain. This is the case for many simplified versions of engineering and management problems. In most situations the objective function is either linear or monotonic (Figure 8.14). Here constraints determine the location of the optimum. A practice that is commonly adopted in engineering is to convert inequality constraints into equalities and then solve for the boundary point. Consider the example in Section 8.2.5.1. The minimum weight design of a simply supported beam of long span is likely to be governed by the serviceability constraint, $\delta \leq \delta_{max}$. Hence the depth of the cross-section is calculated by setting $\delta = \delta_{max}$. After computing the values of design variables using the governing inequality, it is necessary to ensure that other constraints are satisfied for the chosen values. For example, the stress constraint needs to be verified after computing the depth of the cross-section using the serviceability constraint. This is the most common procedure that engineers use to carry out routine design and other traditional engineering tasks.

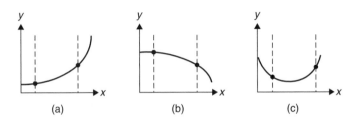

Figure 8.14   Optima are located on the boundaries of monotonic functions. For non-monotonic functions, optima might be in the interior of the domain or along the boundaries: (a) a monotonically increasing function, (b) a monotonically decreasing function, (c) a non-monotonic function

The simplex method (used in linear programming) also searches along domain boundaries for optimal solutions. This method is efficient and can easily accommodate thousands of variables. Most other deterministic methods degrade unacceptably above a few tens of variables. However, the simplex method requires that all constraints are linear.

8.4.2.4 Gradient-based methods

Difficulties associated with the analytical determination of the optimum were discussed in Section 8.2. These difficulties mean that numerical methods are used to determine points of zero slope. As the name implies, gradient-based methods use information about derivatives to move towards optimum points. They assume the objective function is twice differentiable and derivatives can be evaluated at every point within the domain. Gradient-based methods may become trapped in local optima when the objective function contains several minima. Furthermore, there is no reliable method of verifying whether a given local optimum is in fact the global optimum. Therefore they are classified as local search techniques. The optimum that is identified depends on the starting point. When the search is repeated from different starting points, the reliability increases.

For illustration, consider a function in one variable, $f(x) = x^2 - 20\cos(x + 1)$. There are multiple local minima of this function, as can be seen from Figure 8.15. The global minimum is around $x = -1$.

To apply the gradient method, we need to calculate the derivative, which is given by $f'(x) = 2x + 20\sin(x + 1)$. It is not possible to compute local optima directly by setting this equation to zero, since the equation can only be solved numerically. As an alternative to solving the equation through numerical techniques, we use the sign of the derivative to move towards a point of zero slope. An initial starting point and a step size are chosen arbitrarily. The derivative is calculated at each point. If it is positive, the function is increasing, so a negative step size is added to the current point. If the derivative is negative, a positive step size is added, so we move in the direction of decreasing function values. If the derivative changes sign after applying a step size, it means we have crossed the point of zero slope. The algorithm can either be terminated at this point or the step size can be refined if better accuracy is required.

Let us choose the starting point at $x = 0$ and an initial step size of 1. At $x = 0$, the derivative $f'(0)$ is positive. This indicates the function is increasing, hence a negative step

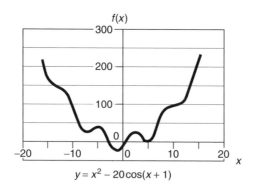

$$y = x^2 - 20\cos(x + 1)$$

Figure 8.15 A sample function with multiple local minima

size is added and the new point is computed as $x = -1$. At this point, the derivative is negative. Since the derivative has changed sign, we reduce the step size by half. The new point is computed as $-1 + 0.5 = -0.5$. The application of this procedure is summarized in Table 8.4. It converges to the global minimum at -0.909. But if the starting point is chosen as $+10$, using the same step size it converges to $+4.784$, which is only a local minimum.

The procedure is generalized as follows:

1. Assume a starting point and assign it to the current point x_i. Evaluate the objective function $y_i = f(x)$ and the gradient vector ∇x_i at this point. The subscript i refers to the iteration number, starting from 1.

2. Assume a step size ΔL.

3. Compute the next point x_{i+1} at a distance ΔL in the direction of the negative gradient. Evaluate the objective function y_{i+1} at x_{i+1}.

4. Evaluate the partial derivatives and the gradient vector ∇x_{i+1}. If all partial derivatives are zero, the current point is a local minimum, so stop.

5. Find the dot product of the gradients ∇x_{i+1} and ∇x_i. If it is negative, reduce the step size by half. The direction of gradient has reversed; the next point has crossed the minimum.

6. Accept the next point as the current point, increment i and repeat from step 3.

Table 8.4 Gradient search for a sample function

x_i	y_i	$\dfrac{dy}{dx}$	Direction	ΔL	x_{i+1}
0	-10.806	16.82942	1	1	-1
-1	-19	-2	-1	0.5	-0.5
-0.5	-17.3017	8.588511	1	0.25	-0.75
-0.75	-18.8157	3.448079	1	0.25	-1
-1	-19	-2	-1	0.125	-0.875
-0.875	-19.0783	0.743495	1	0.0625	-0.9375
-0.9375	-19.082	-0.62581	-1	0.03125	-0.90625
-0.90625	-19.0909	0.059755	1	0.015625	-0.92188
-0.92188	-19.0891	-0.28284	-1	0.007813	-0.91406
-0.91406	-19.0907	-0.11149	-1	0.007813	-0.90625
-0.90625	-19.0909	0.059755	1	0.003906	-0.91016
-0.91016	-19.091	-0.02585	-1	0.001953	-0.9082
-0.9082	-19.091	0.016954	1	0.000977	-0.90918
-0.90918	-19.091	-0.00445	-1	0.000488	-0.90869
-0.90869	-19.091	0.006253	1	0.000244	-0.90894
-0.90894	-19.091	0.000902	1	0.000244	-0.90918
-0.90918	-19.091	-0.00445	-1	0.000122	-0.90906
-0.90906	-19.091	-0.00177	-1	0.000122	-0.90894
-0.90894	-19.091	0.000902	1	6.1E$-$05	-0.909
-0.909	-19.091	-0.00044	-1	3.05E$-$05	-0.90897
-0.90897	-19.091	0.000233	1	1.53E$-$05	-0.90898
-0.90898	-19.091	-0.0001	-1	7.63E$-$06	-0.90897
-0.90897	-19.091	6.57E$-$05	1	3.81E$-$06	-0.90898

Limitations of gradient methods

Gradient methods are limited in practical engineering applications for the following reasons:

- Objective functions are usually not available as explicit mathematical expressions; consequently, derivatives cannot be evaluated.
- They become trapped in local optima.
- Practical problems contain a mixture of discrete and continuous variables; gradient methods cannot accommodate such situations.

There are techniques (such as finite difference approximations) that can be employed when derivatives are not available in explicit forms. However, they suffer stability problems and loss of accuracy due to cancellation and division by small numbers in regions around optimal values.

8.4.2.5   Grid search

Grid Search involves dividing the domain D into a grid of uniform size and evaluating the function at grid points. There are several variations of grid search depending on the schemes that are employed for traversing the grid. A simple method is to move along adjacent points on the grid in a downhill direction until a local optimum is reached. If finer precision is required, another search may be started at the local optimum with a smaller grid size. As with the gradient method, searches may be repeated from multiple starting points and the best local optimum selected.

   As an example, here is a simple grid search algorithm in six steps:

1. Assume a grid size.
2. Start iteration $i = 1$. Set the current point x_i as the starting point.
3. Evaluate the objective function $y_i = f(x_i)$ at the current point.
4. Evaluate the objective function y_{ij} at all neighbouring grid points of x_i.
5. Select the next point x_{i+1} as the neighbouring point j, which has the minimum y_{ij}. If there is no point that gives an improvement, then stop.
6. Increment the iteration count i and repeat from step 3.

In this procedure the neighbourhood of a point may be defined as the set of all points obtained by changing the value of a single variable by plus or minus the grid size. Figure 8.16 shows this procedure applied to a sample function $f(x, y) = (x - 2)^2 + (y - 3)^2$ and Table 8.5 shows the calculations.

8.4.2.6   Line search

Line search methods take advantage of algorithms that are efficient in a single dimension. A minimum is selected from a series of searches along straight lines in different directions from a starting point. Along each direction (i.e. for each line search) the objective function in n variables reduces to a function of a single variable, which is the distance of the point

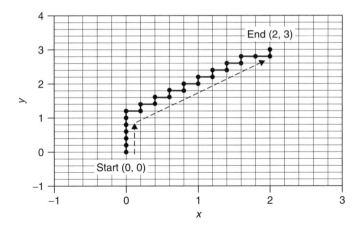

Figure 8.16   Application of grid search technique for the function, $f(x, y) = (x - 2)^2 + (y - 3)^2$. The grid size was chosen as 0.1 and the start point at (0, 0)

Table 8.5   Grid search for a sample function in two variables

x	y	$f(x, y)$	x_j	y_j	$f(x_j, y)$	$f(x, y_j)$
0	0	13	0.2	0.2	12.24	11.84
0	0.2	11.84	0.2	0.4	11.08	10.76
0	0.4	10.76	0.2	0.6	10	9.76
0	0.6	9.76	0.2	0.8	9	8.84
0	0.8	8.84	0.2	1	8.08	8
0	1	8	0.2	1.2	7.24	7.24
0	1.2	7.24	0.2	1.4	6.48	6.56
0.2	1.2	6.48	0.4	1.4	5.8	5.8
0.2	1.4	5.8	0.4	1.6	5.12	5.2
0.4	1.4	5.12	0.6	1.6	4.52	4.52
0.4	1.6	4.52	0.6	1.8	3.92	4
0.6	1.6	3.92	0.8	1.8	3.4	3.4
0.6	1.8	3.4	0.8	2	2.88	2.96
0.8	1.8	2.88	1	2	2.44	2.44
0.8	2	2.44	1	2.2	2	2.08
1	2	2	1.2	2.2	1.64	1.64
1	2.2	1.64	1.2	2.4	1.28	1.36
1.2	2.2	1.28	1.4	2.4	1	1
1.2	2.4	1	1.4	2.6	0.72	0.8
1.4	2.4	0.72	1.6	2.6	0.52	0.52
1.4	2.6	0.52	1.6	2.8	0.32	0.4
1.6	2.6	0.32	1.8	2.8	0.2	0.2
1.6	2.8	0.2	1.8	3	0.08	0.16
1.8	2.8	0.08	2	3	0.04	0.04
2	2.8	0.04	2.2	3	0.08	2.47E−31
2	3	2.47E−31	2.2	3.2	0.04	0.04
2	3	2.47E−31	2.2	3.2	0.04	0.04
2	3	0	2.2	3.2	0.04	0.04

from the starting point. The optimum along a line can be found using deterministic methods since complexity is reduced, because there is only a single variable. Search directions are chosen so they are able to explore the full space of variables. Several schemes have been suggested for the choice of directions so that searching is optimal. A widely used algorithm that employs line search is the conjugate direction method. Here information obtained from previous iterations is used to determine directions for line search.

8.5 STOCHASTIC METHODS

Stochastic methods employ probabilities to find required solutions. They were used as early as 1958 (Brooks 1958). Recently there has been considerable interest in this area, mainly because of the success of genetic algorithms and simulated annealing in solving practical tasks with complex objective functions. In many practical situations the objective function cannot be expressed as a closed-form mathematical equation in terms of its input variables.

Consider the analysis of the slender truss in Figure 8.17. The members of the truss undergo large deformations under the action of the load P, causing the geometry (location of joints) to change. In the changed geometry, the equations of equilibrium formulated for the undeformed shape are no longer valid; this condition is known as geometric non-linearity. New equilibrium equations need to be formulated in terms of the new joint coordinates. The final deflected shape of the truss can be computed only through an iterative procedure. The deflection of the top node d can be computed using this procedure, but it is not possible to express d in terms of P as a closed-form mathematical

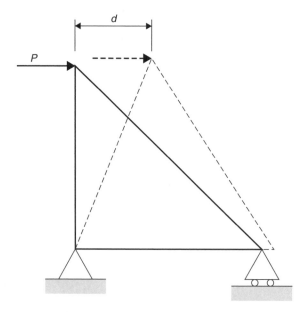

Figure 8.17   A truss undergoing large deformations. The deflected shape is shown in dotted lines

Procedure to compute d

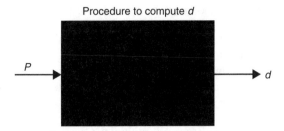

$P \longrightarrow$ $\longrightarrow d$

Figure 8.18   Illustration of a black-box routine. The function produces an output for a given input, however, the details of computation are not revealed to the user

expression. Such procedure are often treated as a black box. The term 'black-box routine' refers to a function in which the method used for computing the output for a given input is not revealed to the user (Figure 8.18).

Suppose that we are interested in finding the value of P_{max} that produces a deflection d_{max}. For a given value of P, d can be computed using the iterative procedure and it can be verified whether d is less than d_{max}. But we are not able to compute P_{max} directly from d_{max}. To find P_{max} we use an optimization (or search) algorithm. The objective function is chosen as the absolute value of the difference between $d(P)$ and d_{max}. Since d is not expressible as a function of P, the necessary preconditions for applying deterministic methods, such as concavity of the function, cannot be established. Stochastic methods such as genetic algorithms and simulated annealing are suitable for such problems since they treat objective functions as black-box routines for testing solutions. These algorithms do not depend on the mathematical characteristics of the objective function. A small selection of stochastic algorithms are presented to illustrate different types of stochastic search.

8.5.1   Pure Global Random Search

Pure global random search is the simplest form of random search. Points are generated randomly in the entire domain and the best solution is selected. This is not efficient, but it is used because of its simplicity when no heuristic is available to guide the search and when the domains are extremely rough and discontinuous.

8.5.2   Local Search with Multiple Random Starts

Local search with multiple random starts is an improvement over local search techniques that converge to local minima. Local search is repeated from multiple starting points selected randomly. Each search might result in a different local minimum, and the minimum of all local minima is chosen. The local search could be deterministic (e.g. using gradients) or stochastic. One method, called random bit climbing (RBC), is a form of local search where neighbouring points are randomly evaluated (Davis, 1991). The first move producing an improvement is accepted for the next stage. This process continues until the point cannot be improved any further.

Local search with multiple random starts is inefficient for the following reasons:

• When there are relatively few local minima, many local searches identify the same final point. Much computation time is wasted.
• Information obtained in previous searches is never reused. A new search may restart from a point very far away and consequently it might take a long time to terminate at a minimum.

Clustering methods are suggested to avoid multiple starts converging on the same point. These methods aim to identify 'regions of attraction' within which local searches terminate at the same minimum. Cluster analysis or pattern recognition methods are used for this purpose.

8.5.3 Simulated Annealing

Simulated annealing (SA) is a generic method analogous to the annealing of metals (Kirkpatrick *et al.*, 1983). During the crystallization of metals, the temperature controls the arrangement of atoms in their lowest-energy configuration. At high temperatures the energy levels of atoms fluctuate rapidly, whereas at lower temperatures only small changes are possible. This process is simulated in SA through a parameter called temperature. The temperature is assigned a high value at the start of the iterations and then gradually brought down. Figure 8.19 shows a scheme for temperature variation called the vanilla schedule.

In a way similar to random local search algorithms, SA attempts point-to-point improvements through randomly generating points in the neighbourhood of the current point. The term 'neighbourhood' indicates the set of points that are obtained by applying a single step and it depends on the definition of the search space. However, it avoids local optima by occasionally allowing movements to worse solution points (uphill moves). A point better than the current one is always accepted. A worse point is accepted with a small probability that depends on the temperature. The probability of accepting a worse point

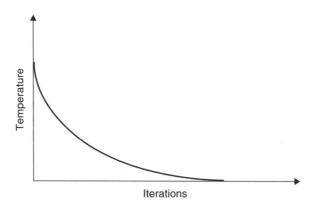

Figure 8.19   Temperature variation during simulated annealing. The form of temperature variation shown here is called the Vanilla schedule. Modified Lam-Delosme Schedule is another popular form

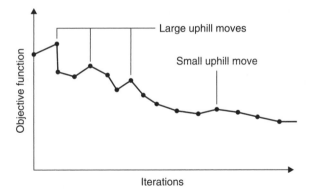

Figure 8.20   Illustration of uphill moves in simulated annealing. In the initial stages, temperature is high; therefore, uphill moves are accepted with higher probability. Towards the end, the temperature is low, and the search is predominantly in the downhill direction

is given by $e^{-\Delta E/T}$, where T is the temperature and ΔE is the difference in the values of the objective function between the next point and the current point (energy difference). At higher temperatures, large uphill moves are accepted with a higher probability. At low temperatures the probabilities are lower, therefore large uphill moves are likely to be rejected. Searching is predominantly in the downhill direction; this results in convergence to an optimal point. The process is illustrated in Figure 8.20.

8.5.4   Genetic Algorithms

Genetic algorithms (GAs) draw analogy from biological evolution. Biological species evolve using genetic operators such as crossover and mutation, and only the fittest survive. In genetic algorithms this process is simulated by encoding potential solutions (individuals) using a chromosome-like data structure. Unlike local search and simulated annealing, genetic algorithms manipulate a population of potential solutions. New individuals (children) are created in the population through reproduction using crossover and mutation operators. These operators ensure that children inherit qualities of parents that are passed on from one generation to the other. Only a certain number of good-quality individuals survive in each generation; this ensures the quality of the population improves with each generation.

Over the years, several improvements have been suggested to the original algorithm introduced by Holland (1975), and the result is a family of algorithms based on evolutionary principles. Currently popular variations of GAs include

- the simple genetic algorithm (SGA) of Holland (1975);
- the steady-state genetic algorithm of Syswerda (1991);
- the CHC adaptive search algorithm of Eshelman (1991).

Since GA is currently the most popular search technique within the engineering community, it is examined in more detail at the end of this chapter.

8.5.5 *Controlled Random Search*

There have been several attempts to improve the convergence of pure random search procedures. The result is a family of controlled random search procedures. A method that improves convergence is the 'random creep' procedure in which exploratory steps are limited to a hypersphere centred on the latest successful point. This procedure can be summarized in four steps:

1. Choose a starting point and set it as the current point x_k.
2. Evaluate a randomly chosen point within a distance d_k from x_k, where d_k is the step size for the current iteration.
3. If the new point is better than x_k, it is chosen as the current point; the step size is updated according to an algorithm-specific rule.
4. If the terminating criteria are not satisfied, repeat from step 2.

Masri and Beki (1980) have proposed an algorithm, called adaptive random search, in which the step size of the random search procedure is optimized periodically throughout the search process. If the steps are too small, the number of iterations required to reach the global optimum will be large, therefore it produces slow convergence. If the steps are too large, they may overshoot the optimum and the probability of improvement will be small. By adapting the step size to the local behaviour of the objective function it is possible to achieve faster convergence without getting trapped in local optima.

Even though controlled random search methods are an improvement over pure random search algorithms, these methods have not been as successful as other methods such as genetic algorithms and simulated annealing. This is reflected by the relatively few full-scale engineering applications that use the technique.

8.5.6 *PGSL*

The Probabilistic Global Search Lausanne (PGSL) algorithm uses a probability distribution function (PDF) to sample the search space and select the best point. A PDF represents the probability of finding a good solution at any given point in the domain. The basic assumption is that better points are more likely to be found in the neighbourhood of good points, hence probabilities are increased in regions where good points are found. This results in more points being generated in those regions. At the beginning of the search, no information is available, so a uniform PDF is used.

Consider the single-variable function shown in Figure 8.21(a). To start with, a uniform PDF is assumed, as shown in Figure 8.21(b). Points generated using a uniform PDF are randomly and uniformly distributed throughout the search space. Points are evaluated, and wherever improvements are observed, the probabilities in those regions are increased. Figure 8.21(c) shows a PDF with higher probabilities in regions where good solutions have been found. With the modified PDF, more points are generated in good regions, further increasing the chance of improvements.

In PGSL the PDF is represented as a histogram. The interval between the minimum and maximum of each variable is divided into a fixed number of sub-intervals and a constant probability is assigned to each interval. These probabilities are updated during the search process.

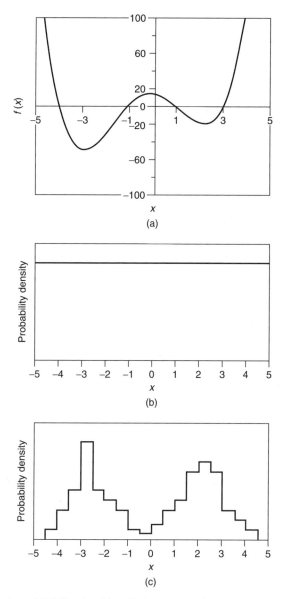

Figure 8.21 Illustration of PGSL algorithm. Points are randomly generated using a PDF. Probabilities are increased in regions where good solutions are found: (a) a function $f(x)$ in a single variable, (b) a uniform PDF, (c) a PDF with higher probabilities in regions containing good solutions

The algorithm includes four nested cycles (Figure 8.22):

- sampling;
- probability updating;
- focusing;
- subdomain.

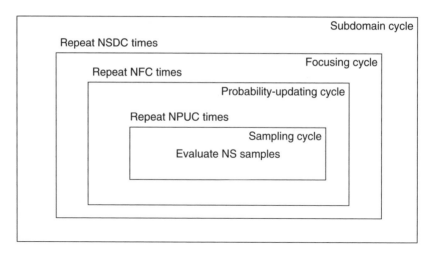

Figure 8.22 Nested cycles in PGSL

In the sampling cycle (innermost cycle), a certain number of points, NS, are generated randomly according to the current PDF. Each point is evaluated by the user-defined objective function and the best point is selected. In the next cycle, probabilities are increased in regions containing good solutions and probabilities are decreased in regions containing less attractive solutions, as in Figure 8.21(c). In the third cycle, searching is focused on the interval containing the best solution after a number of probability-updating cycles, by further subdivision of the interval (Figure 8.23). In the subdomain cycle, the search space is progressively narrowed by selecting a subdomain of smaller size centred on the best point after each focusing cycle (Figure 8.24).

Each cycle serves a different purpose in the search for a global optimum. The sampling cycle permits a more uniform and exhaustive search over the entire search space than the other cycles. The probability updating and focusing cycles refine the search in the neighborhood of good solutions. Convergence is achieved by the subdomain cycle.

Tests on non-linear benchmark functions indicate that PGSL performs better than GAs and SA for most problems. Furthermore, its relative performance increases as the number of variables is increased, hence it is suitable for large-scale engineering tasks.

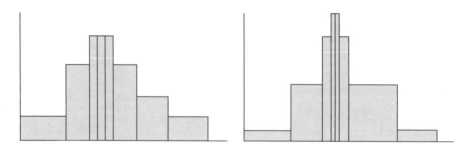

Figure 8.23 PGSL: Evolution of the PDF of a variable after several focusing cycles

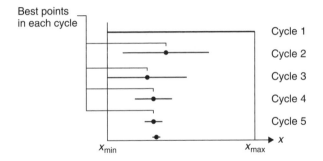

Figure 8.24 PGSL: Changing the sub-domain after each subdomain cycle. The new subdomain (shown in solid line) has a smaller size and is centered around the current best point

8.6 A CLOSER LOOK AT GENETIC ALGORITHMS

Since genetic algorithms are currently used for several engineering applications, they are now examined in more detail. A version of the integer programming problem in Section 8.2.3 with a larger number of variables will be used to illustrate various steps in the GA. This problem can be represented as the following optimization problem:

$$\text{Minimize } f(\mathbf{x}, y) = \text{abs}(x_1^2 + x_2^2 + x_3^2 + x_4^2 + x_5^2 + x_6^2 - y^2) \text{ in the interval } 1 \leq x_i \leq 3,$$

$$1 \leq y \leq 3 \text{ where the components } x_i \text{ of the vector } \mathbf{x} \text{ and } y \text{ are integers} \qquad (8.14)$$

If the minimum value of the objective function is zero, then we can infer there is a solution to the original decision problem. Examining the equation reveals there are multiple solutions. Any vector with any one component of $\mathbf{x}$ equal to 2 and all other components equal to 1 has length 9 and therefore satisfies the equation with $y = 3$.

8.6.1 Representation: Genetic Encoding

The first step is the genetic encoding of all variables into a chromosome. A chromosome represents an individual in a genetic population and corresponds to a potential solution in the solution space. A chromosome is usually (but not always) represented by a binary string. The various methods of encoding and their relative merits and drawbacks are beyond the scope of this book. But note that encoding plays an important role in the success of applying GA to specific problems.

In our example each variable can take the values 1, 2 and 3, so at least two bits (binary digits) are necessary to represent each variable. Without elaborating on the general procedure for binary encoding, let us assume that Table 8.6 provides the mapping between a bit string and its corresponding integer value.

Two bits can represent up to four values, so the number 3 is repeated to ensure that every possible bit string has a corresponding value. This creates a slight bias in the search but it cannot be avoided. Since we have 7 variables, our combined bit string representing the chromosome has 14 bits, the first two representing the value of x_1, the next two representing x_2, and the last two representing y. For example, the bit string

Table 8.6 Genetic encoding of a single variable

Bit string	Value
00	1
01	2
10	3
11	3

01010101010111 represents a solution in which all components of **x** are 2 and the value of y is 3.

8.6.2   Evaluating an Individual

Individuals, each having a different chromosome, are generated during the evolutionary process and need to be evaluated. The process of evaluation requires decoding the chromosomes to obtain the original values of variables. Decoding is the reverse of encoding. In our representation, decoding can be performed by table look-up in Table 8.6. Having obtained the values of all the variables, the objective function is computed using equation (8.14). The value of the objective function is used to evaluate the quality of individuals. Since this is a minimization problem, the smaller the value of the objective function, the better the quality of the individual. Hence the evaluation function can be computed as the negative of the objective function. Negative numbers are avoided by adding a big positive number, 100 in this example, even though this is not essential in general. The evaluation function is computed as $100 - f$, where f is the value of the objective function.

8.6.3   Creating the Initial Population

A population contains a number of individuals. Depending on the type of GA, the population size may be fixed or variable. The size of the population is an important parameter. If the size is too small, the population does not represent the solution space reasonably, so the quality of results will be poor. On the other hand, increasing the population size produces large increases in computational overhead and slows down convergence.

The initial population is usually generated randomly. In our example let us assume a fixed population of 7 individuals and let these individuals be randomly generated as in Table 8.7.

8.6.4   The Fitness Function

The fitness function transforms the evaluation (objective) function into a measure of an individual's suitability for reproduction. The objective function is evaluated independently of other individuals in the population. On the other hand, the fitness function depends on the average quality of the population as a whole. In the original simple genetic algorithm, the fitness of an individual i is computed as $f_i/\overline{f}$, where $\overline{f}$ is the average value of the

Table 8.7 Initial population

Sl No.	Chromosome	x_1	x_2	x_3	x_4	x_5	x_6	y	Objective function	Evaluation
1	01000110110100	2	1	2	3	3	2	1	30	70
2	11000100011010	3	1	2	1	2	3	3	19	81
3	00110100010001	1	3	2	1	2	1	2	16	84
4	01001001011000	2	1	3	2	2	3	1	30	70
5	00011001101001	1	2	3	2	3	3	2	32	68
6	11010100000001	3	2	2	1	1	1	2	16	84
7	01000000010000	2	1	1	1	2	1	1	11	89

Table 8.8 Fitness of individuals

Sl No.	Evaluation	Fitness function
1	70	0.897436
2	81	1.038462
3	84	1.076923
4	70	0.897436
5	68	0.871795
6	84	1.076923
7	89	1.141026

objective function in the population. The fitness function is used in the reproduction process in such a way that the number of offspring generated for an individual is proportional to its fitness. The fitness function of each individual in the initial population is given in Table 8.8.

8.6.5 Reproduction

In most implementations of GA the reproduction is carried out in a two-stage process. The first stage is selection (or duplication) and the second is recombination (or crossover). In the first stage, an intermediate population is created by selecting individuals from the current population and duplicating them using probabilities proportional to their fitness. Hence in the intermediate population there will be more copies of individuals with higher fitness. This ensures that more children are produced for them in the next generation.

Let us assume that individuals 7 and 6 are selected twice in our population (due to their higher probabilities), and individuals 2, 3 and 1 are selected once in our population. The intermediate population is shown in Table 8.9.

Recombination, or crossover, is the process of creating the next population from the intermediate population. Crossover is performed by randomly selecting two individuals from the intermediate population and interchanging parts of their bit strings. There are several variations of the crossover operation. In one-point crossover, strings are cut in two at a randomly chosen position, and the corresponding parts are exchanged. Figure 8.25 illustrates the application of one-point crossover of the chromosomes of individuals 6 and 7 at the ninth bit position. Figure 8.26 illustrates the modification of the values of the variables during this process. It so happens that offspring 1 inherits all good

Table 8.9 Intermediate population

Copied from	Chromosome	Fitness
7	01000000010000	1.141026
7	01000000010000	1.141026
6	11010100000001	1.076923
6	11010100000001	1.076923
3	00110100010001	1.076923
2	11000100011010	1.038462
1	01000110110100	0.897436

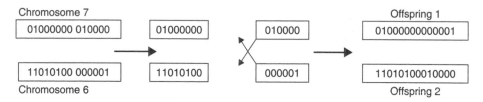

Figure 8.25 1-point crossover at the 9-th bit position

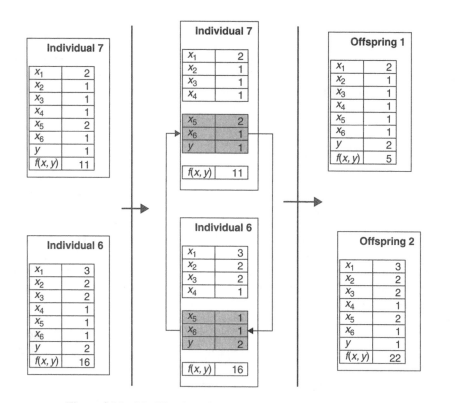

Figure 8.26 Modification of variables during 1-point crossover

values from both parents, producing a considerable improvement in the objective function. Although this does not happen all the time, the success of a GA implementation depends on maximizing the probability of that happening.

8.6.6 *Mutation*

Mutation involves randomly changing bits of the chromosomes with a very low probability. This is done to retain diversity in the population. It might happen that after many generations the same individuals are replicated several times in the solution, making it impossible to improve it any further. This is particularly the case when a small population size is chosen in a large search space. No amount of recombination can produce certain solutions and this is due to 'missing genes' in the population. The situation is rectified by using the mutation operator.

To illustrate mutation, consider offspring 1 obtained after crossover of individuals 6 and 7. This individual has the chromosome 01000000000001 representing variable values $(2,1,1,1,1,1,2)$. Flipping the penultimate bit of the chromosome results in 01000000000011; this corresponds to variable values $(2,1,1,1,1,1,3)$. The value of the objective function for this solution is exactly zero, and this solution is the global minimum for this problem. In practice the probability of obtaining a global optimum by a random flip of bits is very low. However, it might reintroduce certain lost bits into chromosomes, which could produce improvements when combined with crossover operators.

8.7 *SUMMARY OF METHODS*

Method	Best applications	Strengths	Weaknesses
Deterministic			
Exhaustive search	Small tasks	Guaranteed global optimum	Exponential complexity
Branch and bound	Discrete variables	Guaranteed exact solution	Criteria for branching and pruning required
Gradient methods	Mathematical functions with a few local optima	Good convergence to local optima	Becomes trapped in local optima
Grid search	Mathematical functions in a few variables	Easy to implement	Solution identified depends on the grid size
Line search	Non-convex mathematical functions with few local optima	Efficient	Solution identified depends on the choice of search directions

Method	Best applications	Strengths	Weaknesses
Stochastic methods			
Pure random search	Extremely rough and discontinuous domains	Simplicity	Poor convergence
Simulated annealing	Where good heuristics are available for point-to-point movement	Black-box evaluation functions could be used	Global optimum may not be identified
Genetic algorithms	Large combinatorial problems	Black-box evaluation functions could be used	Global optimum may not be identified
Controlled random search	Where heuristics are absent, discontinuous domains	Black-box evaluation functions could be used	Poor convergence
PGSL	Reasonably smooth domains, continuous variables	Good convergence, scalability	Discrete variables

REFERENCES

Brooks, S. H. 1958. Discussion of random methods for locating surface maxima. *Operations Research*, **6**, 244–251.

Dantzig, G. B. 1951. Maximization of a linear function of variables subject to linear inequalities. In *Activity Analysis of Production and Allocation*, T. C. Koopmans (ed.), pp. 339–347. New York: John Wiley & Sons, Inc.

Davis, L. 1991. Bit-climbing, representational bias and test suite design. In *Proceedings of the 4th International Conference on GAs*, L. Booker and R. Belew (eds). New York: Morgan Kaufmann.

Eshelman, L. 1991. The CHC adaptive search algorithm. In *Foundations of Genetic Algorithms*. G. Rawlins (ed.), pp. 256–283. New York: Morgan Kaufmann.

Holland, J. 1975. *Adaptation in Natural Artificial Systems*. Ann Arbor MI: University of Michigan Press.

Kirkpatrick, S., Gelatt, C. and Vecchi, M. 1983. Optimization by simulated annealing. *Science*, **220**, 673.

Masri, S. F. and Bekey, G. A. 1980. A global optimization algorithm using adaptive random search. *Applied Mathematics and Computation*, **7**, 353–375.

Syswerda, G. 1991. A study of reproduction in generational and steady-state genetic algorithms. In *Foundations of Genetic Algorithms*. G. Rawlins (ed.), pp. 94–101. New York: Morgan Kaufmann.

FURTHER READING

Paplambros, P. Y. and Wilde, D. J. 1986. *Principles of Optimal Design: Modeling and Computation*. New York: Cambridge University Press.

Pintér, J. D. 1996. *Global Optimization in Action*. Dordrecht: Kluwer Academic.

EXERCISES

8.1 Find the minimum for each of the following functions:

$$f(x) = x + \cos x \qquad (-5\pi \le x \le 5\pi)$$
$$f(x) = (x + \sin x)^2 \qquad (-5\pi \le x \le 5\pi)$$
$$f(x, y) = x^4 - y^4 \qquad (-2 < x < 2, -2 < y < 2)$$
$$f(x, y) = x^3 - y^3 \qquad (-2 < x < 2, -2 < y < 2)$$
$$f(x, y) = xy + x + y \qquad (-2 < x < 2, -2 < y < 2)$$

8.2 Formulate an objective function to solve the following optimization problem; use a penalty function that is proportional to the degree of constraint violation.

$$\text{Minimize } x^3 - y^3 \text{ such that } x \ge y$$

8.3 A design task involves finding the dimension of a beam with a rectangular cross-section. There are two conflicting requirements. On one hand, deflections need to be made as small as possible. On the other hand, the depth of the beam should be kept low to obtain more clear space between the floors of the building. The equation for the maximum deflection of the beam (in metres) is obtained by substituting the values of design variables as follows:

$$S = \frac{0.0001}{bd^3}$$

Which of the following solutions do not lie on the Pareto-optimal surface?

(a) $b = 0.2$, $d = 0.4$
(b) $b = 0.3$, $d = 0.4$
(c) $b = 0.2$, $d = 0.3$
(d) $b = 0.1$, $d = 0.3$
(e) $b = 0.4$, $d = 0.3$

8.4 Look at the sets in Figure 8.27. Which of them are convex?

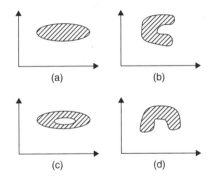

(a)   (b)

(c)   (d)

Figure 8.27   Shaded areas represent the sets

8.5 The problem P is to minimize $f(x, y, z) = xyz$ subject to

$$x + y > 2$$
$$y + z > 3$$
$$x + z > 1$$

where x, y, z are positive real numbers less than 10. Which of the following statements is true?

(a) P is a linear programming problem.
(b) P is a concave minimization problem.
(c) The objective function of P is monotonic.
(d) All constraints of P are linear.

8.6 The following options are available for designing a roof system for a building:

- one-way beam and slab;
- two-way beam and slab;
- flat slab;
- waffle slab.

Attributes and possible values for one-way beam and slab are given below:

beam depth = 20 cm, 30 cm, 40 cm
slab depth = 10 cm, 12 cm, 15 cm
maximum span-to-depth ratio of beams = 15

Attributes and possible values for two-way beam and slab are as follows:

beam spacing = 3 m, 4 m
beam depth = 20 cm, 30 cm, 10 cm
maximum span-to-depth ratio of slabs = 25
slab depth = 10 cm, 12 cm, 15 cm

Possible values for the depth of flat slab are 15 cm, 18 cm, and 20 cm. There are no interior columns within the room, hence the beam span in one-way and two-way beam-and-slab systems is equal to the width of the room (Figure 8.28). The slab span is equal to the beam spacing since the slab is supported by beams on either side. In the case of flat slab, the slab span is equal to the size of the room.

(a) Represent the solution space as a tree.
(b) A roof is to be designed for a room of size 6 m × 6 m. The spacing of beams is restricted to 1 m, 2 m and 3 m in solutions involving beams. How many possible solutions exist if the total depth of the floor system should be less than 25 cm?

8.7 Consider the minimum weight design of a rectangular beam described in Section 8.2.5.1. The maximum permissible deflection is $L/100$. Which constraint is likely to dominate for the following cases?

(a) small values of b and d
(b) small b, large d
(c) large b, small d

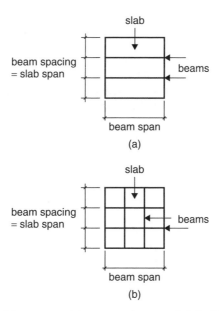

Figure 8.28   Beam and slab systems: (a) one-way beam and slab, (b) two-way beam and slab

8.8 Four cities A, B, C, D are separated by the following distances. How do you find out the coordinates of the cities? City A might be considered as the origin. Formulate it as a minimization problem.

- from A to B is 100 km
- from A to C is 60 km
- from B to D is 50 km
- from C to D is 80 km

8.9 The stress–strain relationship of a certain material is known to follow a non-linear curve of the form $y = ax^p$, where y is the stress and x is the strain; a and p are unknown constants (Figure 8.29). Measured values of stress for different values of

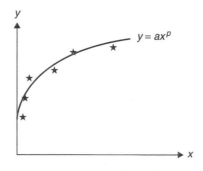

Figure 8.29   Stress-strain relationship of a non-linear material

strain are available in the form of a table. How do you determine the values of a and p from this data? Formulate it as a minimization problem.

8.10 The elongation of a spring is proportional to the load applied to it (Figure 8.30). The relationship $P = kx$ is valid, where P is the load, x is the elongation and k is the spring stiffness. Experiments were conducted to determine the spring stiffness. The data obtained contain human and mechanical errors. Data points that contain large

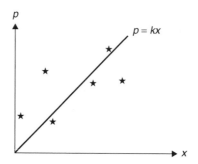

Figure 8.30 Determining the stiffness of a spring

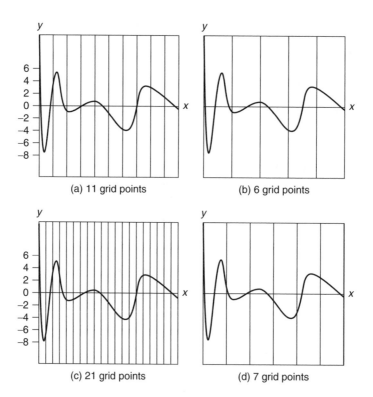

Figure 8.31 Grid search with different grid size. The boundaries of each grid are $x = 0$ and $x = 10$

errors need to be eliminated in the calculations. However, it is not known whether the error is large until k is determined. How do you formulate an optimization problem to minimize errors such that data points containing more than 50% error are not included in the calculation?

8.11 Consider the function $y = f(x)$ in the interval $x = [0, 10]$ as shown in Figure 8.31. Multiple grid searches are performed starting from $x = 0$ (extreme left of each graph) with different grid sizes. What are the values of the optima obtained with each grid?

9

Knowledge Systems for Decision Support

9.1 INTRODUCTION

Engineers' expectations of computers are changing. They see them less as tool-like devices to perform isolated tasks that increase productivity, such as drafting, numerical analysis and communication, and more as instruments that assist innovation and collaboration. Evolution is necessarily slow in most areas because engineers must serve society through processes that involve integrating objectives and finding low-risk solutions. This is where knowledge systems could become valuable assistants. But there are risks as well as opportunities and some of them will be described in this chapter.

Although there can be many reasons for creating a knowledge system (KS), probably the best justification is when the task has exponential complexity and the value for the task size n is likely to be large (Chapter 2). Daily, engineers use their experience to complete exponentially complex tasks in reasonable amounts of time, and such activity stands to benefit from systematic support using, for example, semantic schemas, 'rules of thumb' and previous cases that can be explicitly defined in a knowledge system.

Another justification for a knowledge system is when the task is poorly defined. Then decision-support systems provide information structures that may bring more definition to the task. The creation of new information structures leads to more formalism, therefore decision-support systems are useful for creation and extension of engineering models, objective functions and constraints. Indeed such additional formalism may even be the justification for terminating further use of the decision-support system. In other words, a measure of success for a decision-support system could be its ability to self-destruct after a certain period of use.

Knowledge systems are rarely used alone. They are most often used in combination with other components such as search algorithms, database applications, object-oriented information structures and visualization tools. While some knowledge systems are intended to ensure appropriate use of these other components, others are components of the composite system in their own right.

Knowledge systems have evolved from good and bad experiences with expert systems since the 1970s. This chapter will discuss aspects of this evolution and highlight a few lessons that have been learnt. As far as engineers are concerned, knowledge systems cannot take the place of human decision makers in open worlds (Chapter 1). They can

Fundamentals of Computer-Aided Engineering   B. Raphael and I. F. C. Smith
© 2003 John Wiley & Sons, Ltd   ISBNs: 0-471-48709-0 (HB); 0-471-48715-5 (PB)

make good engineers better, but they can also make bad engineers worse. In any case the decision-making responsibility remains with the engineer. Knowledge systems are analogous to books in that they are collections of knowledge which needs to be used appropriately by the professional user.

This chapter begins with a description of important characteristics and parts of a knowledge system. Each part is then described for a common type of knowledge system. Important issues related to knowledge maintenance are described and a very promising KS strategy called case-based reasoning is introduced.

9.2   IMPORTANT CHARACTERISTICS OF KNOWLEDGE SYSTEMS

There is no fixed and rigid definition for a knowledge system. Indeed one could argue that every engineering software system contains knowledge in some form or another. However, knowledge systems belong to a category of engineering software systems that help perform tasks in ways beyond, for example, providing results of calculations. Although there are no clearly defined boundaries, the following characteristics are usually present:

- Tasks that have many possible solutions are supported.
- The main goal is to help users find good solutions even when the input is incomplete and imprecise.
- There is an explicit representation of knowledge; the term 'knowledge' has a specific definition and this is provided in the next section.
- There is more separation between knowledge and control than with traditional approaches.
- User participation is a key aspect

Parts of a knowledge system are shown in Figure 9.1. The ellipse contains the system, which has two parts: (i) knowledge and data and (ii) control. Knowledge and data are organized into chunks according to characteristics of the task and the available information. The control part contains algorithms that are designed to be as independent as possible from data values and knowledge, and this is the reason for the use of the word 'generic' in Figure 9.1.

Two types of intervention are possible through the human–computer interface of a knowledge system (the ellipse in Figure 9.1). Firstly, the engineer acting as a developer introduces knowledge and data into the system and fixes parameters that determine how the algorithms behave. For example, values of these parameters may determine how many solutions are found at a time and whether or not they are given an order according to comparisons with task criteria.

During this stage, the engineer-developer may consult with other specialists regarding certain aspects. This activity is called knowledge elicitation, and strategies for obtaining knowledge and creating knowledge schemas have been the subject of several books and hundreds of conferences over several decades. In most studies, it is assumed there are experts who interact with a knowledge engineer in order to formalize the knowledge. Much of this work is not relevant to engineering, so this interaction has been omitted from Figure 9.1.

The most successful engineering knowledge systems have been created for situations where engineer-developers were also well acquainted with the subject. Knowledge

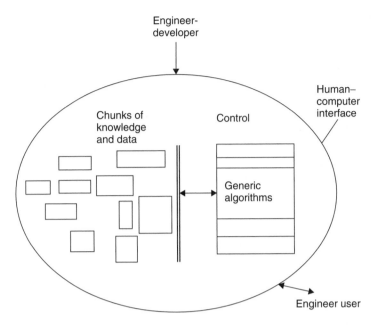

Figure 9.1 Parts of a knowledge system for engineers. Engineers assume roles of developer and user. Successful systems in engineering are possible when the engineer developer is also a domain specialist

schemas in engineering are usually determined by existing formal information schemas and behaviour models rather than by theoretical formalisms and successful applications in other fields. Furthermore, the quality of knowledge maintenance is greatly enhanced when the engineer-developer is able to understand how the knowledge may evolve. In order to have this understanding, the engineer-developer should be a domain specialist.

An engineering user performs the second type of intervention through the human–computer interface. To obtain support for a given task, this user typically employs the knowledge and data in the system along with information specific to the task. This support may vary from advice to complete solutions for consideration. Earlier systems only allowed a user interface to visualize solutions, but more recent systems provide possibilities for engineering users to add and modify knowledge and to make changes in the way the algorithms behave through modifying certain parameters.

The classical separation between the initial developer and the engineering user is weakening. Developers of knowledge systems increasingly recognize that engineering users are professionals, and as specialists in their field they are responsible for their decisions. In an open world (Chapter 1) they may require as much freedom to alter the system as the original developers of the system.

9.3 REPRESENTATION OF KNOWLEDGE

Knowledge has many definitions. Some definitions have broad coverage with vague sociological definitions whereas others are very restrictive. This book adopts a fairly restrictive definition. Nevertheless, from a computer science perspective, it retains enough generality to remain relevant over the whole range of computer-aided engineering (CAE) applications.

We begin with a more common definition with its roots in common English usage, and we need to discuss the ontology that provides its context. A simple definition of *ontology* is 'a hierarchy of the meaning of a group of words'. In the classic ontology set out in the *Oxford Companion to the English Language* (McArthur, 1992), knowledge is part of a scale that begins with the word 'data' and follows with the words 'information', 'knowledge' and 'wisdom'. Data are collections of isolated facts; information is data with 'shape'; knowledge is 'applied and heightened information' such as the specialized information possessed by an expert; and wisdom is 'still more general and valuable'.

There are several difficulties with this classic ontology; here are two important drawbacks. Firstly, there is an implication that not all data are part of information. This would mean that the field of information technology does not include technology that deals with all types of data. This is not compatible with the modern understanding of the word 'information'. Secondly, the borders between information, knowledge and wisdom depend on the context of the situation and the viewpoint of the observer. For example, what is only information to an engineer may seem like knowledge or even wisdom to a person who has no engineering training. Such ambiguity is not helpful to those who wish to increase their understanding of the fundamentals of CAE.

This book adopts a simpler ontology that is less contradictory with modern definitions of information and less ambiguous. Firstly, the word 'wisdom' is not included in this ontology since a precise and context-independent definition for engineering purposes would be at best controversial. Information is defined to include data and knowledge; information is the parent node, and knowledge and data are subclasses of information. Therefore knowledge is a type of information, along with data.

Following a similar start to the first ontology, data are facts about something. Here are some examples: this car is red, that building has five stories, the temperature is 20 °C, his name is Paul. Facts are attribute–value pairs. In relational databases the attributes are the columns and the values are the entries (numbers, symbols) in those columns.

Knowledge is data that are linked together; here are some examples:

- *Causal*:   if the temperature is 100 °C then water boils.
- *Classification*:   this car is a kind of vehicle.
- *Compositional*:   that building is part of a school.
- *Empirical*: $\sigma = E\varepsilon$ implies stress and strain are linearly interrelated through Young's modulus.
- *Physical principles*:   gravitational acceleration is 9.81 m s^{-2} on earth.
- *Semantic*:   Paul is the name of a boy.
- *Heuristic*:   very long bridges are suspension bridges.

Causal knowledge is an important type of knowledge since it is a fundamental element of inference and decision making. Types of inference determine necessary characteristics of CAE since their behaviour is different in 'open' worlds (Chapter 1). Also, most types of knowledge in the above list, such as empirical, physical principles and classification knowledge, can be rewritten in a causal form. Such transformations can be risky (see below).

Classification and compositional knowledge is typically implemented in hierarchies, and these are most explicit in object-oriented languages. Empirical knowledge is knowledge obtained by observing concurrent facts. For example, most material strength formulas are empirical since they come only from laboratory testing. Put another way, empirical knowledge is not reliably deductible from knowledge of atomic forces. Physical principles link data through knowledge of physical laws such as gravity, force equilibrium, conservation of mass and conservation of energy.

Semantic knowledge involves links that provide meanings to words. As such, it originates from links that are often based on culture, context and language. For example, in the UK the word 'boot' is a place to put a suitcase in a car, whereas in the US, the same place is called a 'trunk'. In both countries the word 'boot' is an item of footwear and the word 'trunk' is a part of a tree. Therefore, semantic knowledge is more difficult to implement into systems that are intended for a wide audience. Furthermore, this kind of knowledge often changes over time. For example, the word 'web' was traditionally associated with a spider whereas today most people would think of a computer.

Heuristic knowledge is knowledge based on experience and observation. It is knowledge that helps complete tasks more easily. For example, experienced engineers focus on design solutions that have worked in the past. They would not waste their time on solutions they have determined repeatedly to be undesirable. Although heuristic knowledge is very helpful for tasks that have exponential complexity (Chapter 2) and for tasks that have many possible solutions, it may not be useful in all situations every time. A common synonym for heuristic knowledge is 'rule of thumb'.

In terms of generality, heuristics exist on a wide scale. For example, mathematicians propose heuristics that are helpful for complete classes of problems (such as travel planning), whereas engineers may employ heuristics for specific tasks in specific contexts. In computer-aided engineering, heuristics are usefully applied to all scales of generality. Nevertheless, task- and context-specific heuristics are best accommodated in CAE systems through anticipating user interaction at the right time rather than through attempts to formalize 'tricks of the trade' that change over time.

Engineers often use rules of thumb to do important tasks; they can also disregard them if they suspect they may not be helpful. For example, when a long-span bridge is being designed, an engineer may begin with a study of suspension bridge solutions. If it is determined that it is not practical to have heavy anchorages for the cables at the ends of the bridge, the engineer may disregard the original approach altogether and investigate other design possibilities such as a tunnel or another type of bridge.

Knowledge is also concerned with linking together procedures rather than data. This is sometimes called control knowledge. Much engineering knowledge involves knowing how to proceed in certain situations. Also, successful students know how best to go about studying for an exam. Another example is that if you are reading this book, you probably have a certain amount of control knowledge for learning engineering concepts.

In computer science the field of artificial intelligence is a field that includes studies of explicit representations and uses of knowledge. Many researchers believe that machine intelligence must include predefined knowledge as defined here. Others believe that knowledge can 'emerge' through interaction with the environment during application of very simple starting knowledge. For example, simple robots have demonstrated that links can be initiated and reinforced through use. Nevertheless, our definition still holds: knowledge is data items that are linked together.

9.3.1 *Representation of Knowledge in Knowledge Systems*

Since computer systems are fundamentally employed to link data together, they contain much knowledge. Unfortunately, in traditional systems, this knowledge is implicit in that it forms an inherent part of the system design, and therefore any important modification requires reprogramming, which is both costly and risky. In a knowledge system, important knowledge is made explicit so that it can be examined, modified and augmented more easily than with traditional systems. Such activities are essential, especially when there is semantic knowledge. Here are the most common frameworks for representing knowledge:

- databases;
- object hierarchies and semantic networks;
- rules (IF ... THEN ... statements);
- models;
- cases of solutions to previous tasks.

The identification of relations and the formulation of functional dependencies are important data links. Models could be mathematical formulas, numerical representations (such as finite element models) and other types of simulation. Models are used to transform causes into effects through explicit use of geometry, physical principles, empirical relationships and other links between data.

Early decision-support systems that were developed in the 1970s employed data and rules. This approach is still useful for small systems in well-defined domains where knowledge changes little. Since implementation of rules often requires a transformation of knowledge into IF ... THEN ... statements, important information may be lost. In addition, unwanted dependencies may be added; this is discussed in the next section.

Current systems employ data, objects, rules, models and cases. The number of rules is kept to a minimum; this aspect is discussed in Section 9.6. Models are often a more natural and robust way to represent knowledge, therefore models are usually easier to modify and manage than rules.

9.4 REASONING WITH KNOWLEDGE

In this section the discussion is limited to reasoning with rules. Reasoning with other knowledge structures is partly covered in other chapters. Also, some other representations, such as models, are implemented as rules, hence the following discussion remains valid for these cases.

A rule has two parts: the IF part, also known as the antecedent and the THEN part, also known as the consequent. The antecedent contains a set of conditions that are usually combined using logical AND and OR operators. The consequent contains elements that include information and sets of actions to be taken. For simple representations, the conditions in the antecedent are comparisons (greater than, less than, and equal to) of values of *specific variables*, such as, the span of beam B1. However, more general representations have been developed in which the antecedent consists of patterns in the data that represent generic conditions under which the rule is applicable. Such pattern-matching languages permit generic rules to be defined such as

```
IF no other student has score that is higher than X
THEN student X is the best in the class
```

Generic rules that manipulate data patterns are widely used in data mining, report generation, e-mail filtering and other applications. For simplicity this chapter considers only rules that manipulate values of specific variables.

There are many ways of using rules to support engineering reasoning. Two principal methods are forward chaining and backward chaining. Forward chaining uses the data that is currently available to satisfy the *antecedents* of the rules (`IF ...`). If conditions are satisfied, the rule is fired; this means that *consequences* (`THEN ...`) are added to the data that is currently available. This newly increased data set is then compared with other conditions in other rules to see if other rules allow the data set to increase further. Chaining stops when no rules can be fired.

Backward chaining requires an additional element. This is a goal or a question regarding a fact. For example, a question may be whether a data item has the value true. In backward chaining, a rule is identified that has as its consequence the affirmation of the question. The conditions of this rule are examined to see if they satisfy the data set. If they do not, the conditions of this rule are taken as subgoals for subsequent iterations. Chaining stops when there are no more rules to examine.

Example 9.1

Apply forward and backward chaining to the following example.

Situation   *You are a building inspector for a large insurance company. You are responsible for evaluating their buildings and deciding whether renovation should be carried out. This insurance company has hundreds of buildings scattered around the country. You cannot visit each one on a regular basis. A decision-support system has been created to help you decide which buildings require on-site inspections. The knowledge system contains the rules and data described below.*

Rules

```
R1    IF water damage is possible and if the building has not been
      renovated for 30 years
      THEN an on-site inspection is necessary
R2    IF the plumbing system is suspect
      THEN water damage is possible
R3    IF the building is more than 40 years old
      THEN the plumbing is suspect
```

Data   *Building D450 is more than 40 years old and it has not been renovated for 30 years.*

Question   *The building inspector asks the knowledge system, Is an on-site inspection necessary for building D450?*

Table 9.1 Two rule-chaining methods for the example of the insurance inspector

Rules examined	Rules fired	Data used
(a) Forward chaining		
R3	R3	The building is more than 40 years old
R2	R2	
R1	R1	The building has not been renovated for 30 years
Conclusion Yes, an on-site inspection is necessary for building D450		
(b) Backward chaining		
R1		The building has not been renovated for 30 years
R2		
R3	R3	The building is more than 40 years old
	R2	
	R1	
Conclusion Yes, an on-site inspection is necessary for building D450		

The rows in Table 9.1 are filled out sequentially for the two chaining methods. The number of different combinations of buildings to visit in a given time period is exponential in terms of the total number of buildings, so this is a good task for a decision-support system. If the task does not have an exponential complexity, then a brute-force method may be more reliable, where all possible solutions are evaluated.

The information in the data set has to be compatible with the conditions and consequences of the rules. For example, if the building has *never* been renovated, this information has to be transformed *a priori* into the fact that the building has not been renovated for 30 years. When such transformations are performed, information can be lost.

Addition of rules may require modifications to existing rules. For example, if a rule R4 is added

```
R4    IF the building was built by XYZ contractor
      THEN the plumbing is okay
```

Rule R3 would have to be adjusted to add the condition 'not built by XYZ contractor' in order to avoid inconsistencies. Here the addition of a rule created an unwanted dependency that led to modifications elsewhere.

Changes to rules may require modifications to other rules. The same argument that was developed for addition of rules also applies here. Often comprehensive testing with experts is required to achieve the desired performance. Especially when knowledge is expected to change, rule-based modules are therefore best kept small within knowledge systems in order to reduce the effects of such anomalies.

9.4.1 Rule Selection and Conflict Resolution

Conflicts do not arise if there is only one rule that is applicable at all times. Such situations are possible for small rule sets through examining the preconditions of all rules and searching for variables that are repeated among multiple rules. However, since many rules could be eligible for firing at a time in large rule sets, chaining algorithms contain strategies for rule selection. A simple strategy is to select the first rule according to the order in which rules are put in the rule base. This strategy works only if rules are ordered (such as when read from a text file) and if the order is unaffected by editing operations such as insertion and deletion of rules. Here are some more general conflict resolution strategies:

- *Defining priorities of rules*: a user-defined parameter called salience determines the relative order of rules when there are conflicts.

- *Heuristics for rule selection*: examples of heuristics are recency ordering (selection of the rule that uses the most recent fact) and specificity ordering (selection of the most specific rule, i.e. the one that uses the maximum number of facts).

- *Means-end analysis*: analyse all applicable rules and select the one that contributes the maximum towards the current goal.

When there are many rules, conflict resolution is needed to avoid brittleness. It is extremely difficult to maintain a set of rules that remains consistent under all combinations of input conditions. Inconsistencies frequently arise upon addition of new rules. Conflict resolution strategies are available to make algorithms avoid brittleness when inconsistencies are encountered. This means that performance degrades slowly rather than by a sudden failure.

For practical systems, engineers are nevertheless advised to maintain a small consistent set of rules without relying on generic conflict resolution strategies. Conflict resolution strategies make rule systems difficult to test and debug since system behaviour could be influenced by them in ways that were unanticipated by the engineer-developer.

9.5 IMPORTANCE OF THE USER INTERFACE

A well-conceived user interface is essential. For example, many solutions to a task may be possible. Also, when information is known to be incomplete, unique solutions are not always best. How should multiple solutions be presented to the user? There is no single answer to this question; it depends on the task, the user and the context in which the task is carried out. Here are some guidelines for effective user interfaces:

- Introduce information that is specific to the task.
- Present multiple solutions to the user in an understandable fashion.
- Allow exploration of solutions within the space of good solutions.
- Explain reasoning so the user is better able to understand why certain solutions have been proposed and others have not.
- Provide for adding knowledge to the system.
- Actively 'cue' users to make good choices without trying to guess their next move.
- Signal inconsistent information.
- Evaluate different combinations of choices.
- Teach users how to use the system.

Different combinations of task characteristics, user needs and contexts result in a wide range of appropriate user interfaces. Formal models of engineer–computer interaction are emerging. However, in many engineering areas, developers are currently at the 'craft stage'.

9.6   MAINTENANCE OF KNOWLEDGE

Difficulties associated with knowledge maintenance contributed to the demise of early expert systems. As rule sets grow, the need to check different combinations of relevant rules grows exponentially. So do maintenance costs.

It has already been demonstrated that rule sets may not be able to include all information and may create unwanted dependencies that complicate knowledge maintenance. While such difficulties cannot be avoided altogether, other representations of knowledge require less maintenance.

Many of the maintenance difficulties that were associated with early decision-support systems arose out of a lack of understanding of task analysis and fundamental logic (Chapter 1). Often abductive tasks (e.g. design and diagnosis) were supported by rules that did not maintain the correct causal direction. When rules were formulated, a *causal inversion* was carried out. More specifically, the causal direction

```
IF cause THEN effect
```

was inverted to

```
IF effect THEN cause
```

Developers often did not realize that this inversion did not change the importance of the closed-world hypothesis for abductive tasks (all rules and data are known). Although rule chaining implements deduction, true deduction is carried out only when rules are expressed as `IF cause THEN effect`.

Put another way, rules were formulated for abductive tasks so that deductive mechanisms (chaining) could process them. Such formulation makes an implicit closed-world assumption. Since the possibility of modifications and additions to the rule set implicitly means that all rules are *not* known, difficulties with knowledge maintenance are an obvious consequence.

Modern approaches to knowledge representation involve formulations that maintain the correct causal direction so that when abductive tasks are supported, the closed world assumption is explicit. In general, the number of rules is kept to a minimum. This facilitates knowledge maintenance since fewer unwanted dependencies are created.

Examples of correct formulations are

- `IF environment THEN behaviour`
- `IF loads THEN deformations`
- `IF deterioration THEN less strength`

9.7   MODEL-BASED REASONING

There are many definitions of the word model. For the purposes of this section a model is a relationship between variables that represent causes (Chapter 1) and variables that represent effects. For example, Newton's second law of motion, $F = ma$, is a model that relates the mass m of an object and the forces F acting on it (structure as defined in Chapter 1) to its acceleration a (behaviour). Much engineering knowledge is contained in models and their use is a central topic of most engineering courses.

In model-based reasoning, models are used to support inference through ensuring that important relationships are respected. Since models represent knowledge that is usually based on physical principles, many of them are reversible. Therefore the same model might be used for simulation, diagnosis and control. Models are also helpful when previous cases need to be adapted to a new situation (Section 9.8).

Models are inherent in the mechanism that transforms information during the analysis task (Chapter 1), therefore this task is a natural application for model-based reasoning. Model-based knowledge systems have been successfully applied to situations where it is important to evaluate the results of several simulations using a range of models. They are also useful for diagnosis of complex systems where there are many possible reasons for malfunctioning.

9.8 CASE-BASED REASONING

Case-based reasoning is an attractive technique in computer-aided engineering since its use is intuitively obvious to engineers. Case-based reasoning involves finding solutions to new tasks through reusing good solutions to old tasks. There are many advantages of case-based reasoning; here are some of them:

- Cases are easily understandable and most engineers have already used previous cases to carry out tasks, therefore storing a case in a computer often involves a much lower degree of transformation from reality than is necessary with other representations.

- When there are many possible solutions, a good case is often an easy short cut in the search for good solutions.

- For situations where important information cannot be modelled explicitly (e.g. aesthetics and politics) the closed-world assumption associated with abductive tasks is explicitly and obviously related to the number of cases available.

- When modification of the case for the new solution is small, intrinsic advantages of the case (implicit information such as good aesthetics) are transferred to the new task.

- Cases are often the best way to represent knowledge, particularly in situations where there are no known and reliable models.

- The capability of the system can be enhanced by simply adding a case.

Large case-based reasoning systems exist in practice for applications in diagnosis, maintenance, planning and customer support.

9.8.1 Stages of Case-Based Reasoning

Figure 9.2 shows the five main stages of system implementation and use:

- representation;
- retrieval;

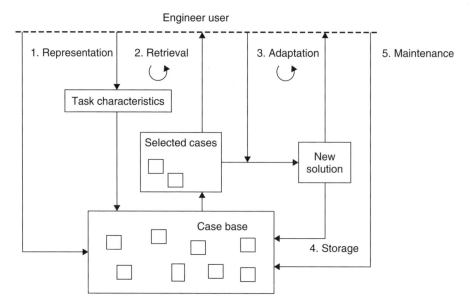

Figure 9.2 Stages of CBR

- adaptation;
- storage;
- maintenance.

Representation

Decisions related to the representation stage are carried out mainly during initial implementation of the system; they are decisions related to what aspects are represented and how the case is stored in the computer. These decisions may depend on the tools that are employed and how cases are used. For example, if cases are to be stored in a relational database, attributes have to be selected a priori since the columns in a table are fixed. Other forms of representation provide better flexibility. Object representations allow case structure to be varied from instance to instance. Semi-structured forms consisting of text and images are the most widely used, but their reasoning capabilities are limited.

Task characteristics and solution aspects need to be represented (Figure 9.3). Before finalizing the case representation, developers should accurately define the required functionality in all other stages, since this is where representational attributes are used. This step can have a critical influence on the quality of support provided by the decision-support system.

Figure 9.3 Case representations include task and solution characteristics

Other desirable aspects to be stored in a case are

- rationale for choosing the solution;
- outcome of the solution (whether the solution met expectations);
- options that were considered and discarded during the process of choosing the solution and reasons for discarding them.

Retrieval

The retrieval stage involves the selection of a case (or cases) having characteristics that are similar to the new task. Here the challenge involves defining the word 'similar'. There are hundreds of ways of defining similarities, called similarity metrics. The most common similarity metrics employ nearest-neighbour methods. Here is a simple example of a nearest-neighbour method for attributes with numerical values (continuous variables):

1. For each task attribute, define a value for the threshold maximum difference, `Max.diff`. This value defines the limit of similarity. Beyond this value, two attribute values are not similar.

2. Define weight factors `wf` according to the relative importance of each task attribute.

3. While there are cases to examine, for each task attribute, calculate the difference (absolute value) between the attribute in the case and the attribute associated with the new task. Divide this difference by `Max.diff`. Values greater than 1 are set to 1. This result is called `Distance`.

4. Calculate values of the similarity variable for each task attribute using
   `Similarity = 1 - Distance`

5. Calculate a weighted overall similarity measure in the interval [0, 1] using

$$\texttt{Overall\_Similarity} = \frac{\sum \texttt{Similarity} \times \texttt{wf}}{\sum \texttt{wf}}$$

   and return to step 3.

6. Report all cases where `Overall_Similarity` is above a preset level.

It is always preferable to report more than one case. Users may then choose to ignore certain cases due to considerations that are not represented in the task attributes. But sometimes one case is all that can be reported.

Adaptation

The adaptation stage is the most difficult to put into practice. Here the solution attributes of the retrieved cases are modified to suit the new task. This is rarely done automatically. User interaction is often essential to bring in the right domain knowledge for creating a useful solution. Although this stage is poorly supported in many commercial systems, it is the defining stage of case-based reasoning. Without this stage, case-based reasoning would be no more than an exercise in information retrieval. There are many case adaptation techniques; here are some of them:

- *User-guided adaptation*:   this is the most common method; even if other techniques are used, successful systems are user guided to some degree.

- *Constraint satisfaction*:   in this technique constraints determine whether and how the case is adapted to a new situation. When constraints are expressed as inequalities, they provide a convenient method for delimiting the space of possible solutions.

- *Adaptation rules*:   here rule inference is used to adapt cases to new situations. It is assumed that rules which adapt solutions are much simpler than rules to generate solutions from scratch.

- *Model-based adaptation*:   models are used to identify parts of the solution that require changes and are then modified using knowledge of relationships.

- *Adaptation by substitution*:   parts of other cases are used to substitute solution parts into the current solution case to meet requirements

- *Derivational replay*:   methodologies used to generate solutions in the absence of case-based reasoning can be used to adapt a case that mostly satisfies requirements. When these methodologies are time-consuming on their own, a combination with case-based reasoning can improve efficiency.

Storage

The storage stage involves storing the newly found solution in the case base for future use. If the solution is within the scope of solutions that were envisaged when case attributes were defined, this stage is straightforward. By storing these cases a system is able to increase its competence with time.

If the solution is outside the scope of solutions that were initially envisaged, a case storage activity could initiate a re-evaluation of how cases are represented and then a change in case representation. If this change has not been anticipated in the development of the system, important revisions to all parts of the system may be required. Indeed each case storage activity should involve an evaluation of the system's scope.

Maintenance

The maintenance stage tries to eliminate cases that will not be relevant to future tasks. Also, the size of a case base may become so large that case retrieval consumes an excessive amount of time. Then case maintenance involves eliminating cases that are not likely to reduce the quality of future solutions. For example, if many cases were similar, a maintenance activity would involve determining their relative importance to the quality of results. Less important cases could be deleted to increase system efficiency. It is important to achieve a uniform coverage of cases across the range of possible attribute values. This helps to ensure the system provides cases of equivalent quality for a range of situations.

Example 9.2   An Example of Case-Based Reasoning

An engineer maintains a case base of road bridges made of concrete box girders of constant cross-section. The following characteristics of each bridge are stored in the case:

- number of traffic lanes;
- maximum span;
- total length of the bridge;
- structural system, i.e. simply supported (simple) or continuous;
- depth of the bridge beam;
- whether the beam is prestressed;
- cost of construction.

The case base is used to obtain a quick estimate for the cost of constructing new bridges. The task characteristics used to retrieve similar cases are

- number of traffic lanes;
- maximum span;
- total length of the bridge;
- structural system;
- whether the beam is prestressed.

The solution characteristics are

- depth of the bridge beam;
- cost of construction.

Similarity is calculated for each attribute using the scheme given in Table 9.2; the term 'target value' refers to the value of the attribute in the new task. The importance of each attribute in the estimation is classified in Table 9.3. A weight factor of 0.8 is used for very important attributes, 0.5 for reasonably important attributes, and 0.2 for less important attributes. The case base consists of the bridges in Table 9.4. The engineer is given the following task characteristics:

- number of traffic lanes = 3;
- maximum span = 70;
- total length of the bridge = 120;
- structural system = continuous;
- whether the beam is prestressed = yes.

The engineer has to find the most similar case. He must adapt the selected case assuming that the cost is proportional to the product of the number of traffic lanes and the total length of the bridge. Here is his solution. The similarity of each case is given in Table 9.5, using the steps on page 199. Case 9 has the maximum similarity and is selected for adaptation. The cost of constructing of this bridge is $7.9 million. The product of the number of lanes

Table 9.2   Scheme for calculating similarity

Attribute	Calculation of similarity
Structural system	Similarity = 1 if the value matches exactly Similarity = 0 otherwise
Number of traffic lanes	Similarity = 1 if the value matches exactly Similarity = 0 otherwise
Length of the bridge	Similarity = 1 − abs(target value − case value)/(maximum difference) with maximum difference = 500
Maximum span	similarity = 1 − abs(target value − case value)/(maximum difference) with maximum difference = 100
Whether the beam is prestressed	Similarity = 1 if the value matches exactly Similarity = 0 otherwise

Table 9.3   Importance of each attribute

Attribute	Importance
Structural system	Very important
Number of traffic lanes	Reasonably important
Length of the bridge	Less important
Maximum span	Very important
Whether the beam is prestressed	Reasonably important

Table 9.4   Bridges in the case base

Case number	Structural system	No. of traffic lanes	Bridge length (m)	Maximum span (m)	Whether prestressed	Beam depth (m)	Cost ($m)
1	Simple	2	60	60	yes	3	2.1
2	Continuous	3	95	45	yes	1.8	4.0
3	Simple	2	30	30	no	2	1.2
4	Continuous	2	300	100	yes	4.15	10.0
5	Continuous	3	150	90	yes	2	7.0
6	Continuous	3	110	50	no	4.15	4.2
7	Simple	4	100	20	no	1.1	4.1
8	Simple	3	120	60	yes	2.4	5.7
9	Continuous	3	200	75	yes	2.9	7.9
10	Simple	3	70	70	yes	2.7	2.7
11	Simple	3	150	30	no	0.9	5.4

and the total length of this case is 580. The corresponding value for the target is 360, therefore the adapted cost of construction for the new bridge is

$$\$7.9 \, \text{million} \times \frac{360}{580} = \$4.9 \, \text{million}$$

Table 9.5 Similarity of each case

Case	Similarity
1	0.5
2	0.93
3	0.23
4	0.71
5	0.94
6	0.76
7	0.21
8	0.69
9	0.97
10	0.71
11	0.42

9.9 SUMMARY

- Knowledge systems have evolved from good and bad experiences with early expert systems.

- Knowledge systems contain an explicit representation of knowledge, and they are developed through efforts to separate this knowledge from generic control algorithms.

- Engineering knowledge systems are usually developed by engineers who are specialists in their fields. This takes away the knowledge elicitation stage between experts and knowledge engineers, typical of knowledge system development in other fields.

- Knowledge is data items that are linked together.

- Small rule sets reduce the risk of update anomalies and other maintenance difficulties.

- Compared with rule-based systems, model- and case-based reasoning do not experience as many difficulties with maintenance.

REFERENCE

McArthur, T. (ed.). 1992. *The Oxford Companion to the English Language*. Oxford: Oxford University Press.

FURTHER READING

Ginsberg, M. 1993. *Essentials of Artificial Intelligence*. New York: Morgan Kaufmann.
Kumar, B. and Raphael, B. 2001. *Derivational Analogy Based Structural Design*. Stirling: Saxe-Coburg Publications.
Leake, D. 1996. *Case-Based Reasoning: Experiences, Lessons, & Future Directions*. Cambridge MA: AAAI Press/MIT Press.
Sriram, R. D. 1997. *Intelligent Systems in Engineering: A Knowledge-Based Approach*. Berlin: Springer-Verlag.
Stefik, M. 1995. *Introduction to Knowledge Systems*. New York: Morgan Kaufmann.
University of Kaiserslautern. *Case-Based Reasoning on the Web*. hyperlink://www.cbr-web.org.

10
Machine Learning

10.1 INTRODUCTION

The proposition that a computer can learn has been around since electronic computers were first built at the end of the 1940s. For the purposes of this book, machine learning involves development, testing and implementation of methodologies that allow computer systems to increase performance with use. This is a broad definition; for example, it includes aspects of case-based reasoning (Chapter 9) since a system may improve as cases are added to its case base.

Machine learning has often been described as the Holy Grail of computing. If computers could really learn, they would eventually be able to exceed human performance in many more areas than they do today. Machine learning has been the fundamental hypothesis behind much science fiction as well as more serious predictions of the future of computing. Learning is often claimed to be an indicator of intelligence. Such claims contributed to the excitement that surrounded the field of artificial intelligence during the final three decades of the past century.

At the same time, the lack of progress related to improving the performance of machine learning has been a disappointment for many observers of artificial intelligence. Especially for engineering tasks, machine-learning algorithms have so far failed to demonstrate permanent increases in performance outside of very restricted and well-defined limits. We are very far from a machine that learns to emulate an engineer; as discussed in Chapter 1, it is unlikely that society would value such a development anyway.

This does not mean that engineers have no use for machine learning. Although progress has been slow, concentrated research activity continues, and this is producing practical systems that show increasing capabilities. The best successes are achieved in areas where there is much implicit knowledge and where models are not accurate. Examples of most promising applications are

- autonomous systems such as robotics;
- recognitions systems for speech, facial features as well as images, handwriting, fingerprints and many other biometrical parameters;
- control of devices such as machines, cars, structures and aircraft.

Machine learning may also improve the performance of decision-support systems (DSS) since most decisions are improved through reference to previous experience. Design and

Fundamentals of Computer-Aided Engineering   B. Raphael and I. F. C. Smith
© 2003 John Wiley & Sons, Ltd   ISBNs: 0-471-48709-0 (HB); 0-471-48715-5 (PB)

diagnostic systems stand to gain the most from machine learning. But they too will never learn to the point where the participation of an engineer is not needed for decisions that require consideration of contextual aspects such as those originating from society, environment and politics.

This chapter describes how performance can be improved through the use of previous experience. Several examples are provided to illustrate important points. Selected learning techniques are classified into categories that are described and illustrated using engineering examples. Together these categories provide engineers with a range of possibilities that continuously improve task support.

10.2   IMPROVING PERFORMANCE WITH EXPERIENCE

Humans learn from experience. If their actions do not produce expected results, they are likely to change their actions when they encounter similar situations in the future. Such behaviour is absent in traditional computer programs, since in general they produce the same output for the same input all the time.

Consider a design system that proposes the dimensions of a bridge beam using a set of equations. The program outputs the beam dimensions using input data that is provided by the designer. If, for example, the span-to-depth ratio is not satisfactory from an aesthetic viewpoint, the designer must manually introduce modifications. Most conventional programs provide no mechanism for treatment of feedback. Also, there is no method for incorporating feedback into future designs. Therefore the design program continues to suggest the same dimensions for the same input, no matter how many times the designer rejects the design.

Another design program asks users if the generated designs are acceptable. If they are not acceptable, the program employs feedback to determine weaknesses associated with the design. Then the program generalizes and adapts its design method to avoid similar output in the future. This process of improving performance with experience is the primary mechanism of machine learning.

Example 10.1   A Tensegrity Structure

A tensegrity structure is a lightweight space structure consisting of compression members surrounded by a network of tension members. It has advantages such as ease of assembly and dismantling, and the absence of strong anchorage forces due to self-equilibrating member forces. Tensegrities adapt their shape by changing their self-stress. Figure 10.1 shows a photo of a tensegrity structure that was built in a laboratory (Fest and Smith, 2002). The shape of the structure is controlled through changing the lengths of compression members that are telescopic bars. The structure deforms in a non-linear fashion when loads are applied. In order to satisfy objectives, such as maintaining a constant slope of the roof, the lengths of telescopic bars are changed.

The control task involves determining which bar lengths have to be changed and by how much. Since there is no closed-form solution for bar lengths given target deflections, potential solutions are generated and then tested for compliance with objectives. Furthermore, due to the non-linear behaviour and uncertainties in the model, such as the influence

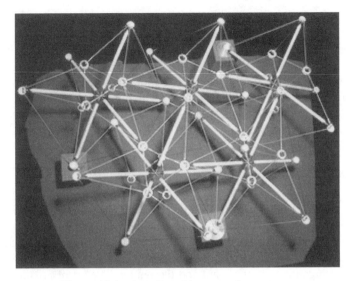

Figure 10.1   An adjustable tensegrity structure

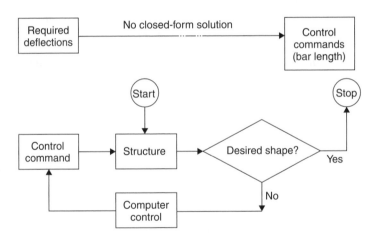

Figure 10.2   Controlling a structure through feedback

of friction in the joints, it is not possible to estimate accurately the effect of each control move. Best results are obtained by analysing the new geometry after each control move and making corrections (Figure 10.2). If the structure 'learns' after each evaluation, the number of iterations required to obtain the control objectives can be reduced. This means that good control commands are identified more rapidly as the structure is used (Domer *et al.*, 2003).

Example 10.2   Autonomous Driving

ALVINN is an autonomous driving system developed at the Carnegie Mellon University. ALVINN learns to control vehicles by observing how a person drives. It receives input from the vehicle's video camera and determines the direction in which the vehicle should travel to keep itself on the road. Since the environmental and weather conditions alter the light patterns obtained through the video camera, it is difficult to develop rules or procedures for determining the direction of the vehicle. Instead, the system employs artificial neural networks (ANNs) (Section 10.5) for learning correct vehicle movements.

ALVINN drives at 70 miles per hour (110 kph) on highways without causing accidents. It is an example of a promising application of machine learning to tasks that conventionally require human intelligence and skill.

10.3 FORMALIZING THE LEARNING TASK

Current learning techniques require a precise specification of what to learn; the learning task has to be well defined. This usually involves defining input and output variables, possible ranges of values of these variables, and methods to compare the output produced with the desired output. In addition, the learning algorithm requires knowledge of possible types of relationships between the input and the output. The set of possible relationships is called the hypothesis space. Apart from defining the variables and the hypothesis space, users need to specify values for several algorithm parameters for good performance.

Consider the task of controlling the tensegrity structure described in Example 10.1. A learning task may be formulated through the following declarations:

- *Input variables*:   changes in the lengths of telescopic bars to be applied to the structure.
- *Output variables*:   the coordinates of the nodes of the structure.
- *Evaluation function*:   the error in the computed coordinates of nodes with respect to the actual values obtained when bar lengths are changed.
- *Hypothesis space*:   the set of possible values of variables used in the model to compute the output for a given input.

Once all the above are defined, the algorithm learns to predict the right output for all input values.

Example 10.3   Defining the Hypothesis Space

This example considers the importance of defining the hypothesis space when formulating the learning task. Consider the tables in Figure 10.3. In each table the first column may be taken to be the input variable (x) and the second column the output variable (y). The first three rows contain a set of values for both input and output variables. The last row contains the value of the input for which we need to predict the output. The first three rows are used for training. More specifically, they are the set of data values used to learn

0	2
10	22
18	38
20	?

0	0
1	1
3	27
4	?

10	10
20	5
25	4
50	?

0	2
1	3
2	5
3	?

Figure 10.3   The learning task is to fill in the missing numbers indicated by question marks

the relationship between the input and the output. This set is known as the training set. The definition of the hypothesis space determines the predicted output values.

Most readers might assume that the missing value of y in the first table is 42. This is because a linear relationship ($2x + 2$) is observed between the input and output. Similarly, a cubic relationship (x^3) is observed in the second table and most readers might guess the answer to be 64. If the 'inversely proportional' relationship that is common in many physical phenomena is adopted ($100/x$), the missing value of y in the third table might be found as 2.

With simple mathematics it is possible to find the missing number in the fourth table as 8. There are three data points and therefore three unknown values may be evaluated by solving three equations. The simplest form of the polynomial equation involving three unknowns is $y = ax^2 + bx + c$, where a, b and c are unknowns. Solving for a, b and c by substituting the values of x and y for the three data points, the coefficients are determined to be $a = 1/2$, $b = 1/2$ and $c = 2$. Then the missing value of y is evaluated by substituting $x = 3$.

The above procedure includes the assumption that y is a polynomial function of x. It is possible to make another hypothesis and obtain different results. For example, we can assume an exponential function of x as follows:

$$y = ax^b + c$$

Using three data points, the unknowns a, b and c are 1, 2 and 2. This leads to a value of $y = 19$.

Discussion   *Predictions made by learning algorithms depend on the hypothesis space that is assumed for the task. Most learning algorithms search in a closed world where the hypothesis space is predefined and finite.*

Example 10.4   Fan and Bulb

A fan and a bulb are connected in parallel as shown in Figure 10.4. Currents I_a is measured at location A and current I_b is measured at location B. The resistance of the fan depends on its speed and is unknown. The voltage of the current source drops as the speed of the fan is increased, due to increased power consumption. The readings of the electric currents in amperes at different times are shown in Table 10.1. This example requires the prediction of I_a when $I_b = 0.183$.

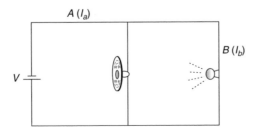

Figure 10.4   An electric circuit. A fan and a bulb are connected in parallel

Table 10.1 Electric currents
in the circuit

I_b (A)	I_a (A)
0.2	0.40000
0.195	0.29250
0.19	0.25330
0.185	0.23125
0.18	0.21600
0.175	0.20467

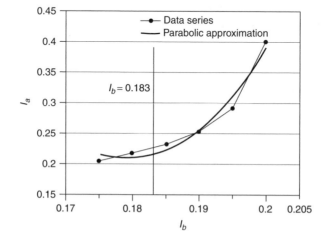

Figure 10.5 Plot of currents I_a and I_b in the circuit in Figure 10.4

The data are plotted in Figure 10.5 along with straight-line interpolation between data points and an approximate parabolic fit. At $I_b = 0.183$ both curves differ considerably. It is not possible to get good results by fitting an approximate polynomial to the observed data. However, it is possible to get very accurate results through the use of domain knowledge (using models). A reasonably accurate model may be constructed as follows.

Let R_{fan} be the resistance of the fan at any time, V be the voltage at any time, and R_{bulb} be the resistance of the bulb; R_{bulb} is assumed to be a constant. The following equations are obtained from Ohm's law:

$$\frac{I_a}{I_b} = \frac{R_{bulb}}{1/R_{fan} + 1/R_{bulb}}$$

$$V = I_b R_{bulb}$$

From knowledge of the behaviour of voltage fluctuations due to increased power consumption, we may assume a linear relationship between V and R_{fan} as follows:

$$V = k R_{fan}$$

where k is an unknown constant.

The learning task is formulated to find the best combination of values for k and R_{bulb} that matches all data points. Through linear regression (see below) the following values are obtained: $k = 0.2$ and $R_{\text{bulb}} = 10$ ohms. It may be verified that with these constants, exact values of I_a and I_b are as shown in Table 10.1. Using these constants, the current I_a corresponding to $I_b = 0.183$ is 0.2246. This differs from the parabolic approximation by 5.2%.

Linear regression (Section 10.4.2) is a statistical technique that finds the best values of parameters through minimizing the error between data points and points obtained through linear approximations. Many learning algorithms use statistical methods for minimizing errors.

Discussion   *Learning tasks can be formulated in different ways. Changing the formulation may alter the results. The most accurate results are obtained by using domain knowledge. Instead of attempting to find hidden relationships between raw data points, it is usually better to reformulate the problem to find values of unknown variables within models that are founded on physical principles.*

10.3.1 Searching Hypothesis Spaces

Learning involves searching a hypothesis space to find hypotheses that best fit the observed data, therefore many of the search techniques in Chapter 8 are used for learning tasks. The choice of search method depends on the representation of the hypothesis space. If the space consists of continuous values of numeric variables (as in Example 10.4), the chosen objective of the learning task may be to minimize errors; optimization methods in Chapter 8 may be used. But in many situations it may not be possible to estimate the best values of unknown parameters, because the relationships themselves might be unknown. Then we need other representations of the hypothesis space. Here is a sample list of hypothesis representations:

- numerical functions;
- symbolic rules;
- decision trees;
- artificial neural networks.

Numerical functions are used where input and output variables are real numbers and where the form of the relationship is not known a priori. For example, it may be observed that the increase in the output from a mechanical plant decreases with the input, but it may not be known whether the decrease is linear, quadratic or exponential.

Symbolic rules connect input and output variables that take symbolic values. Here is an example of a symbolic rule used in the diagnosis of concrete bridge beams

```
IF reinforcement bars have corroded, THEN there might be lon-
gitudinal cracks
```

The hypothesis space consists of all possible rules that connect input and output variables. The learning algorithm finds connections that best match observed data.

Decision trees were discussed in Chapter 3. They are widely used in classifying objects according to their properties. The learning task is to identify the best decision tree that classifies objects. Details are given in Section 10.4.2.4. Artificial neural networks are another way of representing relationships between input and output variables. This is explained in detail in Section 10.5.

10.4 LEARNING ALGORITHMS

Learning algorithms may be classified into four main categories:

- rote;
- statistical;
- deductive;
- exploration and discovery.

These categories are described in the following sections (Figure 10.6).

10.4.1 Rote Learning

Rote learning occurs by remembering facts and information. Much childhood schooling employs rote learning. We learn letters of the alphabet, multiplication tables, historical dates and other useful pieces of information. However, rote learning is not restricted to raw data and facts. Rules and procedures might also be learnt by this technique; for example, the procedure for using logarithm tables is learnt by rote learning.

When rote learning is implemented in a computer system, the machine relies on external sources for improving its performance. The machine does not discover new facts or relationships by itself. It simply applies the knowledge provided to it by humans in the form of facts and rules. Learning in the classical rule-based systems (Chapter 9) is through this technique. Case-based reasoning systems that do not perform generalizations also belong to this category.

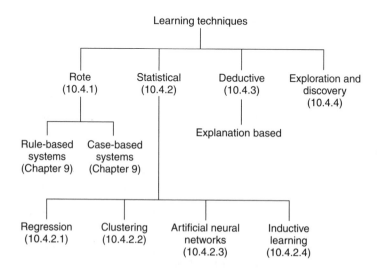

Figure 10.6 A classification of selected learning techniques

A knowledge system consists of a single rule:

If this span is less than 70 metres, then use a cantilever bridge

This system is unable to treat bridges having spans longer than 70 m. Now suppose a new rule is added:

If the span is between 70 and 1000 metres, then use cable-stayed bridge

With the new rule, the system is able to design bridges with spans longer than 70 m. Knowledge systems provide a means for adding new knowledge and incorporating it into the reasoning process, thus they are potentially able to improve their behaviour with time through rote learning. Such potential has attracted much attention.

10.4.2   Statistical Learning Techniques

10.4.2.1   Linear and non-linear regression

Regression techniques identify mathematical equations that are close to observed data. For example, if the form of the equation is known as

$$y(x) = ax^3 + bx^2 + cx + d$$

it is possible to find the values of a, b, c and d such that the curve $y(x)$ is as close as possible to the observed data points. The degree of correlation between the fitted curve and the observations can also be computed, thus relationships in observed data points may be discovered through regression.

10.4.2.2   Clustering techniques

Deflection measurements were taken on a bridge at various times during the day over a period of six months. The objective is to study deflections caused by deformations due to temperature variations. Care is taken to avoid taking measurements when vehicles pass over the bridge. It is not possible to avoid this altogether, so certain measurements include the effect of loads and vibrations due to moving vehicles. Deflections are plotted against the time of the day (Figure 10.7). Which points might have been influenced by vehicle movements?

Visually examining the plot of data, it is clear that the two points at the top between the times 12 and 18 do not follow the trend, therefore it is likely that vehicle movements have influenced them. How does a computer program automatically detect such points? Clustering techniques provide assistance for such tasks.

Clustering techniques group together data points that are similar. Trends in data are examined to classify points into clusters. Each cluster contains points that are similar in some sense. A simple clustering method is hierarchical clustering.

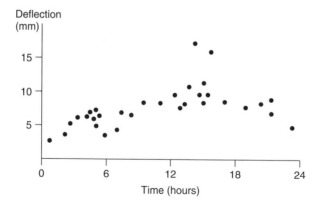

Figure 10.7   Deflection measurements taken from sensors on a bridge

Hierarchical clustering

Let S be a set of N items to be clustered, and M an $N \times N$ distance matrix that specifies the distance between any two items. The method used to compute distances between elements of S is application dependent.

1. Start by assigning each item to its own cluster, so that if there are N items, there are N clusters to start with. Let the distance between two clusters be defined as the distance between the items they contain.
2. Find the closest pair of clusters and merge them into a single cluster, so that now there is one less cluster.
3. Compute distances between the new cluster and each of the old clusters.
4. Repeat steps 2 and 3 until all items are clustered into a single cluster of size N.

Hierarchical clustering implementations differ in step 3, the method used to compute distances between clusters. In single-link clustering, the distance between two clusters is defined as the shortest distance from any member of one cluster to any member of the other cluster. In average-link clustering, the distance between two clusters is defined as the average distance from any member of one cluster to any member of the other cluster.

   This procedure results in a hierarchy of clusters (see below). At the top there is a single cluster containing all the elements. At lower levels there are clusters with varying number of elements.

   Examples of non-hierarchical clustering methods include the K-means method, adaptive K-means method, K-medians method, hard C-means method and fuzzy C-means method. Details are found in specialized textbooks on machine learning.

Example 10.5   Illustration of hierarchical clustering

Table 10.2 contains a list of beams used in a structural frame within a building. In this example a hierarchical cluster is created to group similar beams.

Table 10.2   Beams in a building frame

Identifier	Span (m)	Depth (m)
B1	4.0	0.3
B2	4.2	0.3
B3	6.0	0.4
B4	6.0	0.42

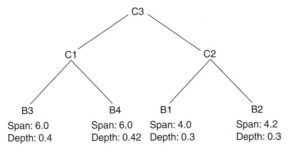

Figure 10.8   A hierarchical cluster of beams in a building frame

The distance d_{ij} between any two items i and j in the list is defined to be

$$\sqrt{(\text{span}_i - \text{span}_j)^2 + (\text{depth}_i - \text{depth}_j)^2} \tag{10.1}$$

where span_i, span_j, depth_i and depth_j are the spans and depths of the beams. The distance between two clusters is defined to be the minimum distance between any two elements of the two clusters.

Using the definitions, the minimum distance is between B3 and B4 (0.02), therefore these two are grouped into a single cluster called C1. In the second step, the minimum distance is between the items B1 and B2 (0.2), so these are grouped together into another cluster called C2. In the third step, there are only two clusters, C1 and C2; they are grouped together into a single cluster C3. The complete hierarchy is shown in Figure 10.8.

The cluster C1 contains small-span beams and the cluster C2 contains larger-span beams. This is a consequence of the distance metric defined in (10.1).

Applications of clustering

Clustering is often used for classification tasks. Classification involves grouping objects together into classes that have distinct properties. Once classes of objects are identified, it is possible to reason about them using knowledge associated with each class. For example, if a beam belongs to the class of 'large span', properties of this class, such as span-to-depth ratio, might be used in the design.

10.4.2.3   Artificial neural networks

Artificial neural networks (ANNs) are inspired by the interconnected, parallel structure of human and animal brains. Since biological neural networks are not treated in this book, the terms 'neural networks' and 'ANNs' will be used interchangeably. A neural network is composed of a number of processing elements called neurons. They are connected to each other and their output depends on the strength of incoming connections. Learning involves adapting the connection strengths so that better output could be produced for the same input by training the net.

ANNs are being applied to a large number of complex practical tasks. Typical applications involve classification tasks such as speech, character and signal recognition, and system modelling where the physical processes are not understood or are highly complex.

ANN is a form of statistical learning since the process involves updating weight factors that are used in computing the output. This is analogous to updating the coefficients in linear regression. Since ANN is the most widely used learning technique in engineering, it is explained in more detail in Section 10.5.

10.4.2.4 Inductive learning

Induction is the process of inferring a rule, 'A implies B', given the facts A and B (Chapter 1). Inductive learning methods are capable of obtaining general domain knowledge from specific examples. From a set of positive and negative examples, inductive learning algorithms create rules. For example, if all instances of large-span bridges in the training set are of type cable-stayed, the learning algorithm might conclude that all large-span bridges are cable-stayed. This rule will be modified whenever new instances of large-span bridges are encountered which are not cable-stayed. When this happens, the algorithm identifies other discriminating features that might be responsible for the change in bridge type.

Induction is a form of human reasoning. Through observing nature, we form rules such as 'birds have wings' and 'dogs have four legs'. By conducting experiments, we conclude 'concrete cracks when tensile stresses exceed limits' and 'presence of chlorides initiates corrosion in reinforcement bars'.

Most inductive learning algorithms attempt to construct decision trees instead of inferring raw rules themselves. Table 10.3 contains a list of slab systems used in buildings. Figure 10.9 shows a decision tree formed using these examples. This decision tree could be used to select slab systems for buildings based on span and room shape.

An algorithm for constructing decision trees was developed by Quinlan (1979). It works by looking for regularities in data and identifying discriminating features. Each data point (sample) consists of a set of attribute–value pairs. To start with, the tree has a single node (root) under which all samples are classified. Then it recursively performs the following operations:

Table 10.3 Slab systems used in buildings

Span	Shape	Slab system
Long	Square	Waffle
Long	Rectangle	Waffle
Short	Square	Two-way
Short	Rectangle	One-way

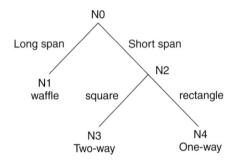

Figure 10.9   A decision tree that was created using examples of slab systems in buildings

1. Select a leaf node with an inhomogeneous sample set. An inhomogeneous set is one in which there are differences in the values of attributes.

2. Replace that leaf node by a test node that divides the sample set into a minimum number of subsets, according to an entropy calculation. Entropy is a measure that characterizes the inhomogeneity of a collection of samples. The entropy is 0 when the set is perfectly homogeneous and 1 when the set is perfectly inhomogeneous.

This procedure terminates when each leaf node is populated by as homogeneous a sample set as possible. Step 2 in the Quinlan algorithm is performed by choosing an attribute that minimizes the entropy. Each attribute is examined and the average entropy of all samples in the set is computed. The attribute that gives the minimum entropy is chosen. That is, the attribute that is likely to produce the best homogeneous set is taken for subdividing the sample set.

Example 10.6   Illustration

Consider the four data points in Table 10.3. At the start of the Quinlan algorithm, there is a single node, N0, in the decision tree. The set associated with this node contains all four data points. This set is not homogeneous since attribute values differ. In the first iteration, an attribute is chosen to divide the set such that there is maximum reduction in inhomogeneity. Since large span results in a homogeneous set of waffle slabs, span is the attribute chosen in this iteration. The root node is split into two nodes, N1 and N2, one for long span and the other for short span (Figure 10.9). The sets associated with both nodes contain two elements each. In the second iteration, node N2 is chosen since its set is inhomogeneous. The attribute shape is chosen to divide the node into two subnodes, N3 and N4.

10.4.3   Deductive Learning

Deductive learning refers to the application of existing knowledge to produce new knowledge. New pieces of knowledge are deduced from existing knowledge. Caching and explanation-based learning are examples of deductive learning. Caching refers to storing computed inferences for quick retrieval in order to avoid the same computations in the future. Examine the following rules:

> IF the support of a beam is fixed THEN there is negative bending moment at the support
> IF there is negative bending moment THEN there are tensile forces on the top of the beam

The following rule might be deduced from the above two rules:

> IF the support of a beam is fixed THEN there are tensile forces on the top of the beam at the support

This rule may be used as a short cut in the reasoning process. Many complex reasoning steps might be omitted and final inferences obtained directly through such short cuts.

Explanation-based learning methods examine the sequence of steps required to perform a task in order to deduce patterns in the context that might result in a success or failure. This is particularly useful for avoiding dead ends in search trees. Dependencies among variables are examined to find out conditions that result in such situations. This information is used in choosing branches to be searched in the future.

10.4.4 Exploration and Discovery

In exploration and discovery, no examples are provided by the user. The search space is defined completely and the learning program explores the space to make discoveries. A famous example in artificial intelligence is a program called AM (Lenat, 1982) to discover concepts in elementary mathematics. AM was written in 1976 in Interlisp. The program was provided with an initial vocabulary of concepts and operators in set theory. Through exploration, AM discovered several important mathematical concepts, including subsets, disjoint sets, sets with the same number of elements, and numbers. AM used heuristics to determine which concepts are interesting in order to prioritize exploration paths.

Random search techniques (Chapter 8) could be used effectively for learning through exploration. Random search methods generate solutions for evaluation. Results of evaluations might be used to determine which solutions need to be stored for reuse.

10.5 A CLOSER LOOK AT ARTIFICIAL NEURAL NETWORKS

Section 10.4.2.3 contains a brief introduction to artificial neural networks (ANNs). Since ANNs are widely used in engineering applications, they are explained in more detail here.

The basic unit of a neural network is a neuron, also known as a processing unit or a node. A node N_j obtains inputs $I_{1j}, I_{2j}, \ldots$ through a set of incoming connections and produces an output O_j (Figure 10.10). The input I_{ij} is equal to the output from the starting node i, multiplied by a weight factor w_{ij}; w_{ij} represents the strength of the connection between the nodes N_i and N_j.

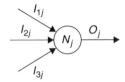

Figure 10.10   A neuron

Input layer Hidden layers Output layer

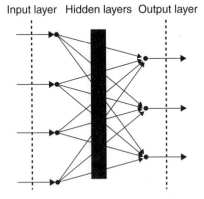

Figure 10.11   Input, output and hidden layers in a neural network

Nodes are grouped into three layers: input, output and hidden (Figure 10.11). Nodes in the input layer represent input variables. Nodes in the output layer represent the output variables. Nodes in hidden layers represent features that are computed using the input variables that affect the output. These nodes may not have any physical meaning in most applications.

The output from a node O_j is computed in two steps. The first step is the computation of the activation level of the node. The activation level is a function of the sum of the inputs arriving at the node. Usually a sigmoid function is employed. The sigmoid function is defined as

$$F(x) = 1/(1 + e^{-x})$$

It produces a value between 0 and 1. In the second step, the output is calculated as a function of the current activation level of the node. It is common to adopt a threshold function so there is no output from the node if the activation level is less than a threshold. Threshold functions produce discontinuities in the output (Figure 10.12). Alternatively, the output function might also be defined to be equal to the activation function.

Example 10.7   Selecting Floor Systems

Figure 10.13 shows a two-layered neural network that has been trained to select floor systems for buildings. The activation function is chosen as the identity function; that is, the activation level is equal to the sum of inputs.

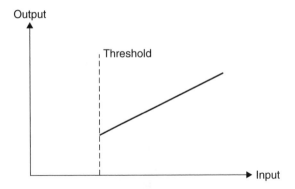

Figure 10.12 A threshold function. Output is zero if the input is less than a threshold

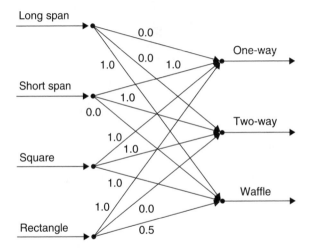

Figure 10.13 Two-layered neural network for selecting the type of floor system for a building

The input layer consists of four nodes representing the span and the shape of the rooms. The first node is activated (activation level = 1) if the span is large. In the case of small spans, the activation level of the first node is set to 0 and that of the second node is set to 1. Similarly, if the shape of the rooms is rectangular, the activation level of the third node is set to 0 and that of the fourth node is set to 1.

The output nodes represent options for the floor system to be adopted. The threshold for the output nodes is taken as 1.0. The nodes do not produce any output if the activation level is less than or equal to 1.0.

Question

What will be the output from the nodes in the case of large span and square shape?

Answer

The sum of the inputs at the one-way slab node is 1.0. Since this is not more than the threshold value (1.0), the output from this node is 0. The output from the node representing two-way slab is also 0. The output from the node representing waffle slab is 2.0 since the net input at this node (2.0) is greater than the threshold.

Example 10.8   A Two-Layered Network for Approximating a Function

Figure 10.14 shows a two-layered network representing a function $z(x, y)$. What should be the values of the threshold t_1 and the weights w_1, w_2 in order to produce the output in Table 10.4? The activation function for the output node is the identity function.

The activation of the output node z is $w_1 x + w_2 y$, where x and y are the inputs from the respective nodes. From the first two rows in Table 10.4, w_1 and w_2 are evaluated to be 1.0 (assuming $t_1 = 0$). These values match the last row in the table, but they are inconsistent with the third row and it is not possible to change the value of t_1 to produce a different result. The only values of w_1 and w_2 that produce the output in the third row are $w_1 = w_2 = 0.0$, but these values are inconsistent with other rows. In fact, the two-layered network is incapable of producing the output given in the table.

The function given in Table 10.4 is known as the exclusive OR operator, XOR. This operator outputs 1 if either of the inputs is 1, but outputs 0 if both inputs are 1. A two-layered network is incapable of representing an XOR relationship. With a three-layered network it is possible to represent this relationship, as can be verified in Figure 10.15. The threshold for the nodes in the hidden layer is 0.0.

Example 10.9   A Multi-Layered Network for Approximating a Function

Figure 10.16 shows a multi-layered network for approximating a function $f(x, y)$. The activation function for each node is the identity function. Write down the expression for

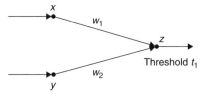

Figure 10.14   A two layered network representing a function $z(x, y)$

Table 10.4   Function $z(x, y)$

x	y	z
1	0	1
0	1	1
1	1	0
0	0	0

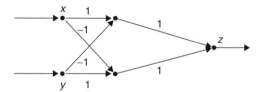

Figure 10.15 A multi-layered network representing a function $z(x, y)$. Weights are shown adjacent to connecting edges

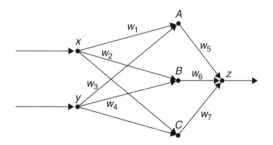

Figure 10.16 A multi-layered network for approximating a parabolic function

Table 10.5 Output function for nodes in a multi-layered network

Unit	$F(a)$
A	a^2
B	a
C	1

the output z in terms of the input variables x and y. The output function for each node in the hidden layer is given in Table 10.5.

The output from each node is as follows:

$$O_a = (w_1 x + w_3 y)^2$$

$$O_b = w_2 x + w_4 y$$

$$O_c = 1$$

$$z = w_5(w_1 x + w_3 y)^2 + w_6(w_2 x + w_4 y) + w_7$$

Thus the network is capable of modelling linear and parabolic relationships between the output variable z and the input variables x and y. In general, through appropriate choices of activation and output functions and a sufficient number of nodes, neural networks are able to represent most continuous mathematical functions. In addition, through the choice of threshold functions, ANNs are capable of modelling discontinuous functions and discrete variables.

10.5.1   Types of Neural Network

Neural networks are classified according to different criteria. Depending on the network topology, they are labelled as two-layered and multi-layered. Limitations of two-layered networks were discussed in the preceding sections. Multi-Layered networks might have one or more hidden layers.

The type of the connections between layers (interlayer connections) determines whether neural networks are classified as fully connected or partially connected. In a fully connected network, each neuron on the first layer is connected to every neuron on the second layer. In a partially connected network, a neuron of the first layer need not be connected to all neurons in the second layer.

The way data is propagated through the network defines neural networks as feedforward and recurrent. In feedforward networks, data proceeds in the same direction; that is, from the input nodes to the output nodes. In recurrent networks, the direction of data flow is not fixed. Neurons in the same layer communicate their outputs with one another many times before they send their outputs to another layer. Neurons of a layer need to achieve specific conditions before they communicate their outputs to another layer.

Within a feedforward network, the mode of communication might be hierarchical or resonant. If a neural network has a hierarchical structure, the neurons of a lower layer may only communicate with neurons on the layer immediately above. In a resonant network, the layers have bidirectional connections, and they may continue sending messages across the connections many times until a predefined condition is achieved.

Depending on the method of learning, ANNs are classified as either supervised learning networks or self-organizing networks. In supervised learning, the output of a neural network is compared to the desired output (as specified in the training samples). Weight factors are adjusted to produce a closer match between the desired output and the actual output. Reinforcement learning is a form of supervised learning in which feedback is continuously provided to the learning algorithm in the process of moving towards the goal for each task.

In unsupervised learning (self-organizing networks), networks use no external feedback to adjust their weights. Instead, they monitor their performance internally. Goals of unsupervised learning include identification of clusters, evaluation of regularities and trends in input signals, and finding possible causes for patterns observed in input data. The information required by the network to organize itself is built into the network topology and learning rules. The adaptive resonance network is an example of an unsupervised learning network. It analyses behaviourally important input data and then detects possible features and classifies patterns in the input vector.

10.5.2   Learning in Neural Networks

Learning occurs by adjusting weights of connections. There are many methods for adjusting weights. They are known as learning laws. Most of these laws are variations of the oldest learning law, Hebb's rule. Hebb's rule states that 'if a neuron receives an input from another neuron, and if both are highly active (mathematically have the same sign), the weight between the neurons should be strengthened'. A variation of Hebb's rule is

Hopfield's law, which states that 'if the desired output and the input are both active or both inactive, increment the connection weight by a constant (known as the learning rate). Otherwise decrement the weight by the learning rate'.

The most widely used learning law is the delta rule. The application of this rule involves iteratively modifying the weights of connections to reduce the difference, the delta, between the desired output value and the actual output of a neuron. This rule changes the weights in a way that minimizes the mean square error of the network. This rule is also known as the Widrow–Hoff learning rule and the least mean square (LMS) learning rule. The rule is applied through the following steps:

1. The delta error in the output layer is computed.
2. Using the derivative of the output function, the delta errors in the nodes of the previous layer are computed.
3. The delta error in the previous layer is used to adjust input connection weights.
4. Backward propagation of errors is repeated until the first layer is reached.

Networks that use the delta rule for backward propagation of errors are called feedforward back-propagation networks.

10.5.3 Summary

ANNs are a computational simulation of biological nervous systems. They offer a method of constructing an approximate function that relates output variables to input variables. Compared with other statistical methods, they have the following strengths:

- They can learn and generalize from large amounts of data.
- They have a high tolerance to noisy input data.
- They adapt easily over time under changing conditions.

And the following limitations:

- There is no explicit knowledge of the real relationships between the input and the output variables. ANNs are often referred to as black boxes.

- It is difficult to determine whether the network has 'learnt' correctly. There is no way of proving that the network will perform reliably in future situations.

- The best topology of the net is hard to fix a priori. The number of layers and nodes is usually established by trial and error. Designing neural networks requires specialized skills.

- A large number of training samples are required to produce reasonable performance.

10.6 SUMMARY

- Machine learning techniques improve the performance of systems through reference to experience.

- Most learning techniques require predefined knowledge of input and output variables as well as prior knowledge about the forms of relationships between them.

- The set of possible relationships between the input and output variables is known as the hypothesis space.

- Rote learning relies on remembering facts and data.

- Statistical learning techniques analyse variations in the values of attributes to identify relationships.

- Deductive learning uses existing knowledge to produce new knowledge.

- Artificial neural networks are a form of statistical learning in which weights of connections between nodes are updated in order to modify the output.

- Artificial neural networks are classified into different types depending on the topology of the network, direction of data flow and method of learning.

REFERENCES

Domer, B., Fest, E., Lalit, V. and Smith, I. F. C. 2003. Combining the dynamic relaxation method with artificial neural networks to enhance the simulation of tensegrity structures. *Journal of Structural Engineering*, **129**(5), in press.

Fest, E. and Smith, I. F. C. 2002. Deux structures actives de type tensegrité. *Construction Métallique*, **3**, 39, 19–27.

Lenat, D. B. 1982. AM: discovery in mathematics as heuristic search. In *Knowledge-Based Systems in Artificial Intelligence*. R. Davis and D. B. Lenat (eds). New York: McGraw-Hill.

Quinlan, J. R. 1979. Discovering rules from large collections of examples: a case study. *In Expert Systems in the Microelectronic Age*. D. Mitchell (ed.). Edinburgh: Edinburgh University Press.

FURTHER READING

Sriram, R. D. 1997. *Intelligent Systems in Engineering: A Knowledge-Based Approach*, Chapter 8 and Section 9.4. Berlin: Springer-Verlag.

Ginsberg, M. 1993. *Essentials of Artificial Intelligence, Chapter 15*. New York: Morgan Kaufmann.

Mitchell, T. 1997. *Machine Learning*. New York: McGraw-Hill.

Russell, S. 1996. *Machine learning. In Artificial Intelligence, M. A. Boden (ed.). New York: Academic Press.*

EXERCISES

10.1 Fill in the missing numbers in the following tables. Is there a unique answer? What does the answer depend on?

1	1
2	3
3	6
4	10
5	?

0	0
1	2
3	6
4	?

10	6
20	11
25	13
50	26
100	?

10.2 Formulate a system of rules that chooses slab systems according to the decision tree in Figure 10.9. What chaining mechanism will be used to determine whether a waffle slab system is suitable in a given situation, forward chaining or backward chaining?

10.3 If there are three input parameters and two output parameters, what is the minimum number of training sets that are necessary for a neural network to perform accurately? Both input and output parameters are of type Boolean (yes/no are the only possible values). *Hint*: examine the number of weight factors that need to be computed.

11

Geometric Modelling

11.1 INTRODUCTION

Modelling of geometry is a fundamental engineering activity. It is impossible to carry out many important tasks without geometric modelling of some form. Design of any product, from nail files to aircraft, requires reasoning related to form. Accurate diagnoses most often require knowledge of the geometry of the malfunctioning object, especially when the trouble is related to mechanical behaviour. Therefore, if computer-aided engineering (CAE) is required to provide support for engineering tasks, geometric modelling is unavoidable. Moreover, the effectiveness of this modelling usually determines the quality of the support a computer can provide.

For many years the impact of geometric modelling was handicapped by the performance of hardware. With limited memory and slow processing power, even the simplest objects were difficult to model realistically. It was often not possible to model complex engineering products in their entirety. These restrictions no longer exist in most cases. Nevertheless, several challenges remain. For a given task, several options for geometric modelling are available. The most appropriate option depends on several factors.

Before computers, physical models of complex objects were often constructed in engineering offices. Scale versions of projects for objects such as new products, buildings, bridges and refineries were created at great cost. While many applications of geometric modelling have eliminated the need for physical models altogether, some engineers employ both computer-generated and physical models for important projects. Each representation has distinct advantages that these engineers do not wish to forgo. In this way, the computer model becomes an additional means for reflection, product development, fabrication and assembly. Once again, in engineering contexts, CAE enhances rather than replaces.

This chapter describes possibilities that are available for use in engineering software. Each approach has positive and negative aspects, therefore the application determines the best combination of modelling techniques. The goal is to present an unambiguous, accurate and consistent representation that can be modified easily.

11.2 ENGINEERING APPLICATIONS

Important engineering applications of geometric modelling are found in CAD/CAM (computer-aided design, computer-aided manufacturing), robotics, computer graphics and

Fundamentals of Computer-Aided Engineering B. Raphael and I. F. C. Smith
© 2003 John Wiley & Sons, Ltd ISBNs: 0-471-48709-0 (HB); 0-471-48715-5 (PB)

structural analysis. These are described briefly here.

- *CAD/CAM*: computer systems are increasingly used to design products and control machinery in manufacturing processes. Such systems require precise product descriptions. Geometry needs to be represented as accurately as possible. CAD systems assist users in creating geometrical descriptions in computers. CAM systems use representations of geometry to control manufacturing processes such as machine-tool operations.

- *Robotics*: robotics is an area of mechanical engineering where machines are programmed to perform tasks such as manufacturing automobile parts and repairing spaceships in outer space. Robots require accurate geometric representations of objects to carry out their tasks.

- *Computer graphics*: the most widespread use of geometric models is in computer graphics (Chapter 12). Graphical views of objects cannot be generated without a suitable geometrical representation.

- *Other applications*: apart from design and manufacture, there are several areas where geometric models are useful. Finite element meshes are automatically generated from geometric models to be used in structural analysis. Cost estimation involves computation of object properties such as volume and mass. Computer simulation of the operation of machines and structures requires geometric data. Such simulations reveal whether components intersect with each other and whether structures are feasible.

11.2.1 Criteria for Evaluating Representations

How does one represent the geometry of the building shown in Figure 11.1? Several schemes are available for representing geometry, but not all representations are suitable for all tasks. Representation schemes are evaluated using the following criteria.

- *Accuracy*: how accurate is the model? Straight-line representations only approximate curved boundaries and may not be suitable where accuracy is important.

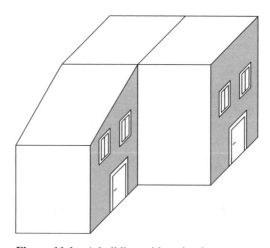

Figure 11.1 A building with a simple geometry

- *Domain*:   what shapes can be represented? A two-dimensional representation is suitable only for an object having a constant cross-section. It cannot accommodate variations along the longitudinal axis of the object.

- *Uniqueness*:   a representation is unique if it can be used to encode any given shape in only one way. This facilitates, for example, testing whether two objects are identical.

- *Closure*:   performing operations such as rotation and translation should maintain the integrity of the shape.

- *Compactness*:   how much memory is required for the representation? Certain representations require more memory than others.

- *Efficiency*:   efficient algorithms exist for processing shapes using certain representations. For other representations, algorithms are not fast.

11.3   MATHEMATICAL MODELS FOR REPRESENTING GEOMETRY

Simple shapes are easily represented by mathematical equations. This section develops mathematical representations of simple curves, surfaces and solids. The next section looks at schemes for representing more complex geometries that do not have simple mathematical equations.

11.3.1   Two-Dimensional Representation of Simple Shapes

A two-dimensional curve is represented in the general form as

$$f(x, y) = 0 \qquad (11.1)$$

This is known as the implicit form since the value of y is not expressed as a function of x explicitly. In simple cases we may express y explicitly as a function of x in the form

$$y = g(x) \qquad (11.2)$$

The form (11.2) has significant advantages over (11.1). The value of y can be computed directly if the value of x is known. The form in (11.1) might require the solution of a non-linear equation. A third form is the parametric form. In this form, both x and y are expressed in terms of another parameter t:

$$x = f(t)$$
$$y = g(t) \qquad (11.3)$$

The main advantage of the parametric form is that both x and y are computed directly from the value of t. All legal values of x and y are obtained by varying t in the permissible range. This is useful in curve tracing. Curve tracing involves generating all the points on the curve by moving from one point to the next. For example, the equation of a circle is expressed in parametric form as

$$x = R \cos t$$
$$y = R \sin t$$

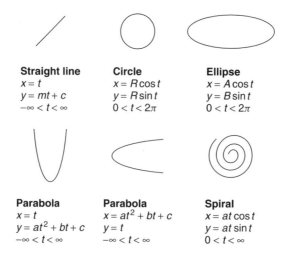

Figure 11.2   Simple 2D Curves expressed in parametric form

By varying the value of t from 0 to 2π, all the points on the circle may be generated. In the explicit form, the equation of the circle is given as

$$y = \pm(R^2 - x^2)^{1/2}$$

This form is not suitable for curve tracing because information related to how the value of x should be varied is also required. Two different values of y exist for each value of x. The complete curve may only be traced in two stages. In the first stage, x is varied from $-R$ to $+R$; during this stage the positive value of y is taken. In the second stage, x is varied from $+R$ to $-R$; during this stage the negative value of y is taken. Ambiguities related to varying parameters do not exist in curve tracing if the parametric form is used.

Figure 11.2 shows curves that are easily represented in parametric form. Using this form, even curves such as spirals, which have multiple values of y for the same value of x, can be traced easily by varying t.

11.3.2   Curves without Simple Mathematical Representations

If curves contain discontinuities, they are broken up into multiple curves for representing them mathematically. For example, a quadrilateral is broken into four straight lines. Figure 11.3 shows simple shapes that are represented by a series of curves.

When curves are too complex and when there is no simple mathematical equation to describe them, they may be approximated by a series of straight lines (Figure 11.4). The accuracy of representation is improved by increasing the number of lines. However, the smoothness of the curve is lost during discretization (breaking into lines).

11.3.3   Bézier Curves

When curves are approximated by a series of straight lines, there are slope discontinuities at the endpoints of each line. The curve is not smooth because there are two values of

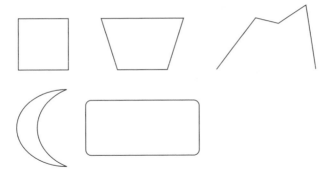

Figure 11.3 Shapes that are composed from simple curves. Each part of the curve has a simple mathematical representation of the form $x = f(t)$, $y = g(t)$

Figure 11.4 The outline of a wine glass approximated by a series of straight lines

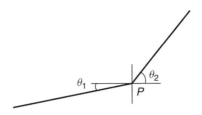

Figure 11.5 When curves are approximated by a series of straight lines, there are discontinuities at intersections of lines. There are two slopes at these points

the slope at these points (Figure 11.5). A smooth curve could be created such that the slope at the endpoint of one segment is equal to the slope at the beginning point of the next segment.

Béziers are smooth curves that are defined using discrete control points. They are named after a French engineer, Pierre Bézier, who used them for the body design of Renault cars in the 1970s. The mathematics of Bézier curves is as follows. Consider $N + 1$ control

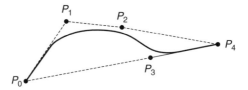

Figure 11.6 A Bézier curve. P_0, P_1, P_2, P_3 and P_4 are the control points. The convex hull of the control points is indicated by dotted lines. All the points on the Bézier curve lie within the convex hull of the control points

points P_k ($k = 0$ to N) in three dimensions (Figure 11.6). The Bézier parametric curve function is of the form

$$B(u) = \sum_{k=0}^{N} P_k \frac{N!}{k!(N-k)!} u^k (1-u)^{N-k} \tag{11.4}$$

Here the parameter u varies from 0 to 1. The first point P_0 is obtained by setting $u = 0$, and the last point is obtained by setting $u = 1$. The curve in general does not pass through any of the control points except the first and the last. The slope of the curve at $u = 0$ is equal to the slope of the straight line between P_0 and P_1. Similarly, the slope of the curve at $u = 1$ is equal to the slope of the straight line connecting the last two points. Slope continuity across multiple Bézier curves is ensured by properly choosing the first and the last control points.

Each term in the summation of equation (11.4) is a polynomial of degree k. These polynomials are called Bernstein polynomials. A third-degree Bézier curve is obtained using four control points. Here is the complete expression for the x-coordinate of any point on the curve:

$$x(u) = x_0(1-u)^3 + 3x_1 u(1-u)^2 + 3x_2 u^2(1-u) + 2x_3 u^3$$

where x_0, x_1, x_2 and x_3 are the x-coordinates of the control points. The equation for y has exactly the same form. All the points on the Bézier curve lie within the convex hull of the control points (Figure 11.6). A convex hull is the smallest convex polygon containing all the control points. See Chapter 8 for the definition of convexity.

11.3.4 *Mathematical Representation of Simple Surfaces*

Surfaces are defined by adding one more parameter to the mathematical representation of curves (Figure 11.7). For example, a circle of radius R is a curve involving a single parameter, t, as follows:

$$x = R \cos t$$

$$y = R \sin t$$

$$0 < t < 2\pi$$

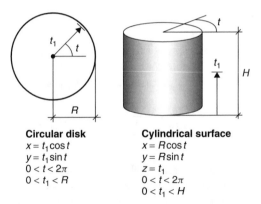

Circular disk

$x = t_1 \cos t$
$y = t_1 \sin t$
$0 < t < 2\pi$
$0 < t_1 < R$

Cylindrical surface

$x = R\cos t$
$y = R\sin t$
$z = t_1$
$0 < t < 2\pi$
$0 < t_1 < H$

Figure 11.7   Regular surfaces that can be represented in parametric forms involving two parameters. All points on the surface can be generated by varying the values of parameters within the bounds

A circular disc of radius R is obtained by adding one more parameter, t_1, using the following parametric equations:

$$x = t_1 \cos t$$

$$y = t_1 \sin t$$

$$0 < t < 2\pi$$

$$0 < t_1 < R$$

A cylindrical surface of height H and radius R is defined by the following equations in two parameters, t and t_1:

$$x = R \cos t$$

$$y = R \sin t$$

$$z = t_1$$

$$0 < t < 2\pi$$

$$0 < t_1 < H$$

Similarly, a spherical surface with radius R is represented using two parameters, t and t_1:

$$x = R \sin t_1 \cos t$$

$$y = R \sin t_1 \sin t$$

$$z = R \cos t_1$$

$$0 < t < 2\pi$$

$$0 < t_1 < \pi$$

11.3.5 Bézier Patches

The Bézier patch is the surface extension of the Bézier curve (Figure 11.8). Whereas a curve is a function of one variable and takes a sequence of control points, the patch is a function of two variables with an array of control points. The general form of the equations is given by

$$Q(s,t) = \sum_i^m \sum_j^n P_{i,j} B_i^m(s) B_j^n(t)$$

where B_i^m, B_j^n are the Bernstein polynomials and $P_{i,j}$ are the control points. The Bézier patch can be viewed as a continuous set of Bézier curves. A patch lies within the convex hull of its control points. A Bézier patch of degree 3 requires 16 control points since 4 control points are used to define the curve in each direction.

11.3.6 Mathematical Representation of Regular-Shaped Solids

Surfaces are obtained by adding an extra parameter to curve representations, and solids are obtained by adding an extra parameter to surface representations. By adding a parameter t_2, a cylinder is obtained from a cylindrical surface (Figure 11.9):

$$x = t_2 \cos t$$

$$y = t_2 \sin t$$

$$z = t_1$$

$$0 < t < 2\pi$$

$$0 < t_1 < H$$

$$0 < t_2 < R$$

where R is the radius of the disk and H is the thickness. New parameter t_2 varies along the thickness of the disc.

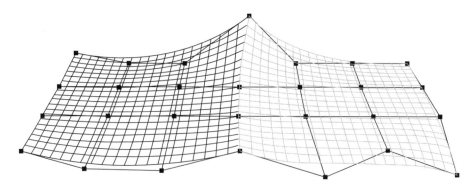

Figure 11.8 Example of a Bézier patch surface

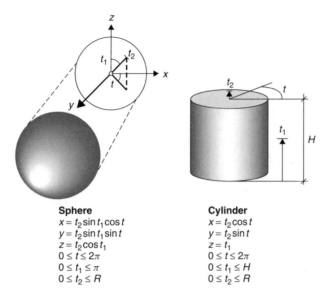

Sphere
$x = t_2 \sin t_1 \cos t$
$y = t_2 \sin t_1 \sin t$
$z = t_2 \cos t_1$
$0 \le t \le 2\pi$
$0 \le t_1 \le \pi$
$0 \le t_2 \le R$

Cylinder
$x = t_2 \cos t$
$y = t_2 \sin t$
$z = t_1$
$0 \le t \le 2\pi$
$0 \le t_1 \le H$
$0 \le t_2 \le R$

Figure 11.9 Mathematical representations of solids are obtained by adding an extra parameter to surface representations. Regular solids are represented in parametric forms involving three parameters. All points within the solid can be generated by varying the values of parameters within the bounds

Similarly, a spherical solid is obtained from a spherical surface by adding parameter t_2 that varies along the radius:

$$x = t_2 \sin t_1 \cos t$$

$$y = t_2 \sin t_1 \sin t$$

$$z = t_2 \cos t_1$$

$$0 < t < 2\pi$$

$$0 < t_1 < \pi$$

$$0 < t_2 < R$$

All the points within the volume of the solid are obtained by varying the parameters within the specified bounds.

11.4 REPRESENTING COMPLEX SOLIDS

Simple mathematical representations are not adequate for most engineering artefacts. Several schemes have been used which are broadly classified as follows:

- primitive instancing;
- mesh representations;

- sweep representations;
- boundary representations;
- decomposition models;
- constructive solid geometry.

11.4.1 Primitive Instancing

Primitive instancing schemes provide a library of all possible object shapes, called primitives. Each primitive is described by a set of parameters. Users create instances of these primitives by providing values to parameters. Only objects corresponding to one of the predefined types in the library can be modelled, because operations for combining instances are not defined. Primitive instancing is supported by many CAD and modelling systems for the representation of common parts.

11.4.2 Mesh Representations

In the mesh representation, a solid is approximated by the union of a number of smaller elements (Figure 11.10). The mesh representation of solids is analogous to representing a curve using a series of straight lines. Each straight line may be considered as an element that approximates the curve.

A mesh representation involves two entities, nodes and elements. Nodes represent points within and on the boundary of the solid. Elements are defined with respect to corner nodes. Usually, the shape of each element is approximated by the straight lines that connect the corner nodes. However, it is possible to use curved elements that approximate the shape using higher-order polynomials that pass through corner nodes as well as nodes within the element (internal nodes). Figure 11.11 shows an embankment which has a constant shape for its cross-section. Tables 11.1 and 11.2 describe the mesh.

The most widespread application of mesh representation is in finite element analysis, where meshes are used for representing the geometry of structures as well as for interpolating properties such as temperature and stresses that vary from point to point. Figure 11.12 shows a finite element mesh used in the stress analysis of an automobile body.

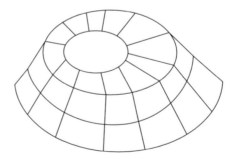

Figure 11.10 A mesh representation of an irregularly shaped mechanical component

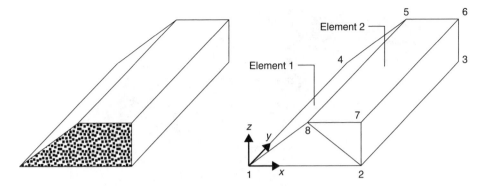

Figure 11.11   Mesh representation of an embankment

Table 11.1   Nodes of the mesh shown in Figure 11.11

Node	x	y	z
1	0	0	0
2	10	0	0
3	10	10	0
4	0	10	0
5	5	10	5
6	10	10	5
7	10	0	5
8	5	0	5

Table 11.2   Elements of the mesh shown in Figure 11.11

Element	Nodes connected to the element					
1	1	2	8	4	3	5
2	2	7	8	3	6	5

Advantages of mesh representation

- Accuracy is improved by reducing the size of the element.
- Meshes are useful for interpolating continuously varying properties over the volume of the solid.

Disadvantages of mesh representation

- A large number of nodes and elements might be required to represent complex shapes. Computer memory requirements can exceed practical limits of the hardware.
- Special skill is required to create appropriate meshes for complex shapes.
- It is difficult to verify the validity and accuracy of meshes.

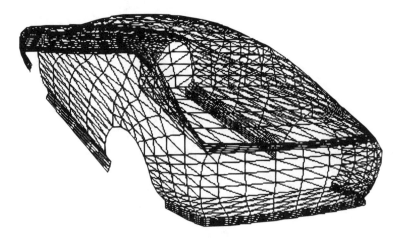

Figure 11.12 A mesh representation of an automobile body © 2002 Silicon Graphics, Inc. Used by permission.

11.4.3 Sweep Representations

Sweeping an object along a path through space defines a new object called a sweep. Sweep representations are useful where axial symmetry is present. For example, the water tank in Figure 11.13 is symmetrical about the vertical axis. Only five points are required to define the shape of the structure. Sweeping the curve about the vertical axis generates the entire volume.

There are several ways of creating sweeps. Extrusions, or translation sweeps, are made by sweeping a polygon along a straight line normal to the polygon. The trajectory is not perpendicular to the plane of the polygon in oblique sweeps (Figure 11.14). Rotational sweeps are made by rotating about an axis (Figure 11.13). General sweeps are made by sweeping along an arbitrary curve (Figure 11.15). The object that is swept need not be two-dimensional.

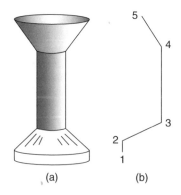

(a)

(b)

Figure 11.13 A symmetrical water tank: (a) is modelled by rotating a curve (b) through 360 degrees

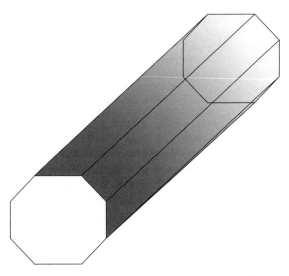

Figure 11.14   Oblique sweep. A polygon is moved along a straight line not necessarily perpendicular to the polygon

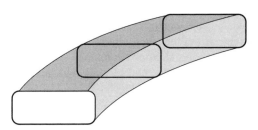

Figure 11.15   General sweep. The shape of the handset of a telephone is obtained by sweeping a rounded rectangle along its longitudinal axis

11.4.4   Boundary Representations

In boundary representations only the external boundaries of the solid are represented. The boundaries are usually represented by lists of vertices, edges and faces along with their topological relations. Boundary representations are based on a surface-oriented view of solid objects – an object is considered to be represented completely by its bounding faces.

Figure 11.16 shows part of a spread footing of a column. The boundary representation involves storing the details of 14 faces, 28 edges and 16 nodes. Even though this part of the structure can be conveniently represented by a mesh involving three 8-noded tetrahedral elements, the boundary representation has advantages in visualizing the structure through removing hidden lines and faces.

A disadvantage of boundary representations is that it is difficult to verify the validity of the solid. Here are three essential criteria for a valid solid:

- At least three edges must meet at each vertex.
- Edges must connect two vertices and be shared by two faces.
- Faces must not interpenetrate.

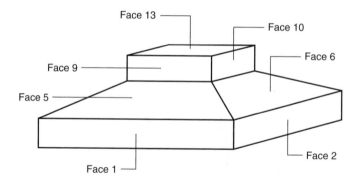

Figure 11.16 A part of a spread footing of a column using boundary representation. It has 14 faces, 28 edges and 16 nodes

While the first two are easily verified, checking the last criterion is computationally intensive.

11.4.4.1 Solids with holes

Even though in the boundary representation the entire volume contained within the bounding faces is considered to be part of the solid, objects with holes are also represented easily. This is done by defining the inner and outer boundaries. Figure 11.17 depicts a plate with a hole. A boundary representation is created by making a fictitious cut that connects the outer and inner boundaries.

11.4.4.2 Operations on boundary representations

Two or more solids may be combined into a single solid through defining Boolean set operations such as union, intersection and difference (Section 11.4.6) on the boundary

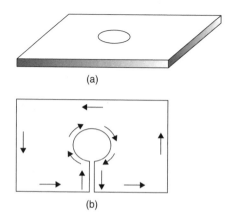

Figure 11.17 Boundary representation of a plate with a hole: (a) a plate with a hole, (b) top face of the plate with a hole shown in (a). The boundary consists of an outer loop and an inner loop

representation. Even though these are simple operations at the user level, at the implementation level they are complex. The main difficulty is in creating a valid representation by modifying the nodes and connectivity of the constituent objects.

11.4.5 Decomposition Models

Decomposition models involve breaking up the volume of the solid into cells. Each cell is labelled as full, partially full, or empty depending on how the cell is occupied by the solid. The occupancy of cells may be defined either sequentially (voxel representation) or hierarchically.

11.4.5.1 Voxels

Primitive cells that have the same size and shape (usually cubes) are used to enumerate spatial occupancy sequentially. The cells are called voxels and their size is called the grid size. In two dimensions this representation is known as a bitmap and is commonly used in 2D graphics (Chapter 12).

A bitmap defines the properties (such as colour) of each cell. Colour is analogous to the level of occupancy. Black indicates an empty cell, white indicates a fully occupied cell, and other colours indicate varying levels of occupancy. Figure 11.18 shows the bitmap representation of a circle. The occupancy level is discretized into two values: 1 indicates that the cell is more than 50% occupied; 0 indicates that the cell is either empty or less than 50% occupied.

Spatial resolution is determined by the grid size. A more accurate representation is possible by decreasing the grid size, but this considerably increases the memory requirements.

Two advantages

- *Simplicity*:   an object is represented by an array of cells.
- *Boolean operations*:   it is easy to perform Boolean operations such as the union of two objects.

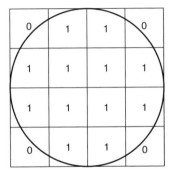

Figure 11.18   A bitmap representation of a circle. 1 indicates cells that are more than 50% occupied, 0 otherwise

Two disadvantages

- *Redundancy*: many cells might have the same properties and there is considerable redundancy. Voxel representations require much storage space on computers. For example, if a 3D solid is discretized into 100 cells in each direction and it requires 1 byte to represent the property of each cell, 1 million bytes are needed to represent the complete solid.

- *Topological information*: topological information is not contained in voxel models, therefore operations such as geometric transformations are costly. For example, if a rectangular solid is rotated by 45°, the properties of all cells have to be recomputed.

11.4.5.2 Hierarchical decomposition

In hierarchical decomposition the space representing a solid is divided recursively into cells having varying sizes. The most common form of hierarchical decomposition is an octree, in which each node represents a cube or a box. If the properties are uniform within a cube (either completely occupied or not occupied at all), the cube is not further decomposed. Otherwise, the cube is subdivided into eight, which form the child nodes. A quadtree is the same idea in two dimensions; here each node is a rectangle (Figure 11.19). More general decomposition methods use cells of different shapes, positions and sizes. These simple cells are glued together to describe the solid object.

Figure 11.20(a) shows the part of a city that is affected by groundwater pollution. To represent the area as a quadtree, it is initially decomposed into four cells, as in Figure 11.20(b). Partially occupied cells are further divided, as in Figure 11.20(c). The quadtree representation of this coarse decomposition is given in Figure 11.20(d). Figure 11.20(e) contains the final decomposition into cells having a minimum dimension of 0.125 km.

Advantages

- Storage requirements are reduced through varying the cell sizes. Since cells are not subdivided if the properties do not change, information is not repeated in multiple cells (unlike in the voxel representation).

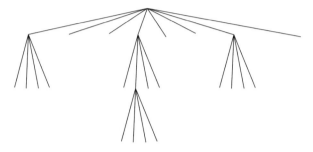

Figure 11.19 A quadtree. Each node represents a box. Leaf nodes have uniform properties throughout. Other nodes are subdivided

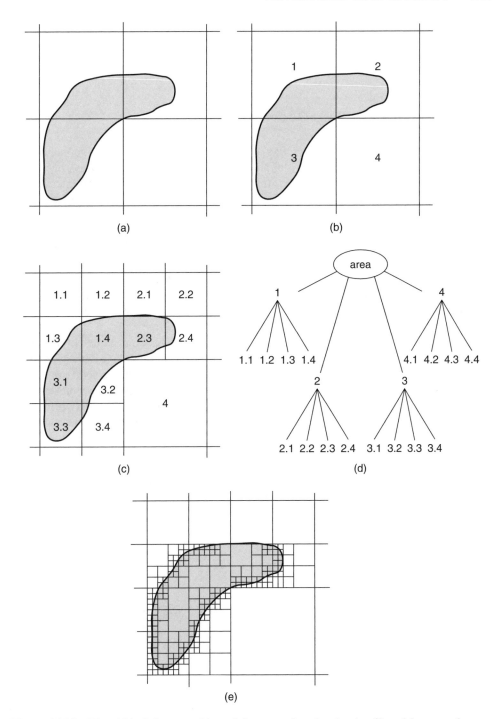

Figure 11.20 Hierarchical decomposition of the area of a city that is affected by ground water pollution

- It is easy to represent objects by removing hidden surfaces for graphical display.

- Efficient algorithms exist for storing and processing quadtrees and octrees; for example, Boolean set operations are straightforward.

11.4.6 Constructive Solid Geometry

Constructive solid geometry (CSG) refers to the creation of complex solid geometries by combining primitives such as boxes, tetrahedrons and pyramids. The process of combination involves Boolean set operations, for example, union, difference and intersection. If the input objects are valid solids, these operations result in objects that are also valid. An example of an invalid solid is one that contains dangling boundary points, lines and faces.

Figure 11.21 illustrates Boolean operations used in CSG. Complex solids are created through the repeated application of these operators. CSG operations are usually represented by a tree structure which stores the generation history of the solid. The leaf nodes of the tree are primitives such as boxes, tetrahedrons and pyramids. Intermediate nodes are Boolean set operators or geometric transformation operations such as translation and rotation. Figure 11.22 shows an object created using a CSG tree.

The CSG representation is unambiguous but not unique. That is, each CSG representation models exactly one object, but an object might have different CSG representations.

Certain tasks such as detecting whether a point lies inside or outside a solid are carried out easily using CSG. However, visualization requires deriving a boundary representation from a CSG model. This operation is called boundary evaluation. The CSG primitives have to be converted into boundary models and then these models have to be combined using the Boolean set operations. This is a complex process.

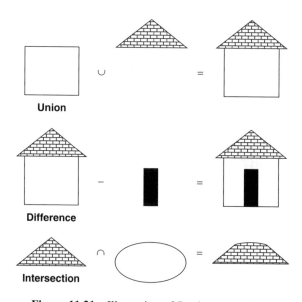

Figure 11.21   Illustration of Boolean operations

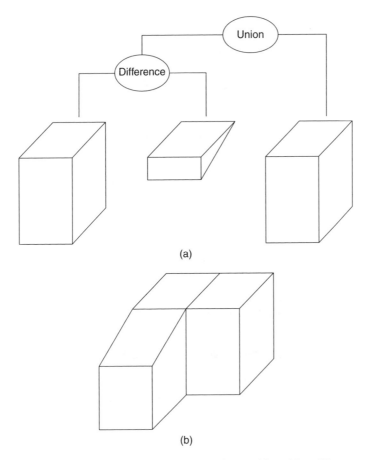

Figure 11.22   A CSG tree (a) and the resulting object (b)

11.5   APPLICATIONS

11.5.1   Estimation of Volume

The cylindrical water tank in Figure 11.23 is represented using CSG as the subtraction of two cylinders (difference operator). These cylinders have the dimensions given in Table 11.3.

Question

What is the volume of concrete required to construct the water tank?

Answer

The second cylinder is contained entirely inside the first cylinder; that is, the union of the two cylinders is equal to the first cylinder. Therefore the volume of the resulting solid is

Figure 11.23 A cylindrical water tank

Table 11.3 Dimensions of the primitives used in CSG

Cylinder	Diameter (m)	Height (m)
1	4.5	3.2
2	4.3	3.0

equal to the difference between the volumes of the two cylinders. In general, computation of volume using CSG is straightforward.

Example 11.1 Finite Element Mesh for a Spread Footing

The spread footing in Figure 11.16 is to be analysed for stresses due to loads acting on the structure. This requires creation of a finite element mesh by discretizing the solid into elements. Generating a valid mesh using a boundary representation is difficult. Meshing of complex solids is usually performed through interactive graphics. To explain why this operation needs to be performed systematically, here is a sample procedure.

Step 1

- Define a tetrahedral block, `block-1`, consisting of faces `face-1`, `face-2`, `face-3` and `face-4`.

Step 2

- Insert nodes and elements in `block-1`
- Select `face-1`. Insert nodes from 1 to 12 as shown in Figure 11.24.
- Select opposite face, `face-3`. Insert nodes from 37 to 48.
- Connect each node j on `face-1` to the node $j+36$ on the opposite face with a straight line. Insert nodes $j+12$ and $j+24$ along this line (Figure 11.25).
- Create tetrahedral elements connecting these nodes.

Step 3

- Define a tetrahedral block, `block-2`, consisting of faces `face-9`, `face-10`, `face-11` and `face-12`.

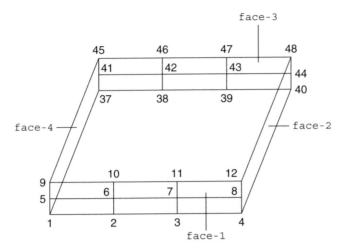

Figure 11.24 Creation of a mesh from a boundary representation: Steps 1,2. Creation of nodes on opposite faces

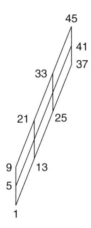

Figure 11.25 Creation of a mesh from a boundary representation (continued): Step 3. Creation of nodes along lines connecting nodes on opposite faces

- Insert nodes and elements in `block-2` as in step 2. Nodes from 49 to 96 are created (Figure 11.26).

Step 4

- Define a hidden face, `face-15`, consisting of nodes on the upper layer of `block-1`. Define another hidden face, `face-16`, consisting of nodes on the lower layer of `block-2`.
- Define a tetrahedral block, `block-3`, consisting of faces `face-5`, `face-6`, `face-7` and `face-8`; `face-15` and `face-16` are at the bottom and top of this block.
- Insert nodes and elements in `block-3` by mapping nodes on `face-15` to corresponding nodes on `face-16` (Figure 11.27).

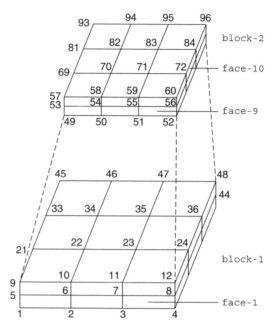

Figure 11.26 Creation of a mesh from a boundary representation (continued): Step 4. Creation of nodes from 49 to 96

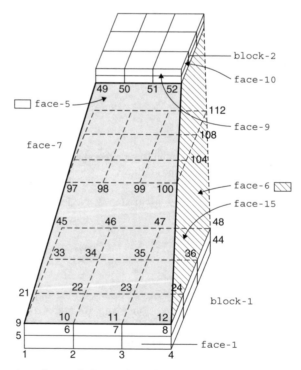

Figure 11.27 Creation of a mesh from a boundary representation (continued): Step 5. Creation of nodes from 97 to 144

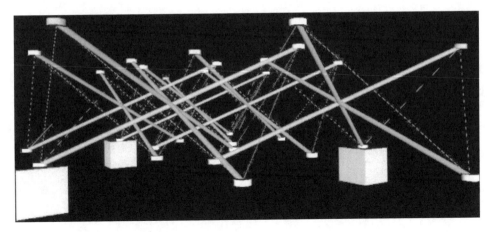

Figure 11.28   A 3D view of a tensegrity structure described in Chapter 10

In the above steps, a solid model similar to that used in CSG is implicitly created from the boundary representation. This procedure could be automated through algorithms that determine which faces might be combined to create regular-shaped regions.

11.5.2   3D Graphical View of a Structure

An important application of geometrical modelling is in computer graphics. Figure 11.28 is a 3D view of the tensegrity structure in Chapter 10. It was generated using a graphics package that uses a 3D geometric model.

11.6   SUMMARY

- Geometric modelling involves representing the geometry of physical objects.
- Geometrical models are used in visualization, computer-aided design and manufacture, estimation and analysis.
- Many representation schemes are available. These are evaluated using criteria such as accuracy, versatility, uniqueness, operations that may be performed, compactness and efficiency.
- Mathematical representations are used for simple shapes where accuracy is important. More complex shapes are broken up into simpler ones. Equations in parametric form are used to represent curves, surfaces and solids.
- Primitive instancing is used to represent variations of predefined shapes by assigning values to parameters.
- Mesh representations approximate objects into a finite number of regular-shaped elements.
- Sweep representations are often used when axial symmetry is present.
- Boundary representations permit efficient processing of shapes for visualization.
- Solids are composed of partially and fully occupied cells in decomposition models. Decomposition models facilitate modification of shapes through Boolean operations.

12
Computer Graphics

12.1   INTRODUCTION

Computer graphics is a branch of computer science that deals with the theory and technology of computerized image synthesis. While all applications of computer-aided engineering (CAE), require some form of computer graphics, the most demanding fields are computer-aided design (CAD), and scientific visualization. In CAD the principal goal is to produce the most realistic image of the product at all design stages and from all design perspectives. For example, the design of a new aircraft would result in thousands of computer graphics images, and these images would vary greatly depending on whether they were intended for electrical engineers, mechanical engineers or structural engineers.

Computer-aided drafting has slowly replaced manual drafting in engineering design, mainly because it is easier to make modifications. This means it is essential for engineers to understand the basics of computer graphics.

The principal goal of scientific visualization is to present data to engineers in the format they find most understandable. Data include results of studies such as numerical simulations and experimental programs. Good visualization software helps to develop insights about data that would not have been possible otherwise.

Other demanding uses of computer graphics include advanced computing applications in areas of diagnosis, control, task planning and facility management. Abductive tasks that are carried out in open worlds (Chapter 1) often require intermediate representations so that engineers are able to introduce new information. Good computer graphics may facilitate engineer–computer interaction, identify feasible solution spaces, and assist the search for the best solutions. Finally, computer images that are realistic and that increase understanding have the potential to provide support for engineering creativity.

This chapter gives a brief description of the key mechanisms in computer graphics. It describes the sequence of steps that transform a geometric model into an image on a display device. The last section provides a strategy for developing software that does not require specific knowledge of input devices.

12.2   TASKS OF COMPUTER GRAPHICS

A method for modelling the geometry of the building in Figure 12.1 was discussed in Chapter 11. Having modelled the building, what is required to display it on a computer screen? Display involves tasks such as

Fundamentals of Computer-Aided Engineering   B. Raphael and I. F. C. Smith
© 2003 John Wiley & Sons, Ltd   ISBNs: 0-471-48709-0 (HB); 0-471-48715-5 (PB)

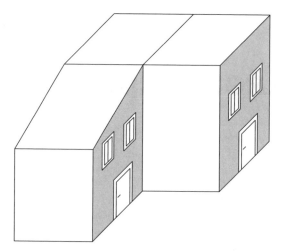

Figure 12.1   A building with a simple geometry

- fixing orientation and perspective parameters (called viewpoint parameters);
- removal of hidden lines and surfaces;
- projection of the three-dimensional shape of the building onto two dimensions;
- discretization of continuous curves and lines into points of finite sizes to be shown on the computer screen.

Computer graphics is the area of computer science that deals with the theory and application of these operations.

12.3   DISPLAY DEVICES

While geometric modelling techniques (Chapter 11) permit accurate representations of real objects, hardware technology is capable of displaying only primitive objects such as points and straight lines. Transformations are required from higher-level geometric models to forms that display devices are able to manipulate. Even if hardware devices were able to display higher-level geometric representations directly, composing these representations into images of complex engineering objects would require similar transformations. Characteristics of display devices influence mechanisms that are associated with these transformations; we now look at two types of display device.

12.3.1   Types of Display Device

There are two main types of display device, raster and vector. Raster devices are based on traditional television technology. A raster display is a two-dimensional matrix of light sources (Figure 12.2). Each light source is called a pixel and it can be turned on or off through sending appropriate electrical signals to the device. More precisely, the state of each pixel is defined by the colour of the light it emits. A black colour indicates the

Figure 12.2   Images are represented in raster devices as matrices of points called pixels. Each pixel is turned on or off or set to different colors in order to produce images

Figure 12.3   Images are represented in vector devices as a series of straight lines

pixel is turned off. In general, the colour of a pixel is composed of the components red, green and blue. The computer's video memory stores the pixel values of the display area. This memory is scanned several times a second to refresh the display. Low-level graphics routines change the contents of the video memory to modify the display.

Vector devices draw straight lines instead of individual pixels (Figure 12.3). Instead of storing the state of each pixel, they maintain a list of line segments to be drawn. The display list memory limits the number of line segments that may be viewed simultaneously. In vector displays, an electron beam moves from the beginning of a line to the end, producing a line on the screen. Oscilloscopes are used to display output from analogue devices; they are examples of vector displays. Traditional pen plotters also use vector technology for producing graphical output.

12.3.2   *From Geometrical Representations to Graphical Displays*

Since display devices are capable of drawing only straight lines or points in two dimensions, all geometric data have to be converted to this form. Since most displays are of raster type, pixel-based representations are particularly important. The process of converting higher-level representations to device-level representations involves a sequence of steps known as the graphics pipeline. This is explained in Section 12.5, following a discussion of graphical representation.

12.4   REPRESENTING GRAPHICS

Graphical representations should be

- as device-independent as practicable so that the same representation can be used on different types of device;
- close to device-level representations so that images are displayed rapidly.

These requirements are conflicting, so trade-offs will have to be made. For example, devices differ with respect to characteristics such as resolution (the number of pixels per unit length), the position of the origin of the coordinate system, and the number of possible colours. Such device-dependent characteristics should be avoided in the representation. However, if graphics primitives are stored in terms of coordinate systems that correspond to the application (instead of device coordinates), it might be computationally intensive to process them for display. Graphical file formats are part of a trade-off resulting from these conflicting requirements. Three aspects of graphical representations are colours, coordinate system and primitives. These are described below for the case of raster devices.

12.4.1   Representing Colours

If display devices are not capable of showing multiple colours (monochrome devices), only two values are possible for each pixel. By convention, 1 indicates white and 0 indicates black. This representation is compact since a single bit is sufficient for each pixel.

Colour devices require more storage space than monochrome devices. Since each pixel might have a different colour, more than two values are possible for each pixel. There are two schemes that are used for representing colours; they are the indexed colour scheme and the RGB (red, green, blue) scheme.

In the indexed colour scheme, each colour is given an index. For example, the index 1 might be defined as red, 2 as green, 3 as blue, etc. If a single byte (8 bits) is used to store one pixel value, 256 indexed colours are possible.

In the RGB model, different colours are obtained by combining the values of the basic colours: red, green and blue. Arithmetic performed using the RGB colour model produces the right effect of mixing colours similar to mixing light of different colours. If 1 byte is used to represent each colour component, a pixel requires 3 bytes. The first byte represents the level of red in the given colour, the second byte represents the level of green, and the third byte represents the level of blue. Some 16.8 million (2^{24}) colours are obtained by specifying different values of red green and blue.

In addition to the basic colours, it might be necessary to store information related to the brightness so as to produce a realistic view of a physical object. There are display devices that can produce different levels of brightness for the same colour. The level of brightness (or intensity) is known as the gamma value. An extra byte might be used to store the gamma value. Although these data may not be useful on a printer, they might be used to enhance the display on an electronic display device.

Another related concept is transparency. We are able to see through certain materials. In computer graphics if we place a transparent object above another object, we should be able to view the object underneath. The level of transparency is called the alpha value. In transparency-supported image formats, usually a single byte is used to store the alpha value. Then 0 indicates a completely opaque pixel and 255 (the highest number represented by 8 bits) indicates complete transparency.

12.4.2   Coordinate System

In engineering we use a right-handed coordinate system (Figure 12.4). In two dimensions the origin is at the bottom left corner. The value of x increases to the right, and the

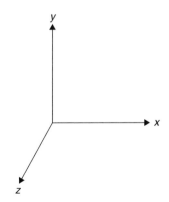

Figure 12.4 A "right-handed" coordinate system used in engineering

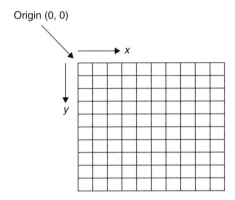

Figure 12.5 The coordinate system of a display device

value of y increases to the top. Unfortunately, most computer devices have their origin at the top left corner (Figure 12.5). The x-coordinate increases from left to right, and the y-coordinate from top to bottom. In the past, this has been confusing to engineers using graphics software that was developed by computer scientists.

Another major difference between reality and device coordinates (coordinate systems used by devices) is that the coordinates are integers and not real numbers. This requires transformation from world coordinates (coordinates that correspond to applications) to device coordinates. The maximum values of x and y on the device depend on the resolution of the device, so appropriate scaling is also necessary. The choice of coordinate system on computers has been dictated by the efficiency of graphical operations. However, for engineering, a graphical representation that employs a right-handed coordinate system in the real number space is most appropriate.

12.4.3 Bitmap Representations

Bitmap representations store pixel values sequentially. The number of bits used to represent a pixel depends on the number of possible colours and whether alpha and gamma values are stored. Two-dimensional bitmaps and their variants are most widely used. It is extremely fast to display bitmapped images since this mainly involves copying bytes to the video memory of the computer.

Bitmaps have several drawbacks. They take too much memory since every pixel value is stored. Information related to primitives such as lines and curves is lost when converted to pixels. It is difficult to identify and delete a straight line from a bitmap. Furthermore, when bitmaps are changed in size, curved edges are distorted. Smoothing algorithms are used to prevent such distortions.

12.4.4 Higher-Level Representations

If higher-level primitives, such as lines and curves, are stored in a graphics representation, operations such as translations and rotations of objects within an image can be carried out easily. This is essential for engineering applications where changes are often frequent.

Higher-level graphics representations are mostly defined in a declarative manner. They contain 'what is' information rather than 'how to' information. They do not specify how to draw the objects, but they do specify the objects' properties. For example, the texture of a surface might be specified as a set of values. The graphics software determines how the texture is rendered on a display device.

Higher-level representations can be generic, application-specific or hybrid. Generic representations (used by drafting packages) usually involve only mathematical shapes such as lines and curves. These can be used by all applications. Application-specific representations involve objects that are custom-made for a particular use. Objects are parameterized and stored in a similar way to those in geometric models. Graphical information such as luminosity and transparency might be stored in addition to geometric data. The high-level representations are usually device-independent and require a number of transformations for display.

12.4.4.1 Generic graphics primitives

Complex graphical objects are a combination of graphics primitives. Here are some standard graphics primitives in two dimensions:

- polylines;
- shapes;
- fill areas;
- markers;
- text.

A polyline is a series of line segments, each starting at the endpoint of the previous one. Circles, ovals, rectangles and Bézier curves are examples of the shape primitive. Fill area refers to a filled shape. Markers are symbols that are used to indicate points. The text primitive is a character string. Figure 12.6 illustrates these primitives. Each primitive has a set of attributes that affect its display. Table 12.1 shows a sample list of attributes for each primitive.

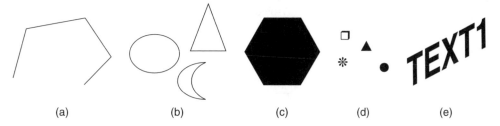

(a)   (b)   (c)   (d)   (e)

Figure 12.6 Graphics primitives: (a) a polyline, (b) shapes, (c) a fill area, (d) markers, (e) text

Table 12.1 Graphics primitives and their attributes

Primitive	Attribute	Meaning
Polyline	Style	Dotted, dashed, plain, etc.
–	Thickness	Thickness of the line
–	Colour	Colour of line
Shape	Same as polyline	–
Fill area	Style	Solid, patterned, etc.
–	Colour	Colour of fill
–	Gradient	Change in colour along each direction
–	Texture	Pattern with which area is filled
Marker	Style	Cross, dot, etc.
–	Colour	Colour of marker
–	Size	Size of the symbol
Text	Typeface	Times Roman, Arial, Courier, etc.
–	Colour	Colour of text
–	Size	Size of text
–	Style	Bold, italic, etc.
–	Inclination	Angle at which text is inclined

12.5 THE GRAPHICS PIPELINE

The sequence of steps involved in converting higher-level representations to device-level representations (usually bitmaps) is known as the graphics pipeline. A simplified graphics pipeline is shown in Figure 12.7. Relevant steps are explained in the following subsections.

12.5.1 Modelling Transformations

Geometric models are usually described by two- or three-dimensional coordinates (x, y, z) in the units of the application. Modelling primitives might be solids, surfaces or curves. There are usually many objects that are composed of these primitives and each object is described using a local coordinate system called the object space.

In the modelling transformation stage, the coordinates of all objects are transformed from their object space to a common coordinate system called the world space or global

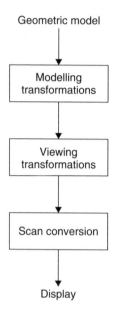

Figure 12.7   A simplified graphics pipeline

coordinate system. During modelling transformations, complete graphical models are composed from individual objects. Important modelling transformations are

- translation;
- rotation;
- scaling;
- skewing (shearing).

12.5.1.1   Translation

Translation is the process of shifting coordinates. The transformation equation is

$$\mathbf{x}^g = \mathbf{x}^l + \mathbf{x}_0$$

where $\mathbf{x}^g$ is a vector containing the global coordinates, $\mathbf{x}^l$ contains coordinates in the object space and $\mathbf{x}_0$ contains the origin of the object space with respect to the global coordinate system.

Example 12.1

The cross-section of a T-beam consists of two objects, a vertical plate called the web and a horizontal plate called the flange, as shown in Figure 12.8(a). The coordinates of

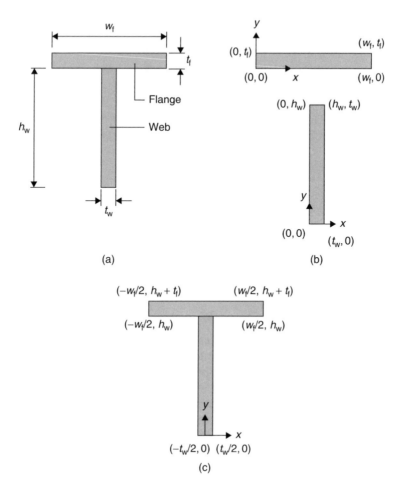

Figure 12.8   Modeling a translation: (a) cross-section of a T-beam, (b) local coordinates of plates, (c) resulting coordinates

both plates in their respective object spaces are shown in Figure 12.8(b). The complete T-beam is composed through the following transformations:

- Translate the flange by a distance $-w_f/2$ along the x-axis and h_w along the y-axis.
- Translate the web by a distance $-t_w/2$ along the x-axis.

The resulting coordinates are shown in Figure 12.8(c). The origin of the global coordinates is chosen to be at the middle of the web in order to preserve symmetry about the y-axis. Describing objects in their local coordinate systems (also known as their natural coordinate system) is convenient and easy to understand since these descriptions do not depend on the relative positions of other objects. Such coordinates are easily transformed into global coordinates.

12.5.1.2 Rotation

Rotational transformation involves the following matrix equations:

$$\begin{bmatrix} x^g \\ y^g \end{bmatrix} = \begin{bmatrix} \cos\theta & -\sin\theta \\ \sin\theta & \cos\theta \end{bmatrix} \begin{bmatrix} x^l \\ y^l \end{bmatrix} \qquad (12.1)$$

Where x^g, y^g are the global coordinates obtained by rotating the object through an angle θ about the local coordinate system that is denoted by the superscript l.

Example 12.2

The body of a vehicle is schematically represented as two circles and a rectangle (Figure 12.9). The rectangle has dimensions (l, t) and the circles are of diameter d. When the vehicle is moving along a slope of angle θ, what are the coordinates of the rectangle and the circles?

The local coordinates of the rectangle are $(0, 0)$, $(l, 0)$, (l, t) and $(0, t)$. Through rotational transformation about the bottom left corner of the rectangle, the global coordinates are

$$(0, 0)$$

$$(l\cos\theta, l\sin\theta)$$

$$(l\cos\theta - t\sin\theta, l\sin\theta + t\cos\theta)$$

$$(-t\sin\theta, t\cos\theta)$$

The coordinates of the centres of the circles are calculated in a similar way.

12.5.1.3 Scaling

Objects might be described in different units, so they need to be scaled during the composition. The scaling transformation is defined by

$$\begin{bmatrix} x^g \\ y^g \end{bmatrix} = \begin{bmatrix} s_x & 0 \\ 0 & s_y \end{bmatrix} \begin{bmatrix} x^l \\ y^l \end{bmatrix},$$

where s_x and s_y are the scale factors in the x and y directions, respectively.

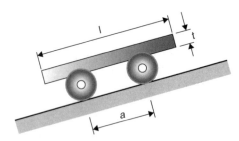

Figure 12.9 Schematic representation of a vehicle moving along a slope

12.5.1.4   Skewing or shearing

The shearing transformation deforms an object (Figure 12.10). An example of the shearing transformation along the x-axis is

$$\begin{bmatrix} x^g \\ y^g \end{bmatrix} = \begin{bmatrix} x^l + sy^l \\ y^l \end{bmatrix},$$ (12.2)

where s is the shearing constant. In general, shearing involves modifying coordinates along a direction by adding a linear combination of the values of coordinates in the other directions.

12.5.2   Viewing Transformations

Viewing transformations involve transformations of object coordinates according to users' viewing parameters. Two important viewing parameters are eye position and viewing angle. Transformations from three dimensions to two dimensions are carried out at this stage.

12.5.2.1   3D-to-2D transformations

Two commonly used projection techniques are parallel and perspective. Figure 12.11 shows a cube displayed after parallel projection. Figure 12.12 shows the same cube

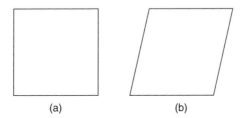

(a)   (b)

Figure 12.10   Shearing transformation: (a) a cube, (b) the cube after shearing

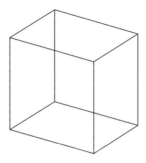

Figure 12.11   Parallel projection

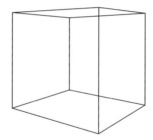

Figure 12.12 Perspective projection

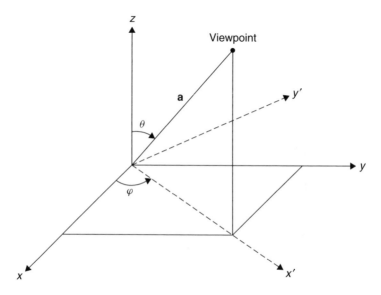

Figure 12.13 Parallel projection: Rotation 1

displayed after perspective projection. In parallel projections, lines that are parallel in the original object remain parallel after projection. In perspective projections, the sizes of objects reduce with distance from the viewpoint and parallel lines do not remain parallel.

To explain the method of parallel projection, let **a** be a vector from the origin of the coordinate system to the viewpoint (Figure 12.13). Let P be a plane perpendicular to **a** passing through the origin. The original coordinate axes are rotated such that the new z-axis coincides with **a**, and the new xz plane lies along the plane defined be **a** and the original z-axis. This is done through two rotations. First, the x and y axes are rotated about z through an angle φ, as shown in Figure 12.13. The resulting coordinate axes are x', y' and z.

Next the z and x' axes are rotated by an angle θ, about y' in the vertical plane defined by the z and x' axes (Figure 12.14). The resulting coordinates are x'' and z''. All the points of the objects to be drawn are projected onto the plane $x''y'$. That is, the z''

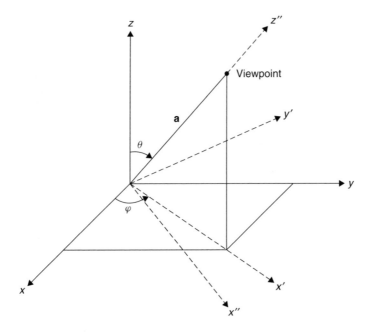

Figure 12.14   Parallel projection: Rotation 2

coordinate is ignored and the coordinates x'' and y' are plotted on the screen. The complete transformation matrix is defined below; it is obtained by multiplying the transformation matrices of the individual rotations:

$$\begin{bmatrix} x'' \\ y' \\ z'' \end{bmatrix} = \begin{bmatrix} \cos\theta\cos\varphi & -\cos\theta\sin\varphi & -\sin\theta \\ \sin\varphi & \cos\varphi & 0 \\ \sin\theta\cos\varphi & -\sin\theta\sin\varphi & \cos\theta \end{bmatrix} \begin{bmatrix} x \\ y \\ z \end{bmatrix}$$

12.5.2.2   Window-to-viewport transformations

Entire world spaces are rarely displayed on screens. It is usually necessary to view a part of the world space in order to carry out engineering tasks. This is carried out through window-to-viewport transformations. In computer graphics, a window refers to an area in the world space that is selected for viewing; a viewport refers to an area on the screen where the window is displayed. Window-to-viewport transformation maps the points in the window to those in the viewport (Figure 12.15).

Usually the transformation from window to viewport is defined using an intermediate coordinate system called the normalized device coordinate (NDC), which takes values from 0.0 to 1.0. NDC is used to specify coordinates in a device-independent manner. For example, if a picture is to be drawn on a device with a 10% margin on the left and right, the viewport coordinates are specified as 0.1 and 0.9 in the x-direction. Without NDC, viewport parameters need to be specified in device coordinates (pixels). Applications should be independent of the characteristics of devices such as the screen size and resolution.

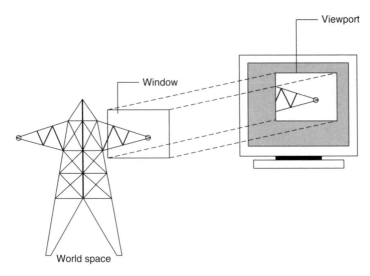

Figure 12.15   Window to viewport transformation

Transformation equations

Let (x_{min}, y_{min}), (x_{max}, y_{max}) be the coordinates of the window and (vx_{min}, vx_{max}), (vy_{min}, vy_{max}) be the coordinates of the viewport (Figure 12.16). A point (x, y) in the world coordinates is converted to a point (vx, vy) in the viewport coordinates using the following equations:

$$vx = \frac{x - x_{min}}{x_{max} - x_{min}}(vx_{max} - vx_{min}) + vx_{min}$$

$$vy = \frac{y - y_{min}}{y_{max} - y_{min}}(vy_{max} - vy_{min}) + vy_{min} \qquad (12.3)$$

Preserving aspect ratio during window-to-viewport transformations

When the aspect ratios of windows and viewports are not the same, the application of (12.3) results in distortion. Squares appear as rectangles and circles appear as ovals. To

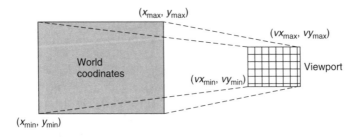

Figure 12.16   Window to viewport transformation

prevent this effect, the ratio of width to height should be the same for the window and the viewport.

Example 12.3

A house is shown in Figure 12.17(a). It has to be displayed on the top right corner of a display device of resolution 800 pixels × 600 pixels, as in Figure 12.17(b). What are the necessary window and viewport settings? If the same window and viewport settings are used on a display device of resolution 1280 × 1024, where will the image appear?

Solution

The total width and height of the object are 6.6 m. and 4.2 m, therefore the window coordinates (x_{min}, y_{min}), (x_{max}, y_{max}) are (0, 0), (6.6, 4.2). The ratio of width to height is $6.6/4.2 = 1.57$. Since only one quadrant of the screen is available for display, the maximum width and height of the display area are 400 and 300 pixels, respectively. Leaving a margin of 20 pixels on all sides, the size of the display area is chosen as 360 pixels × 260 pixels. To preserve the aspect ratio, the height is modified using the aspect ratio of the window coordinates. That is, dividing 360 by 1.57 gives the height of the display area as 230 pixels. To vertically centre the image on the display area, the margin on the top and bottom are increased to $(300 - 230)/2 = 35$ pixels. Since the top left corner is the origin of device coordinates, the viewport coordinates are set equal to (420, 35), (780, 265). Figure 12.18 shows the appearance of the image with these window and viewport settings on a device of higher resolution.

12.5.2.3   Other transformations

Modern graphics software provides a rich set of viewing transformations. These include hidden line and surface removal (Figure 12.19), culling, lighting and shading (Figure 12.20), and texturing. Details are found in textbooks on computer graphics.

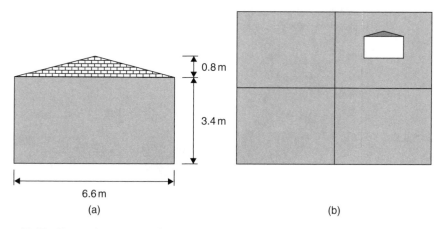

0.8 m

3.4 m

6.6 m

(a)

(b)

Figure 12.17   Preserving aspect ratio in window-viewport transformation: (a) elevation of a house, (b) a display device

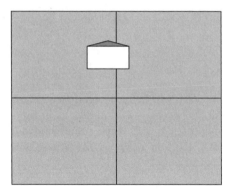

Figure 12.18 Application of the window-viewport settings used in Figure 12.17 to a device of higher resolution

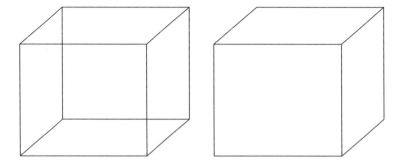

Figure 12.19 Illustration of hidden line removal

Figure 12.20 Illustration of lighting and shading

12.5.3 Scan Conversion

In the scan conversion stage, also known as rasterization, we convert primitives into pixels. It is the process of determining which pixels to illuminate to draw various shapes. It involves approximating infinitely thin mathematical points to finite-sized pixels on display devices. This process needs to be efficient and should not involve an excessive amount of floating-point computations to produce a good display.

Consider this algorithm for the scan conversion of lines, known as Bresenham's line-drawing algorithm. Figure 12.21 shows how to draw the line using pixels, here denoted by dots. The scan conversion algorithm determines which pixels to illuminate in order to show the line such that there is a continuous appearance with uniform thickness. The line starts from the point (x_0, y_0) and ends at (x_1, y_1). The slope of the line is given by

$$m = \frac{dy}{dx}$$

where

$$dy = y_1 - y_0$$

and

$$dx = x_1 - x_0$$

Since x and y are integers, there are multiple values of x for the same value of y when the slope is less than 1 (Figure 12.21). However, there is only a single value of x for a given value of y. When the slope is more than one, the condition is reversed: there is a single value of x for a given value of y. This condition is treated through interchanging the x and y coordinates. In the following discussion it is assumed that the slope is less than one. Here are the key parts:

- Assign the starting value of y to be y_0.
- Repeat for values of x from x_0 to x_1:

  - Increment the value of y by 1 if the condition $m \times ix \geq 1$ is satisfied, where ix is the total increment in x since the last change in the value of y.

- Turn on the pixel at the point (x, y).

Since operations on integers are faster than operations on real numbers, the condition $m \times ix \geq 1$ for incrementing the value of y is converted into an integer expression by

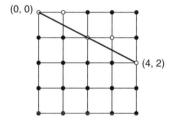

Figure 12.21   Scan converting a line. Approximating a continuous line to a set of pixels

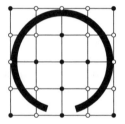

Figure 12.22   Scan converting fill area

multiplying both sides by dx. The condition then becomes $dy \times ix \geq dx$. In computer implementations this condition is further modified to avoid truncation errors.

In Figure 12.21 $dx = 4$ and $dy = 2$, so $dy \times ix$ is equal to dx when $ix = 2$. Therefore the value of y is incremented after every two increments in the value of x.

Scan conversion of fill area is more complex. Figure 12.22 shows an open tubular section used in the construction of aircraft components. It reveals obvious difficulties with scan conversion. First of all, reasonable approximation of the original shape is not possible with low resolution. Secondly, it is difficult to determine whether a point lies within the shape or outside the shape when the area is non-convex. Details on scan conversion of fill areas can be found in specialized textbooks about computer graphics.

12.6   INTERACTIVE GRAPHICS

Good engineering software allows for good user interaction. Graphics is not used for visualization only. It permits users to interact with objects. An essential requirement is graphical input. One of the most significant developments in interactive graphics has been the development of a pointer device to locate points on a graphical display. Today graphical input devices include light pens, mouse pads and touch screens.

Since new devices are always emerging, there is a need to develop applications that do not require knowledge of specific types of input device. Applications need to work without changing the code when new input devices are developed. This need leads to the concept of logical input devices. A logical device is a model of an input device for performing a specific task. These are mapped to physical devices that exist on the computer. Applications are developed for logical devices and they are automatically mapped to physical devices by graphics libraries. Examples of logical input devices are

- locator;
- pick;
- valuator;
- text input;
- choice.

A locator is a device to input a point on the screen. A mouse is a physical device that belongs to this category. A pick is a device that locates an object on the screen. Whereas the locator returns a point in (x, y) coordinates, a pick returns a reference to an object selected by the user. A valuator is a device for inputting a number. Keyboards and thumbwheels are examples. Text input refers to a device that allows users to enter a string. Keyboards and microphones are physical devices that allow text input. A choice is a device used to make a selection from a list of options. Menus and checklists are special cases of choice input.

Logical input devices are useful for developing applications that do not rely on the characteristics of specific input devices. This concept has considerably increased the useful lifespan of software. If a graphics tool provides options to manipulate physical devices directly, these options should be avoided whenever possible.

12.7 SUMMARY

- Graphics capabilities are limited largely by hardware. Limitations of hardware dictate how objects are displayed on devices.

- There is a wide spectrum of schemes for representing graphics. Low-level representations permit fast display since they require less transformation to data forms required by devices. But they do not usually permit easy modifications to images. Higher-level representations require a sequence of transformations for generating graphical output.

- Geometric models are input to computer graphics. Engineers need graphics tools that allow them to manipulate geometric models rather than low-level representations.

- The sequence of steps involved in converting high-level representations to device-level representations (usually bitmaps) is known as the graphics pipeline. An understanding of the steps involved in the graphics pipeline is necessary to develop high-quality graphics.

- Interactive graphics permit development of useful applications that increase the capacity of engineers to carry out complex tasks. The concept of logical input devices is important for increasing the useful life of software.

FURTHER READING

Foley, J. D., Dam, A. V., Feiner, S. K. and Hughes, J. F. 1993. *Introduction to Computer Graphics*. Reading MA: Addison-Wesley.
Xiang, Z. and Plastock, R. A. 2000. *Theory and Problems of Computer Graphics*. New York: McGraw-Hill.

13

Distributed Applications and the Web

13.1 INTRODUCTION

Complex computer-aided engineering (CAE) tasks are rarely performed on one computer. Important information sources, such as databases that provide information related to material properties, costs, availability and delivery times are usually geographically separated. Furthermore, it is rarely justifiable to carry out all computations on one machine, since this precludes opportunities for improving performance through sharing tasks and for reducing the impact of hardware failure.

In spite of these clear advantages, distributed applications were not implemented when computers first became available. In the beginning, computers from different manufacturers could not communicate with one another. There were few physical links between computers, no generally accepted data transfer protocols and no easy framework for linking documents. The best way to transfer information from one computer to another was by copying information from one machine onto floppy disks and then inserting them into the floppy disk drive of another machine. Even then, there were compatibility problems related to document formats, especially when the operating systems were not the same.

It was cumbersome to transfer information using floppy disks. Large files could not easily be transferred. Document exchange was time-consuming and this made them inappropriate for information that was often subject to change. Collaborative engineering using computers was indeed limited. Furthermore, software upgrades required tedious interventions at each and every machine.

The development of the Internet and local area networks (LANs) provided many opportunities. Network protocols such as TCP/IP (Transmission Control Protocol/Internet Protocol) facilitated transfer of documents. The advent of the World Wide Web (WWW) is an important milestone for distributed systems. The mixture of textual links between and within documents significantly reduced difficulties associated with machine compatibility. In many practical situations, interoperability between heterogeneous hardware and software platforms became feasible for the first time.

As with most technological advances, these developments offer opportunities as well as risks. This chapter describes several examples. The client-server (C/S) architecture, as exemplified by the Web, is the most widespread approach to distributed computing. This architecture introduces complications that do not exist in non-distributed computing.

Fundamentals of Computer-Aided Engineering   B. Raphael and I. F. C. Smith
© 2003 John Wiley & Sons, Ltd   ISBNs: 0-471-48709-0 (HB); 0-471-48715-5 (PB)

Other architectures, such as peer-to-peer configurations, have also had much success in selected applications and these are described briefly. Concepts in this chapter are illustrated through examples in collaborative design, information publishing and project management. All of these areas have tremendous potential for improved performance through judicious application of computer-aided engineering.

13.1.1   A Simple Example of a Client-Server System

A construction firm is involved in the task of estimating the cost of construction of residential buildings. Employees of the firm use a program to estimate these costs. The program uses this formula:

$$\text{cost estimate} = (\text{total plan area}) \times (\text{the average cost per unit area})$$

In the initial version of the program, this formula is hard coded–written into the program itself.

Users input the plan area of the building and the program computes the estimate by multiplying it with the average cost per area. The average cost per unit area is also stored in the program. This leads to cumbersome maintenance. Whenever the company wants to update the average cost per unit area, the program needs to be recompiled and reinstalled on all the machines. After networking all its computers, the company has a better idea. The average cost per unit area used in the estimation shall be stored in a data file on a central computer. Programs running on multiple machines read this file through the network and use it in the computation. This avoids the need to reinstall the program each time the average cost per unit area is changed.

Although this new feature is an improvement, there remain some cumbersome aspects. For example, the company decides to use a more sophisticated method for computing the estimate. The formula used in the estimation program is too simple and is replaced by a formula that includes more variables. Once again, the program has to be recompiled and reinstalled on all the machines within the organization. After a few updates and inevitable problems due to version mismatches, the company realizes it needs a better software architecture. The solution it identifies is a client-server system.

Instead of a single program, the application is now split into two different parts: a client program which interacts with the user, and a server program which performs the computation. The client is installed on every machine, whereas the server program, which performs the computations, is installed on only one machine.

Since the procedure for computing the estimate is contained only in the server program, whenever the computation logic changes, only one machine needs to be updated. The client programs continue to execute exactly in the same manner on every machine. However, they provide new results to the user because of the changes to the server program. This system of client and server working together makes updates simple and easy to implement.

The architecture of the new program is shown in Figure 13.1. The client program takes input from the user and sends a request to the server to compute the construction cost. It sends the plan area of the building and other details that are needed by the server. The server program performs the computation and sends back the result to the client program.

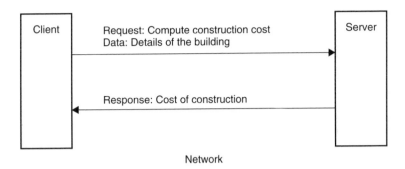

Figure 13.1   An example of message passing between client and server

13.1.2 Definitions

- *Processes and programs*:   to understand the client-server architecture, it is necessary to distinguish between a program and a process. The term 'program' refers to an executable file whereas the term 'process' refers to an instance of the program in execution. A programmer might write a C program called `compute.c` and compile it into an executable program `compute.exe`. The file `compute.exe` is an executable program. When the program is executed, a process is created in the working memory of the computer. Multiple processes can be created by executing the program several times and this leads to multiple instances of a program in execution at the same time. The term 'program code', or simply 'code', will be used in this chapter to denote statements and procedures as well as declarations of variables, classes and objects.

- *Client*:   a client is a process that sends requests over the network to a server to obtain a service.

- *Server*:   a server is a process that receives requests from clients and services them by performing required computations and operations, returning any results to the client.

- *Service*:   a service could be any specialist task, such as computing an estimate of construction costs for residential buildings.

- *Middleware*:   a middleware item is a software component that exists between the client and the server and allows them to interact.

- *Client-server (C/S)*:   this is an approach to application design that decomposes application functionality into two distinct components, the client and the server. These components work together over a network (Figure 13.2).

13.1.3 Trends Driving C/S Architecture

There are several reasons for the widespread use of client-server programs. Here are some trends that have driven the use of client-server systems:

- *Downsizing* is the downward migration of applications from super minis and mainframes to the desktop. Users like to work on their personal computers and they like

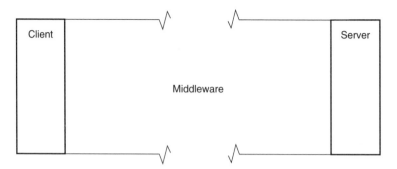

Figure 13.2 Separation of computation into client and server parts

to have easy access to information that was traditionally stored on mainframes and super minis.

- *Upsizing* is the networking of stand-alone desktop computers; it creates a need to store huge amounts of information and to make it accessible by everyone.

- *Rightsizing* means moving applications to the most appropriate platform. Not all applications are suitable for all platforms.

13.1.3.1 Downsizing

In the past, computers were expensive, so organizations wanted to make maximum use of the central processor (CPU). It was important that the CPU never remained idle. The solution was to execute all the programs on a single computer within an organization. People submitted their programs to the central computer and collected the output after execution had completed. Not much CPU time was wasted interacting with the user. This mode of operation is known as batch processing.

As computers became less expensive, wastage of CPU time no longer became an issue, and users wanted programs to be more interactive. They wanted to modify programs and data interactively. User productivity improved through better interaction with computers. People no longer had to wait for long hours to see the results of their programs. They could quickly correct any mistakes and immediately see the results. Employees wanted personal computers that could be used with greater freedom.

13.1.3.2 Upsizing

The proliferation of personal computers leads to difficulties within organizations. There is a need to store data in a central place and share this data with multiple users. One solution is computer networks. Networking enables people to use the resources stored on other computers. For example, it is not necessary to install every application on every computer. Instead it is possible to execute programs that are installed on other computers through the network. In this way, storage requirements on individual computers are considerably reduced.

13.1.3.3   Rightsizing

Not every application is suitable for every platform. Desktop computers are suitable for delivery of graphical user interfaces (GUIs) that are custom-made for the application. But they are not suitable for heavy numerical computations because they do not have enough computing power. It is better to move applications to the most appropriate platform. This involves splitting the application functionality into different parts and implementing them on multiple platforms. For example, systems that manage inspection and maintenance activities of bridges are implemented such that the GUI runs on desktop computers whereas data is stored on more powerful server machines.

13.2   EXAMPLES OF CLIENT-SERVER APPLICATIONS

There are several client-server applications that are in wide use. Some are described in the following subsections. They serve as case studies for understanding client-server architectures and are potential models for developing client-server applications in engineering.

13.2.1   File Servers

File servers are used for common storage of files to be accessed from multiple machines. A traditional file server is a process that listens to requests from clients for manipulating the file system (Figure 13.3). Currently, file servers are integrated into operating systems and therefore users do not perceive them to be separate processes. When a user accesses a file over the network, the file manager running on the local machine acts as the client and the operating system running on the remote machine acts as the server.

13.2.2   FTP Servers

An FTP (File Transfer Protocol) client is a common application, especially in the Unix environment. FTP servers perform functions similar to file servers. An FTP client running

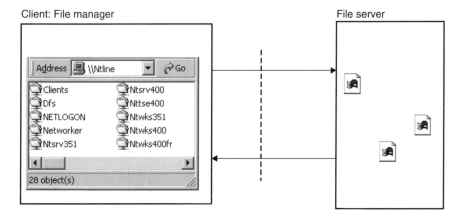

Figure 13.3   A client-server application

on the local machine communicates with an FTP server running on the remote machine. The client sends requests for operations such as `get`, `put` and `delete`. These operations are carried out by the server.

13.2.3 Database Servers

Database servers perform database management operations. Database servers are usually processes running on remote machines that listen to requests from clients. In the case of relational database management systems (DBMS) requests are normally SQL statements to be executed by the server (Chapter 5) and the resulting relations (tables) are returned to the clients for display or further local processing.

13.2.4 Groupware Servers

Groupware servers are used to exchange unstructured information such as documents and electronic mail. For example, a mail browser (client) may connect to a groupware server to send a message to another user. Groupware applications have advanced beyond sending electronic messages and now automate several tasks in workflow management, such as scheduling meetings and processing forms related to project planning.

13.2.5 Object Servers

Object servers enable communication between distributed objects. Objects are created on multiple machines and they need to interoperate over the network. Object servers facilitate this interoperability. Servers make remote objects accessible to client processes as if they were stored locally.

13.2.6 Operating System Servers

Operating system (OS) servers perform tasks related to the operating system. Clients are usually processes that interact with users for manipulating files and processes. An illustrative example is the use of a terminal emulator (Figure 13.4).

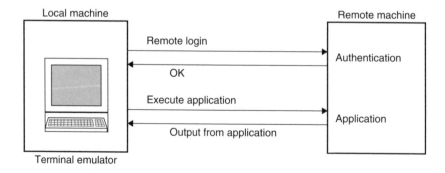

Figure 13.4 Functioning of operating system servers

A terminal emulator is a program that emulates the terminal functioning of a remote machine. The user receives the impression that he or she is working directly on the remote machine, whereas actually the terminal emulator program is producing output that resembles the workings of the terminal. Users are able to log in remotely and execute programs on the remote machine through the terminal emulator. Terminal emulators connect to operating system servers on behalf of users. The commands typed in by users are submitted to the operating system and the results are displayed on users' machines.

13.2.7 Display Servers

Display servers are an interesting application of C/S technology. They were inspired by the need for operating systems to execute graphical programs through remote login (Figure 13.5).

A common example involves a user who connects to a Unix server using a text-based terminal emulator. The user executes a program that creates graphical windows. The terminal emulator is usually capable of displaying only text output. Any graphics produced by the program are only displayed on the screen of the remote machine. In order to obtain graphics on the screen of the local machine, the program running on the remote machine needs to send a request to the local machine. This is possible only if there is a process running on the local machine for servicing these requests. The process that accepts requests to produce graphics on the local machine is called the display server. In the case of the display server, the roles of client and server are reversed. The display server runs on the local machine whereas the client (the graphics program) runs on the remote machine.

13.2.8 Web Servers

With the exponential growth of the World Wide Web (WWW), the terms 'web browser' and 'web server' have become widely known. Perhaps less familiar is the idea that the Web conforms to the classical client-server architecture. The web browser is the client and the web server is the server. The browser sends requests for files to the web server. The web server supplies the files requested by the browser. Browsers usually have a GUI for properly displaying files and letting users interact with them. More details are given in Section 13.7.

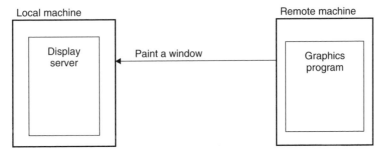

Figure 13.5 A display server

13.2.9   *Application Servers*

Application servers perform custom applications developed for specific requirements. An example is the cost computation server discussed earlier.

13.3   *DISTINCTIVE FEATURES OF C/S SYSTEMS*

Client-server systems are a form of distributed computing. There are other forms such as those used in parallel processing machines and machine clusters. Two features that distinguish client-server from other forms of distributed computing are an asymmetrical protocol and a message-based mechanism.

13.3.1   *Asymmetrical Protocol*

The term 'asymmetrical protocol' implies these three properties:

- Clients always initiate the interactions; servers are passive listeners.
- Servers remain alive for a long time; clients are usually short-lived.
- There is usually only one server but multiple clients (Figure 13.6).

This architecture is similar to the model that we follow in shops and restaurants. Shops remain at the same location for a long time, whereas clients come and go. Shop owners

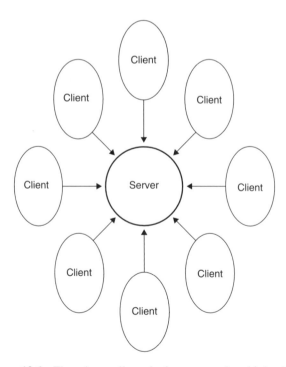

Figure 13.6   There is usually a single server and multiple clients

advertise their products, but it is the client who initiates a transaction by requesting a product or service.

13.3.2 Message-Based Mechanism

Within a conventional stand-alone program, information is exchanged through the computer's main memory. For example, when computing the sum of a set of numbers, a program might make a procedure call and pass the numbers as parameters. The parameters of a procedure are stored at some location within the computer's working memory. The procedure obtains the values of all parameters by reading this memory. The result of the procedure is also returned to the calling function in a similar manner. This approach differs from a C/S program that performs computations by sending messages.

In client-server architectures the calling function might exist on a different computer, therefore parameters cannot be read from a known memory location. Instead the client program prepares a message (request string) describing the operation to be carried out. This message is then passed on to the server program through the network. The server program interprets the message, performs the computation and prepares a response string to be sent to the client.

The client and server programs must agree on a common protocol so that requests and responses are interpreted correctly. The protocol defines the format of messages and responses. A typical message structure is shown in Figure 13.7.

String-based messaging formats are used in many client-server applications, especially on the Web. To appreciate the issues in using such application-level protocols, here are two examples.

Example 13.1

A server program provides a single service–it computes the square root of a number. Design a messaging format for requests and responses.

Message format for the request string

Since the server performs a single operation, it is enough to send only the data without header information. That is, the only data to be sent is the number whose square root needs

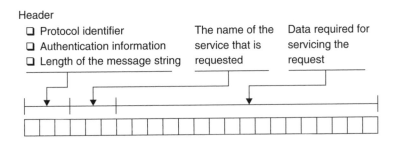

Figure 13.7   A typical message string exchanged between a client and a server

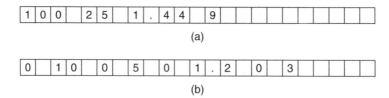

Figure 13.8   An example of messaging format: (a) request string, (b) response string

to be completed. But since the same client might send multiple requests, it is necessary to separate numbers using delimiting characters. Let us use a space as a delimiting character. Thus we have a simple protocol that consists of numbers separated by spaces. A sample string sent from a client to the server appears as shown in Figure 13.8(a). Each number is followed by a space. This is a simple ASCII format and is easy to understand. It is possible to use binary format to compress the volume of data that is exchanged.

Message format for the response string

Initially we might think we could use the same format for the response string—a sequence of numbers separated by spaces—but this format cannot accommodate errors. Suppose the client asks to compute the square root of a negative number, the server should send back an error-code. Therefore, the following format may be used

```
error-code space result space
```

If there is no error then the error-code is set to 0, otherwise the error code is set to 1 and the result is set to 0. Figure 13.8(b) shows the response to the request string in Figure 13.8(a).

Example 13.2

A server program offers two distinct services: (1) computation of the square root, and (2) computation of the average of a set of numbers. Design a messaging format for this application.

Solution

Since the server performs multiple operations, it is no longer possible simply to send the data. A client has to specify three things:

- the service required;
- the length of the data;
- the actual data.

Let us assume that `service-id` uniquely specifies the type of service: 0 indicates computation of the square root, and 1 indicates computation of the average. For the first service, there is only one piece of data, hence the length of the data may be omitted. For the second service, the length of the data needs to be specified. The server reads the request string and performs computation according to the following algorithm:

```
Read service-id
If service-id is zero
   Read a number
   Compute square root
   Send the response
Else if service-id is 1
   Read the length of data
   Read all data
   Compute average
   Send the response
Else
   Send an error message as the response
```

The request format becomes more and more complex as the number of services offered by the server increases. In order to manage this complexity, generic application-level protocols have been developed. Their primary aim is to structure data using formats that are independent of applications, so applications need not be concerned with syntactic details of requests and responses.

13.3.3   Why Are Protocols Important?

Why are protocols important? This question is similar to the question, Why do we need product models? (Chapter 4). Client-server architecture has given rise to open systems in many domains. People and enterprises are launching services that are potentially accessible to everyone. However, this accessibility cannot be achieved unless protocols are published.

For example, consider a server maintained by a government organization to publish rates for subcontract work. Contractors send requests to the server to obtain rates for the type of work that interests them. To use this service, the contractors need to describe the work in terms that the server can understand. If the server requires additional information, it needs to be able to ask for it when it sends back a response. This mode of conversation is defined by the application-level protocol. A poorly designed protocol limits the capabilities of an application. Examples of bad designs are demonstrated by applications such as instant messaging systems.

13.4   CLIENT-SERVER SYSTEM DESIGN

The client-server system is an abstract architecture for distributed computing. In practical applications the main design issue is to decide how to split the application functionality between the client and the server.

The most common C/S architecture used in business applications is where the server performs only data management. All other application functionality is incorporated into the client program. The client program usually has a GUI and performs operations such as accepting data from users, processing data and presenting results. The server is contacted only when data needs to be saved or retrieved. The server is comprised of a DBMS and user-defined stored procedures. This architecture, where data management is separated from the rest of the application, is usually called a two-tier architecture.

Example 13.3   A Two-Tier Cost Computation Program

Suppose we want to convert the cost computation program of Section 13.1.1 into a two-tier architecture. The only data item that is permanently stored is the cost per unit area; this is stored in a database on the server machine. Data for the building to be estimated are input by the user. These data items are used to compute the total plan area. The estimate of cost per unit area is obtained from the server. The returned result is then multiplied by the total plan area to obtain the final result that is presented to the user. Therefore the application functionality is split as follows. The client carries out most of the operations, hence this distribution of tasks is called a fat-client model.

Client

- Input the building data.
- Compute the plan area.
- Obtain the unit cost from the server.
- Compute the cost estimate.
- Display the computed cost to the user.

Server

- Retrieve the unit cost from the database and send it to the client.

13.4.1   Three-Tier Architecture

Applications consist of the following three parts:

- presentation layer;
- data management layer;
- application logic layer.

The presentation layer contains the user interface; this includes methods that process user inputs and display results of computations. The part of the program code that stores and retrieves data belongs to the data management layer. Task-specific knowledge used in computations is stored in the application logic layer.

In conventional stand-alone programs, all three layers are usually intermixed and it is not possible to make a clear separation between the presentation, application logic and data management code. The same function might read user input, check the validity of user input and perform computations. This is an instance of a single-tier application.

In the two-tier architecture, data management is clearly separated from the other two layers. The main advantage is that data is stored and managed in an application-independent manner and could be shared among several programs. For example, the unit cost data is accessible to the cost computation program as well as another program that compares the unit costs of different types of building.

A three-tier architecture is an improvement over the two-tier architecture. In a three-tier architecture all three layers are clearly separated. The presentation layer interacts with the user. This layer does not contain code that depends on the application logic. When needed, the presentation layer communicates to the application logic layer to perform computations according to the needs of the application. The application logic layer does not contain any code related to data storage and retrieval, both of which are handled by the third layer.

This explicit separation between layers improves maintenance reliability. For example, if the GUI needs to be changed, there is no need to modify the code in the other two layers. A user interface that is developed in Visual Basic may be replaced with a web interface without knowing the details of the application logic. A DBMS from a particular vendor might be replaced by another DBMS without affecting the application logic and the user interface.

13.4.2 Application Partitioning

Even when a three-tier architecture is used, the layers need not be physically separated, just logically separated. All three layers could exist only on two machines. This leads to an important design issue: How should the three layers be distributed between the client and server machines? Several models exist; here are some of them:

- The GUI is on the client side. All the other layers are implemented on the server. This option is useful in cases where both the application logic and the data change frequently. Since the application logic and the data are stored centrally, updates are easily made.

- The GUI and a part of the application logic are on the client side. The part of the application logic that is likely to change is on the server. The part of the application logic that is likely to remain unchanged for a long time is incorporated into the client program, so this computation may be performed locally without contacting the server. This architecture reduces the amount of data exchanged between the client and the server. The client program executes faster because there are fewer communication exchanges.

- The GUI is split into two parts: a part that runs independently of the server and a part that interacts with the server. For example, the server decides on the sequence of screens shown to users depending on their profile. The logic related to the navigation in the GUI is updated dynamically through feedback from users or from saved preferences.

- The GUI, the application logic and a part of data management are on the client side. The only data items that are likely to be changed by multiple users are stored on the server side. The data items that are managed locally are typically changed only by the local user. This reduces the extra load on the server, and it improves performance due to fewer data exchanges with the server.

Many other combinations are possible. Client-server design could adopt any of the above patterns. The design task should consider characteristics such as

- whether data is likely to be changed by multiple users, and which items;
- the amount of data that can be exchanged between the client and server in unit time, called the communication bandwidth;
- whether the application logic is likely to be changed frequently;
- the amount of computation time taken for the application of each unit of application logic;
- the number of expected users.

Example 13.4

Consider the two-tier program in Example 13.3. Assume the following data:

- The procedure to compute the cost takes 100 milliseconds (0.1 s) of CPU time.
- This computation is likely to be performed by 100 users per minute.
- Each computation requires 100 bytes of data to be exchanged.
- The network connection from the server can transfer 8 kilobytes of data per second.

Is it a good decision to implement the cost computation logic on the server side?

Solution

Since 100 users perform the computation per minute and each computation takes 0.1 s of CPU time, the total CPU usage is 10 s per minute. So this procedure alone is likely to take 16% of the server's computation capacity. Whether this is justified depends on the other applications that are hosted by the server. From the viewpoint of data transfer, this two-tier solution might be adequate since it requires only 0.16 kilobyte of data transfer per second. This is a simple example that involves a single operation. In practical applications the working scenario is usually very complex, hence it may not be possible to calculate how to partition the application.

13.5 ADVANTAGES OF CLIENT-SERVER SYSTEMS

The advantages of client-server systems may be summarized in the acronym MISA: manageability, interoperability, scalability and accessibility.

- *Manageability*: since data and logic that are likely to change are stored centrally, updates are easily made. Applications are easier to manage and maintain.

- *Interoperability*: since the interface between the client and the server is well defined, different applications could interoperate by conforming to this interface. For example, a drafting program and a computer-integrated manufacturing (CIM) system could communicate with the same server that performs design calculations.

- *Scalability*:   since the load is distributed among multiple machines, applications are easier to scale. For example, if the load on a server increases, multiple servers could be brought up for serving clients from different geographical regions. Alternatively, the computations performed by a single server might be distributed to multiple servers.

- *Accessibility*:   hardware and software compatibility issues do not hinder accessibility. For example, engineers who prefer to work on Unix machines are able to collaborate with architects who use Apple machines, and they are able to exchange information easily.

13.6   DEVELOPING CLIENT-SERVER APPLICATIONS

Software developers need to make several choices related to programming languages, databases, third-party libraries, etc. In addition, client-server application developers have to make an important decision about the choice of middleware. Many engineers consider this an implementation detail for the computer scientists, but there are good reasons why engineers should know about some aspects of middleware:

- Certain options work only on limited platforms. Porting to different platforms might require complete redevelopment.

- Protocols might limit possible operations. Middleware products based on these protocols restrict application functionality. For example, certain protocols are stateless. That is, a connection from the client to the server is made whenever it is necessary, and the server does not record details of previous connections. This makes it difficult to enforce security.

To understand the mode of communication in client-server applications, we now examine a selected set of middleware options.

13.6.1   TCP/IP Sockets

The main requirement for the development of a client-server system is a reliable network. All client-server communication mechanisms are built on top of a low-level communication protocol. A widely used protocol is TCP/IP (Transmission Control Protocol/Internet Protocol).

Most middleware implementations based on TCP/IP use a concept called a socket. A socket is a mechanism for a full-duplex communication between two applications separated by a network. A full-duplex connection means that an application can simultaneously send and receive data. (A half-duplex connection is able to perform only a single operation at a time.) A socket is a software concept and not related to any hardware device; however, its operation is analogous to a telephone (Figure 13.9). Users are able to communicate in both directions at the same time. A socket has two endpoints. Two applications send and receive data from the two endpoints. The first application writes data on one end. The second application reads exactly the same data at the other end. Data written on one side is transmitted to the other end by TCP/IP.

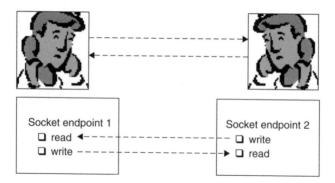

Figure 13.9 A TCP/IP socket is analogous to a telephone

Client-server applications may be developed by using low-level communication through sockets. Here are the steps involved:

1. The server program creates a socket (server socket) that listens on a specific port number. A port is a TCP/IP concept and is not related to any hardware device. A port is used to distinguish between multiple applications on the same machine that communicate through the same network connection. The combination of IP address and port number uniquely identifies a communication endpoint. Creation of a server socket is similar to installing a telephone and obtaining a telephone number from an operating utility.

2. The client program creates a socket and connects to the server socket by specifying the host name (or IP address) and the port number. This is similar to making a telephone call by ringing the number.

3. The server program may or may not decide to accept the connection from the client. If it accepts, a full-duplex connection is established between the client and the server. This step is similar to picking up the phone when it rings.

4. The client program writes a message to the socket and the server reads it. The server responds by writing the results to the socket and the client reads them. This conversation could continue until either party decides to terminate the connection.

13.6.2 *Other Middleware Options*

TCP/IP communication through sockets may be considered as the most basic middleware option. Applications using this option have to design and implement their own application-level protocols to facilitate proper communication. Instead higher-level middleware tools might be used. Examples include remote procedure call (RPC), object request broker (ORB) and remote method invocation (RMI).

13.7 THE WORLD WIDE WEB

The Web was created to enable free exchange of scientific documents across the globe. Originally it was a simple client-server application. The web server creates a server socket

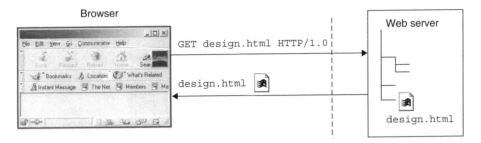

Figure 13.10   Illustration of client-server communication on the WWW

and listens on a standard port. The browser connects to this port and communicates with the server using Hypertext Transfer Protocol (HTTP). HTTP was designed to be a stateless protocol; this means that once the browser requests a file and the web server supplies the file (Figure 13.10), the socket connection is broken. The web server does not maintain a memory of previous connections from the same client. This architecture is only capable of exchanging static information.

Hypertext Markup Language (HTML) was introduced to enable easy navigation through the contents of the Web. HTML permits a webpage to have links to documents that might exist on other servers. Browsers connect to appropriate servers when users activate these links.

13.7.1   Limitations of Exchanging Only Static Information

When there is only static information exchange, the Web is like a bookstore where there is no one to assist in the selection of books. Customers have to browse through catalogues and locate the books they want. As the amount of available information on the Web increased exponentially, it was difficult to find relevant documents. This led to a basic requirement for the ability to run processes that accept input from users. Users need to be able to input queries and web servers need to provide relevant responses.

Without the ability to run programs on the server side, the role of the Web is limited to information publishing. Any processing of information has to be performed on the client side, and this has drawbacks. Consider a cost estimation program that uses government rates published on the Web. Since the web server is only capable of sending raw HTML pages containing all the data, the client program needs to parse the page and locate the relevant data. Often this requires downloading huge volumes of data and complex parsing. This is avoided if web servers are allowed to accept input from the client, process the input and send back data that is more relevant to their needs. The common gateway interface (CGI) is a solution that was adopted very early in the development of the Web.

13.7.2   Common Gateway Interface

The CGI model works as follows. Executable programs, called CGI programs, are stored on the same machine as the web server at specific locations. Through the web server configuration, the server recognizes that these programs are not ordinary documents. When clients request these files, instead of sending files directly, the web server executes the programs and sends back the output produced by them. CGI defines the mechanism for sending input to the CGI program as well as the format for sending back results. CGI is not a programming language; it is only a specification for writing programs to be executed on the server side using input data obtained from clients. The programs themselves can be written in any language.

Users input data through HTML forms. HTML forms contain GUI elements for inputting different types of data. There are text boxes, buttons, check boxes, list boxes, etc. All data that are input by users are sent by the browser to the CGI program in the form of a string consisting of attributes and values. Attributes and values are text strings. Other types of data are not supported. The CGI program reads this request string and separates it into variables and values. It performs the necessary computations and sends back the result usually in the form of an HTML file. This file is displayed to the user by the browser.

Example 13.5 CGI Example

Suppose we want to take the cost computation program of Section 13.3.1 and implement it using the CGI model. At the front end there is an HTML form and at the back end (the server side) there is a CGI program. Only three GUI elements are required in the HTML form:

- a message to users requesting them to input the data;
- a text box for entering the data;
- a submit button.

When the user clicks on the submit button, the data entered by the user are sent to the CGI program. No error checking is performed by the browser. HTML does not contain any mechanism for performing error checks on the client side. This is possible through scripting languages such as JavaScript. All data are processed on the server side by the CGI program. The cost computation CGI program converts the text string into a number, computes the estimate using its application logic and prepares an HTML document displaying the computed result.

13.7.3 Engineering Applications on the Web

Engineering applications are complex and might require interaction with multiple servers. Consider a more complex cost estimation program than the one in Example 7.5. This program obtains product models from another server, consults government rates from websites published by government organizations and also queries application servers of subcontractors (Figure 13.11). Such multi-tiered architecture can be implemented using CGI, since a CGI program might act as a client to other servers.

13.7.4 Other Models for Dynamic Information Exchange

CGI is a fat-server model. Since all processing is performed on the server side, the server tends to be overloaded, especially when there are many simultaneous clients. Also, error

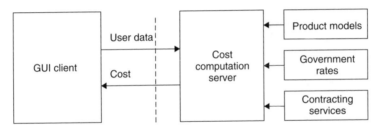

Figure 13.11 A complex Client-Server application. Full scale engineering applications require much more than static information sharing

checking is difficult since no processing is performed on the client side. Many other models are available; they are classified into two main types:

- client-side computing, e.g. Java, JavaScript;
- server-side computing, e.g. CGI, templates, server-side scripting, servlets.

In the client-side computing architecture, programs written in special-purpose languages are downloaded from the web server and executed locally on client machines. This procedure avoids several problems associated with traditional client-server systems. Since the client-side code is also maintained on the server machine, updates are easy.

In the server-side computing architecture, processes are executed on the server machines that produce the relevant dynamic content. New architectures concentrate on generating dynamic content with minimum programming effort. For example, server-side scripting languages allow special tags to be embedded in webpages; these tags are processed by the server for standard operations such as inserting dates and including other documents within a page.

13.8 PEER-TO-PEER NETWORKS

Peer-to-Peer (P2P) networks distribute information among member nodes instead of concentrating it on a single server. P2P architecture offers a mechanism for information sharing that is different from client-server. Consider a client-server implementation of a system for collaborating between an engineer and a contracting firm (Figure 13.12). Details of designs performed by the engineer are uploaded on the central server. Employees of the contracting firm download this data from the central server. All exchange of information takes place through the central server. When there are multiple collaborators, parties that make modifications upload on the server and parties that use the information download it from the server (Figure 13.13).

Now consider another architecture that does not involve a central server (Figure 13.14). The exchange of design data takes place directly between the engineer and the contracting firm. Each party locally maintains data that are modified by it, and the other party obtains the data through direct connection instead of through a central server. When there are multiple users, there are information interchange links between each pair of users (Figure 13.15). Such a network is called a peer-to-peer network. Each node in the network is called a peer. Links in the network are bidirectional since each peer publishes

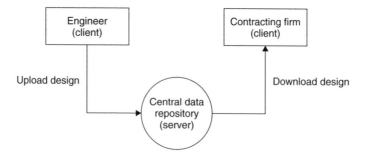

Figure 13.12 Exchange of information through a central server

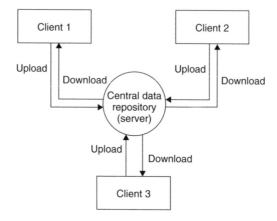

Figure 13.13 Multiple parties collaborating through a central server

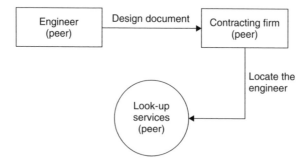

Figure 13.14 Exchange of information without a central server

information as well as obtains information from other peers. In addition there might be look-up services on the network that help peers locate other peers. This is important since a peer might shift location and then their connectivity parameters such as their host name and port number would change. The look-up server maintains a list of active nodes and their addresses. Look-up services are sometimes replicated on every node. Nodes that do not host look-up services store the location of a reliable look-up server.

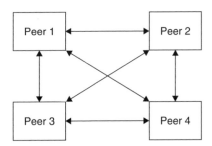

Figure 13.15   A peer to peer network

13.8.1   Information Interchange through P2P Networks

An analogy that helps to understand the mode of information interchange through P2P networks is the use of shared folders on a Microsoft Windows network. Users on a network are allowed to share folders on their local machines so they are accessible to other users. Assume that two users, A and B, collaborate in a project. User A prepares a document and puts it in his shared folder. User B makes a copy of this document, makes modifications to it, and saves the modified version in his shared folder. User A reads the modified version and the exchange of information continues.

P2P networks extend the concept of file sharing to include mechanisms that enable easily searching and finding information and to include users that do not belong to the same local area network. Users of a P2P network are geographically separated. Potentially, anybody can join a P2P network. Sometimes P2P networks have policies to restrict admissions to interest groups and to remove peers who violate terms and conditions of the network. Once a peer is admitted to the network, they become a node like any other node in the network and they are able to publish and receive information. All nodes in the network are notified about the existence of the newly admitted node, and look-up servers update the list of currently active nodes.

An essential aspect of P2P networks is searching for information. Searching for information on the Web requires connecting to search engine websites. Search engines periodically index information located on known websites, and this information is then made available to other users. On P2P networks there are no central search engines. Instead each peer maintains an index; ideally all peers maintain the same index and are automatically updated when new information arrives. Searching can start on any peer and then propagates to other peers until the required information is located. During this process, information may be duplicated on multiple sites and indices may be updated. For users on a P2P network, all nodes appear to be a single repository with a single index even though, in reality, sources of information physically exist on multiple sites. Redundancy resulting from information duplication improves reliability of access when one or more nodes become inactive.

13.8.2   P2P Networks for Engineering Applications

P2P is not only an architecture for sharing files; it could also be used for building scalable distributed applications. The concept of file sharing is easily extended to sharing data,

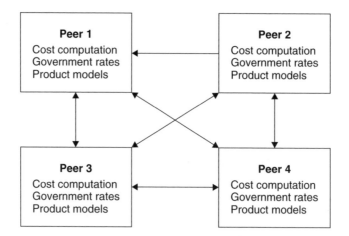

Figure 13.16   A P2P network that performs cost computation calculations. All nodes appear to provide all services, even though computations are physically performed on selected nodes

knowledge and computations. Shared and distributed databases and knowledge bases are possible with the P2P architecture. Another possibility is to distribute scientific and engineering computations among multiple peers.

Consider the client-server application in Figure 13.11. A P2P version of the application is shown schematically in Figure 13.16. All nodes maintain a list of available services. Data and services are replicated on multiple nodes. When a peer X requests another peer Y for a service, peer Y routes the request to an appropriate peer, if the service is not provided by itself directly. When multiple nodes are capable of servicing a request, a node is selected so that the load is evenly balanced.

13.8.3   Advantages of Peer-to-Peer Networks

The traditional client-server architecture employed by the Web does not permit easy dissemination of information. Only users who are granted permissions to modify files on the website are able to publish information. Other users are only able to consume information. Granting permissions to multiple users to modify files on a website has security implications and makes the website difficult to maintain in a consistent state. In any case, anonymous users (as opposed to trusted and authenticated users) are not allowed to contribute to the information published on a website. P2P architecture alleviates the need to provide permissions to modify a website to multiple users. Each user publishes information using a peer process running on his local machine, and he assumes responsibility for the content.

A client-server system becomes non-operational if the server breaks down. A P2P network continues to operate even if multiple nodes fail. Such fault tolerance is possible through redundancy resulting from the replication of information. Since information is available on multiple peers, the load is dynamically distributed. Depending on traffic, demand for information and usage patterns, information is replicated to produce the best performance.

13.8.4   Issues and Challenges

Here are three challenges in building effective P2P networks:

- *Security*: since there is no central control, security is difficult to enforce.

- *Intellectual property*: the P2P architecture permits dynamic replication of information and provides easy access to all members of the network. Protecting intellectual property and copyrights is difficult in such an environment.

- *Objectionable content*: since peers are able to update content freely, some content may not be suitable for some members of the network. P2P networks are easily abused by individuals.

13.9   AGENT TECHNOLOGY

A software agent is a computational entity that acts on behalf of a user and performs tasks that are conventionally performed by users themselves. There are software agents that place auction bids on behalf of the user and filter e-mail messages according to the user's rules and preferences. There are software agents that collaborate with each other for scheduling meetings and for performing more complex tasks such as air traffic control. OASIS is an agent-based system that has been used for air traffic control since September 2000, according to the US Department of Transportation.

A defining characteristic of agents is autonomy. Wooldridge and Jennings (1995) define an agent as 'a computer system that is situated in some environment that is capable of autonomous action in this environment to meet its design objectives'. Autonomy refers to an agent's ability to take decisions by itself for progressing towards its goal. To take decisions autonomously, an agent might require explicit representations of its goals and constraints. The term 'agent' is often confused with the term 'object', as in 'object representation' (Chapter 4), but there are significant differences between them.

Objects act only when messages are passed to them. The state of an object is modified only when other objects send messages to it or when other objects directly modify its public attributes. An agent, on the other hand, reacts to changes in the environment autonomously, without other agents sending messages to them. Agents continuously monitor the state of the environment as well as their own internal states and take appropriate actions. For example, a procurement agent constantly checks prices of relevant items and sends purchase requests whenever prices become low. In fact, agents do more than reacting to changes in the environment; they proactively initiate actions. For example, if an agent does not receive any communication for a long time, it might suspect that the network is malfunctioning and inform the user about it.

When a message is passed to an object, it executes a method consisting of a fixed sequence of steps. The sequence of steps is specified by the programmer and remains the same throughout the life of the object. The behaviour of an agent is more dynamic. Actions taken by an agent, upon receiving a request, depend on current goals, the state of the environment and prior experiences of the agent. Agents employ a procedure known as means-end analysis for moving towards their goals. This goal-directed and adaptable behaviour is achieved through the use of machine learning techniques (Chapter 10), and agents that employ these techniques are sometimes known as intelligent agents.

Computer programs that exhibited agent behaviour were developed long before the agent architecture became widely known. Several background processes that run on the Unix operating system qualify as agents. For example, the traditional mailbox program monitors a user's mailbox and notifies them about incoming mails. The program is autonomous in the sense that it takes actions without the intervention of the user. Modern software agents perform more complex tasks in increasingly challenging environments. The ability to perform in complex environments requires representations that allow behaviour to adapt to changing conditions.

An agent is a server and a client at the same time. Similar to a server process, it continues to execute indefinitely until the user stops it. It receives and services requests from other agents. Similar to a client process, an agent sends requests to other agents (as well as non-agent server processes) for gathering data and information. But unlike a client process in a traditional client-server system, there are very few interactions with users and the behaviour is more autonomous.

Agent systems are classified according to several criteria. Depending on the number of agents, they are classified into single-agent and multi-agent systems. Multi-agent systems are further classified into communicating and non-communicating systems. Multi-agent systems are either cooperative or competitive. Cooperative agents support each other to reach a common goal, whereas competing agents attempt to maximize their own goals without considering the effects on other agents. Depending on the nature of collaboration, the organization of agents might be hierarchical or flat. In a hierarchical organization, tasks carried out by agents are controlled from top to bottom, similar to the organization of personnel in an enterprise. In a flat organization, agents perform tasks without any central control. Agents are classified as static when they operate on a single machine and mobile when they are active on multiple machines. Mobile agents transport themselves to remote machines that accept them, and perform tasks using the CPU of the remote machine. In static agent architecture, an agent may only send requests to agents on remote machines to perform tasks for them.

13.9.1 Issues in Multi-Agent Systems

13.9.1.1 Global system control

Since there is no central control of agents, it is difficult to ensure that the overall system functions correctly. Similar to messaging loops in object representations (Chapter 4), agent interactions might result in never-ending cycles. Although agents might be programmed to detect such cycles, corrective action is reliable only when the complete context is known.

13.9.1.2 Trust and competence

Delegating all responsibilities to an agent requires considerable trust. For example, at the beginning an agent might not have sufficient competence to be granted complete autonomy. There is an intermediate stage in which an agent acquires knowledge by observing the user and through interactions with other agents. At this stage, decisions taken by the agent need to be approved by the user. Full autonomy is granted only when the user is confident about the decision-making capabilities of the agent. However, it is difficult to judge an agent's capabilities, and it is impossible to ensure that an agent takes correct decisions under all circumstances.

13.9.1.3   Updating information

Interrelated data are difficult to update when several agents generate data. In a collaborative environment, the agent that makes modifications should ensure that the constraints of other agents are satisfied. This would require detailed representations of constraints and the implementation of constraint-solving capabilities in all agents.

13.10   SUMMARY

- There are different ways of distributing and processing information.

- Engineering applications require complex information-sharing architectures

- A client-server application is partitioned into two distinct components, client and server, that work together over the network. Clients request data and services; servers supply data and perform computations to service the requests.

- Protocols are important in client-server communications. Service providers publish protocols so that others are able to develop client programs for accessing their services.

- Applications need to be designed carefully for manageability, interoperability, scalability and accessibility

- P2P networks distribute information and services without using a central server. P2P networks are more fault-tolerant than client-server systems.

- Software agents perform useful tasks for humans; one of their defining characteristics is autonomy. Agents can initiate actions themselves, unlike objects that act only when messages are sent to them. Agents monitor the state of the environment as well as their own internal state and adapt their actions to suit changing situations.

- Cycling, competence and information updating create challenges for the development of robust agent systems.

REFERENCE

Wooldridge, M. and Jennings, N. R. 1995. Intelligent agents: theory and practice. *Knowledge Engineering Review*. **10**, 2, 115–152.

FURTHER READING

Orfali, R., Harkey, D. and Edwards, J. 1999. *Client/Server Survival Guide*. New York: John Wiley & Sons, Inc.

Index